A Historical Syntax of English

T0373778

Edinburgh Textbooks on the English Language - Advanced

Visit the Edinburgh Textbooks in the English Language website at
www.euppublishing.com/series/ETOTELAdvanced

A Historical Syntax of English

Bettelou Los

EDINBURGH
University Press

© Bettelou Los, 2015

Edinburgh University Press Ltd
The Tun, Holyrood Road,
12(2f) Jackson's Entry,
Edinburgh EH8 8PJ
www.euppublishing.com

Typeset in 10.5/12 Janson by
Servis Filmsetting Ltd, Stockport, Cheshire,
printed and bound in Great Britain by
CPI Group (UK) Ltd, Croydon CR0 4YY

A CIP record for this book is available from the British Library

ISBN 978 0 7486 4144 4 (hardback)
ISBN 978 0 7486 9456 3 (webready PDF)
ISBN 978 0 7486 4143 7 (paperback)
ISBN 978 0 7486 9457 0 (epub)

Contents

List of figures and tables

Abbreviations

7	for the *Tironian Sign* ET 'and'
A	adjective; aspect
ACC	accusative
AgrS	subject agreement/head of AgrSP
AcI	accusative-and-infinitive
AP	Adjective Phrase
AUX	auxiliary
C	Complementiser
c.	*circa*, about (of dates)
cf.	compare
CP	Complementiser Phrase (clause)
DAT	dative
dual	dualis
ECM	Exceptional Case-Marking
edn	edition
e.g.	for instance
eME	Early Middle English
eModE	Early Modern English
f.	feminine
GEN	genitive
ibid.	in the same work
i.e.	*id est* 'namely'
IND	indicative
INF	infinitive
I	inflectional element/head of IP
INST	instrumental
IP	Inflection Phrase (clause)
Lat.	Latin
lit.	literally
lME	Late Middle English
lOE	Late Old English

m.	masculine
M	modality
ME	Middle English
n.	neuter
N	noun
NEG	negation/head of NegP
NICE	negation, inversion, code, emphasis
NOM	nominative
NP	noun phrase
O	Object
OE	Old English
OV	Object-Verb
P	preposition
part.	participle
pass	passive
p.c.	personal communication
PDE	present-day English
phi	person, number, gender features
PIE	Proto-Indo-European
pl	plural
PP	prepositional phrase
pres	present
pret	preterite, past tense
PRT	particle
R	Recipient
REL	relative clause
RP	Recipient Phrase
subj	subjunctive
sg	singular
SOV	Subject-Object-Verb
Spec	specifier
SVO	Subject-Verb-Object
T	tense
TMA	tense, modality and aspect
TP	Tense Phrase
trans.	translation
V	Verb
VO	Verb-Object
Vv	non-finite complement-finite verb
vV	finite verb-non-finite complement
VP	verb phrase
vs.	versus

wh	interrogative
X	any category
X'	X-bar
XP	any phrase

Note on data references

Entries in < > brackets correspond to the system of short titles as employed in Healey and Venezky ([1980] 1985) (in turn based on the system of Mitchell et al. 1975, 1979). This is identical to the TEI reference in the Dictionary of Old English Corpus (DOEC or Toronto Corpus), which means that line numbers refer to the beginning of the sentence rather than the line in which the relevant structure occurs.

Entries in [ ] brackets refer to the Helsinki Corpus, and refer to the filenames; the full reference for the material in these files can be found in Kytö (1993).

Entries from the *OED* (*Oxford English Dictionary*) and the *MED* (*Middle English Dictionary*) have the reference as given in those sources.

Data quoted from other sources will have the reference as given in those sources, augmented with a reference to the edition or concordance used by that source. An exception is data from Visser's data collection, where the reader is referred to Visser (1969) for the full reference.

Corpora in the references refer to:

BNC: The British National Corpus <http://www.natcorp.ox.ac.uk>.
CEMET: CEMET (Corpus of Early Modern English Texts), precursor to the CLMETEV, covering the period 1640–1710. The CLMETEV is The Corpus of Late Modern English Texts (Extended Version), 2006. Compiled by Hendrik De Smet, Department of Linguistics, University of Leuven.
Helsinki Corpus (HC) refers to a set of tagged and parsed corpora: YCOE: York-Toronto-Helsinki Parsed Corpus of Old English Prose (Taylor et al. 2003).
LC: The Lampeter Corpus of Early Modern English Tracts <http://www.ota.ox.ac.uk/id/2400>.
MED: Middle English Dictionary Online.

Michigan Corpus: The Corpus of Middle English Prose and Verse, <http://quod.lib.umich.edu/c/cme/>.

OED: Oxford English Dictionary Online.

PPCME2: Penn-Helsinki Parsed Corpus of Middle English, 2nd edn (Kroch and Taylor 2000b).

PPCEME: Penn-Helsinki Parsed Corpus of Early Modern English (Kroch et al. 2004).

PPCMBE: Penn Parsed Corpus of Modern British English (Kroch et al. 2010).

Switchboard Corpus: The Switchboard Corpus (Godfrey et al. 1992) is a preliminary version of the Penn Treebank Corpus.

Preface

This book presents an overview of the major changes in English syntax from Old English times until the present day. Students are assumed to be familiar with syntactic functions (subject, object, adverbial, etc.) and constituent form (NP, PP, finite and non-finite clause, etc.), although the first chapter is intended to serve as a refresher course. Although students will find it easier to cope with such unfamiliar languages if they have had some exposure to them, they are not assumed to be familiar with Old or Middle English.

The changes dealt with in this book include two major word order changes: the loss of Object-Verb orders and the decline of Verb-Second. As much of the research into these losses has shown that a finely-articulated clause structure makes sense of the various positions in Old English, Chapters 6 and 7 – which deal with these losses – will make reference to this structure, and provide some formal syntax to model it. In preparation of this, some of the formal machinery that is required in Chapters 6 and 7 will be introduced in Chapters 2 and 4. The X'-structures in the book are there primarily for the insights they offer into the connection between morphology and syntax, and how movement of a syntactic head like the verb may serve to demarcate certain areas of the clause. For the reason why speakers might want to make such demarcations, we turn to other fields: information structure and discourse.

I would like to thank Heinz Giegerich for inviting me to write this book, and for his reading of the final draft. Of the many colleagues and students who were subjected to the various earlier drafts, my thanks go to Ans van Kemenade, Sanne van Vuuren, Erwin Komen and especially Linda van Bergen, whose meticulous annotation of yet another unsatisfactory version pointed the way to the final version of this book. I would like to acknowledge with gratitude the incredible patience of Gillian Leslie, Michelle Houston, Laura Williamson and Richard Strachan at

EUP who remained unruffled while one deadline after another whizzed past. Thanks are also due to James Dale, the managing desk editor, and Geraldine Lyons, for her careful copy-editing.

To my teachers
Geert Booij
Johan Boswinkel
Jet van Dam van Isselt
John Eadie
Roger Eaton
Olga Fischer
Ans van Kemenade
Willem Koopman
Amanda Lacy
Frederike van der Leek
Margaret Locherbie Cameron
Andries Vos

1 Introduction

1.1 What is syntax?

When we learn our own language as young children, the task ahead of us is to construct the rules of our language on a number of different levels: the sound system (phonology), the internal structure of the words (morphology), how words are combined into clauses (syntax), and how clauses can be strung together to form longer stretches of discourse in such a way that our hearers can keep track of what we want to communicate, and what the various participants in our narrative are doing (discourse). Each level has its own 'building blocks' that combine into larger units, and each level has its own set of rules to build these (see Table 1.1).

The output of one level in Table 1.1 is the input of the next. Phonemes combine into morphemes, morphemes into words, words into clauses, clauses into (spoken or written) text. We tend to take it completely for granted that our languages are constructed from sounds that we make with our mouths and vocal chords, but the fact that our speech has this oral 'modality' has consequences for the rule systems of the linguistic levels. The building blocks need to be lined up linearly, as the information can only leave our mouths sound by sound (and morpheme by morpheme, word by word, etc.) – unlike, for instance, the visual/gestural modality of sign language, where it is possible to make two signs simultaneously. Much of the rule systems of oral languages is concerned with getting the order of the elements right on all levels.

Table 1.1 Four levels of linguistic description

Rule system	Building blocks	Creates as output
Phonology	Phonemes	Morphemes
Morphology	Morphemes	Words
Syntax	Words	Clauses
Discourse	Sentences	Text

Syntax, the rule system that combines words into sentences, operates on (at least) two levels: words are grouped into constituents
(noun phrases like *a lovely bunch of grapes*, prepositional phrases like
in the morning, etc.), and these constituents then 'slot' into designated
spaces in the clause. For noun phrases (NPs), designated spaces are for
instance the subjects (1a) or objects (1b) of verbs, or the complement of
prepositions (1c), building a prepositional phrase (PP).

(1)   a. **The boys next door** bought a lion cub in a department store.
      b. The boys next door bought **a lion cub** in a department store.
      c. The boys next door bought a lion cub in **a department store**

In turn, a PP may appear as an adverbial, encoding additional information about place (2a), time (2b) and manner (2c) of the action or event
encoded by the verb.

(2)   a. The boys next door bought a lion cub **in a department store**.
      b. The boys next door bought a lion cub **in the sixties**.
      c. The boys next door bought a lion cub **on a whim**.

We will use the short narrative in (3) to discuss this process in more
detail.

(3)   Anthony and John lived in London in the sixties. They bought a
      lion cub in Harrods. They named him Christian. Christian grew
      into an adult lion. Anthony and John could no longer keep him
      in the basement of their London house. Visitors to the house put
      them in touch with George and Joy Adamson. The Adamsons
      had reintroduced a female lion to the wild some years earlier.
      With their help, Anthony and John released Christian into a
      national park in Kenya. Anthony and John visited Kenya a year
      later. Christian still remembered them. Forty years on, the
      footage of their reunion became a hit on the internet.

The first verb, *live*, requires someone who does the living, in other words,
an AGENT, and this role is here taken by the subject and expressed in the
form of coordinated NPs (*Anthony and John*). There are two additional
constituents, both PPs, and they contain information about the place
and the time at which this *living* takes place.
    The second verb, *buy*, requires an AGENT who does the buying, and a
PATIENT who is being bought, and both of these roles are associated with
particular syntactic functions: the AGENT role is encoded by a subject and
takes the form of an NP, this time a pronoun (*They*), because Anthony
and John are by now known to the reader/hearer, while the PATIENT
role is encoded by a direct object, also in the form of an NP (*a lion cub*).

The third verb, *name*, requires these same two roles for the same two syntactic functions of subject and object, and also expresses them as pronominal NPs (*They* and *him*) because both Anthony and John – *they* – and the lion cub – *him* – are now both known to the reader; there is a third NP, *Christian*, but this NP does not refer to a new entity or role but to a property of an entity, an attribute, in this case a label, a name, that is given to the lion cub. The syntactic function of this label is referred to by some approaches as object complement, by other as object predicate or object attribute.

The fourth verb, *grow*, also connects an attribute to an entity: Christian is associated with being an adult lion, and as such *grow* accommodates a subject, in the form of an NP, and the attribute, here encoded by an NP inside a PP. The syntactic function of this PP is referred to by some approaches as subject complement, by other as subject predicate or subject attribute.

The fifth verb, *keep*, again has an AGENT role expressed as subject and a PATIENT role expressed as object, and both of these functions have the form of NPs; there is also a PP, *in the basement of their London house*, which gives the place where the lion was kept, and a phrase that consists of a negation and a time adverb, *no longer*, that indicates that the entire 'action' – two young men keeping a lion in such an unsuitable place – is not sustainable and will have to end. *No longer* and the PP *in the basement of their London house* both have the syntactic function of adverbial, as they do not express a role of the verb *keep*.

1.2 What is syntax for?

Syntax creates slots for certain kinds of information, and provides routines for lining this information up word by word. The verbs are particularly helpful for the hearers or readers of the message because they show them what information to expect: AGENTS, PATIENTS, attributes, etc. The syntax in the short narrative in (3) is quite basic. Every verb is accompanied by all the roles it requires; there are no passives that might serve to obscure the identity of the AGENT role. Each sentence contains a single verb, and hence a single clause. This means that there are no complex sentences containing clauses-within-clauses. This simple syntax does not necessarily make the short narrative in (3) easy to read, however.

A text like (3), whether it is written down or narrated as part of a face-to-face conversation, tries to communicate a narrative to its hearer or reader, and it does so by asking the reader to construct a mental model of the setting and the players, and to update this model according to the information s/he receives from the text. A helpful analogy here might be a game of blindfold chess, where the chess master has to visualise the board in his or her mind's eye and keep track of all the pieces, only in this case the chessboard is more like a stage, as in a theatre, which the text peoples with entities that do things. As with the chess pieces, the challenge is to keep track, and the more entities there are, the more difficult the challenge will be.

The stage in (3) is populated first by Anthony and John, then by the lion, by visitors coming to the house, by the Adamsons, and by a film. They interact in a number of different settings: a basement in London, Kenya, the internet. With such a crowded stage, we need the linguistic equivalent of a followspot to know who we should focus on, and who we can forget about. This is where passives may be very useful, as they remove entities from the limelight. A sentence like *They were put in touch with George and Joy Adamson* gets rid of *the visitors to the house* that do not have a part to play in the rest of the narrative and are only taking up valuable memory space, with the added benefit that we keep focused on Anthony and John, who have now become the subject (*They*). *With their help, Anthony and John released Christian into a national park in Kenya* may be similarly streamlined by using a passive: *With their help, Christian was released into a national park in Kenya.* This reduces the number of entities to two: the Adamsons, who are the referents of *their*, and the lion Christian.

The other problem with a narrative of single-clause-sentences is that some clauses belong to the actual narrative, while the function of other clauses is to give background information about some of the new characters that the story introduces. This is, again, a burden for the focus of our attention as we have to make out the story from a welter of background details. These background details also force us to travel backwards and forwards in time, from the present of our story to events in the past: *The Adamsons had reintroduced a female lion to the wild some years earlier*, whereas the storyline itself proceeds linearly from the purchase of the lion cub, its year in the basement, its release into the wild, the reunion a year later, and *YouTube* Hall-of-Fame forty years on, taking us to the present of the actual writing. One way to help the reader sort out foreground, the storyline, from background could be a rewrite of (3) as in (4):

(4)   When Anthony and John lived in London in the sixties, they bought a lion cub in Harrods and named him Christian. When Christian grew into an adult lion, and they could no longer keep him in the basement of their London house, they were put in

touch with George and Joy Adamson, who had reintroduced a female lion into the wild some years earlier. With their help, Christian was released into a national park in Kenya. When Anthony and John visited Kenya a year later, Christian still remembered them. Forty years on, the footage of their reunion became a hit on the internet.

What this revision has done is to group the eleven clauses that were presented as eleven simple sentences in (3) into five sentences, three of which are complex. The storyline is still encoded by main clauses: *they bought a lion cub in Harrods and named him Christian; they were put in touch with George and Joy Adamson; Christian was released into a national park in Kenya; Christian still remembered them; Forty years on, the footage of their reunion became a hit on the internet.*

The background material is now encoded by subclauses, either as adverbials of time to a main clause (*When Anthony and John lived in London in the sixties; When Christian grew into an adult lion; When Anthony and John visited Kenya a year later*), or as an adverbial that gives a reason (*and they could no longer keep him in the basement of their London house*), or as a relative clause providing background information about the Adamsons' expertise, showing why they are relevant to the story (*who had reintroduced a female lion into the wild some years earlier*).

Making active sentences passive, 'promoting' a clause to main clause and 'demoting' a clause to subclause, are optional syntactic operations that we can use to focus the attention of our hearers and readers, as if we are operating a follow-spot on our mutual mental stage. This does not mean that all subclauses convey backgrounded information. Subclauses that are objects of verbs as in (5) often belong to the main storyline:

(5)   a.   They discovered to their surprise that Christian still remembered them.
       b.   They were thrilled to discover that Christian still remembered them.
       c.   They had not believed it possible that Christian still remembered them, but he did.

In (5a–b), what used to be a main clause in (3) now appears as a subclause in the complement of the verb *discover*. In (5a) there is a main clause (with *discover* at its core) and a subclause (with *remember* at its core), in (5b) there is a main clause (*were thrilled*) and two subclauses (*discover, remember*), so that the *remember*-clause is even more deeply embedded, a clause-within-a-clause-within-a-clause. In (5c) the *remember*-clause is the object of the verb *believe*, and *possible* is the object complement (*They had not believed [that Christian still remembered them] possible*).

The subclause has undergone a further syntactic operation in (5c) in being moved to the end of the clause, with *it* slotted into its earlier position as a kind of syntactic placeholder (**extraposition**). Note that *Christian still remembered them* remains part of the storyline, whether it is a main clause or a subclause, or a subclause-within-a-subclause as in (5b).

A fairly extreme example of such embedding at the level of syntax is (6), uttered on 8 March 1860 at the hundred-and-twenty-second anniversary of the Royal Society of Musicians, which was celebrated in the Freemasons' Hall, with Charles Dickens in the chair.

(6)   When the Grace had been sung, there were the usual loyal toasts;
       after which the chairman continued: 'Ladies and Gentlemen,
       I suppose I may venture to say that it is pretty well known to
       everybody that all people, whenever they are brought together at
       dinner in private society for the declared purpose of discussing
       any particular matter or business, it invariably happens that they
       never can by any ingenuity be brought to approach that business,
       and that they invariably make it the one sole object and ground
       on which they cannot be trapped into the utterance of a syllable.
       This being the curious concurrent experience of all mankind, it is
       the cautious custom of this particular dinner to place its business
       in the very front of the evening's engagements. It commits it
       to paper, and places it in black and white before the unhappy
       chairman whilst he speaks. [Laughter]'. (Fielding 1988: 294)

The first sentence of the actual speech ('Ladies and Gentlemen . . .') is nearly seven lines long. The same simple rules as in (3) underpin the formation of this long sentence: a lexical verb *suppose* creates slots for entities with certain roles (AGENT, PATIENT, etc.) and certain syntactic functions (subject, object). What makes it different from (3), and more like (4), is that the object is expressed by a clause rather than by a phrase. This clause has another lexical verb, *venture*, at its core, which in turn creates a slot for another object, which is also expressed by a clause, which has a verb *say*, at its core, which creates a slot for another object, which is another clause, this time one in which the subject rather than the object is expressed by a clause (*[that all people, whenever they are brought together . . . never can by any ingenuity be brought to approach that business] is pretty well known to everybody*), and as in (5c), this clause is extraposed to the end and a placeholder *it* appears in the subject position instead. The rules of English syntax quite happily allow this complex clause-within-a-clause-within-a-clause-within-a-clause construction, but it strains the capacity of human memory. Note that the sentence goes off the rails here: *all people* starts another clause that is abandoned halfway through, as a dropped stitch in an intricate piece of knitting, and a new start is made by *it invariably happens that.*

What syntax offers is routines, templates, automatic ways of doing things. When hearers are decoding messages, syntax allows them to have expectations about how the sentence will develop:

(7) a. They [verb]
     b. They discovered [object]
     c. They discovered to [NP] [object]
     d. They discovered to their surprise that [subject]

These predictions make the message easier to process. The templates allow speakers to construct sentences from scratch – strings of words that have never been uttered before in that particular combination – and still be understood by their hearers. But fixed routines also benefit the speaker, as they automate the sentence-construction process. Many combinations of words or phrases come in ready-made chunks. Examples in (6) are *Ladies and gentlemen* and *black and white.* Much of a speaker's output, spoken or written, has been shown to consist of such conventionalised 'prefabs' (Ermann and Warren 2000: 31). At the same time, syntactic operations like passivisation, extraposition, or subordination provide the speaker with various means to focus the attention of the hearer, and facilitate communication, as we saw in (4).

1.3 Three dimensions of syntax

1.3.1 Introduction

We saw in the previous sections that syntax serves a number of functions: (1) providing routines to facilitate production (for the speaker); (2) providing routines to guide processing (for the hearer). The routines include syntactic operations that help to focus the hearer's attention by going from what is familiar to the hearer to what is new and unfamiliar, and by providing clues as to what information pertains to the main storyline and what is background. The routines also help the reader to keep track of the entities involved in the story. The role of the verb is pivotal in keeping track of who is doing what to whom, as verbs come with semantic roles to match the entities in the utterance. Adverbials express the when, where, how and why of an event.

What aspects of how these functions are expressed may vary from language to language, and hence, from language stage to language stage? It is clear that the lexicon, the combinations of sounds that make up the individual words and morphemes, will differ from language to language, and from language stage to language stage. If we abstract away from the lexicon, we are left with the system, the structure of the language. The variation we find there represents aspects of three domains:

1. How the information about the relationships between the verb and its semantic roles (AGENT, PATIENT, etc.) is expressed. This is essentially a choice between expressing relational information by endings (inflections), i.e. in the morphology, or by free words, like pronouns and auxiliaries, in the syntax.
2. The expression of the semantic roles themselves (NPs, clauses?), and the syntactic operations languages have at their disposal for giving some roles higher profiles than others (e.g. passivisation).
3. Word order.

As any variation between languages can also characterise variation between different stages of a single language, these three dimensions indicate where we can expect to find syntactic *change*. We will discuss each of these in turn, and how relevant they are for the history of English.

1.3.2 Morphology or syntax?

The semantic roles are part of the **lexical** content of the verb, the sort of information that comes with the verb when the verb is retrieved from our mental lexicons to be used in an utterance, or recognised when heard in the utterance of another speaker. The verb also contains **grammatical** information: when it is slotted into its position in an utterance, it will show agreement with one of the entities that express its semantic roles (the subject). When the subject changes from plural (8a) to singular (8b), or from third person singular (8b) to first person singular (8c), the verb changes with it:

(8)   a. Anthony and John live in London.
      b. Anthony lives in London.
      c. I live in London.

In English, this marking is minimal; in the past tense, person-and-number marking on the verb is absent, which is why the tense of the examples in (8) is given in the present. In other languages, this marking is much more extensive, as it was in earlier English:

(9)   Why **shouldest** thou do so, seeing how thou was not far from thine own shore? (*OED*, 1671 H. M. tr. Erasmus Colloquies 326)

The second person singular pronoun *thou* would trigger an -*est* ending on the verb, not only in the present but also in the past tense; when *you* supplanted *thou*, this ending was lost with it, as *you*, originally a second person plural, did not have an ending – or, better, had a zero-ending, as having no ending is meaningful if other combinations of person-and-number do have endings. Languages with extensive person-and-number marking have less need for subject pronouns; in a narrative like (3), the marking on the verb of a third person plural would suffice to pick out Anthony and John as the subject of *were put in touch*, and the pronoun *they* would not be necessary.

Person-and-number agreement is not the only marking on verbs. Although the specifics of the *when* of the event expressed by the verb can be expressed lexically, by e.g. an adverbial like *in the sixties*, the verb itself is also marked for tense. This grammatical marking conveys information about the time of the events in the narration relative to the time of narrating: all the verbs in the narrative in (3) were in the past tense. English verbs are only marked for present and past; all other tenses (perfect, future) require the addition of an auxiliary. Other languages may mark these additional tenses on the verb, too, as well as other categories that are expressed by auxiliaries in English, like passives.

Only finite verbs carry subject-agreement and tense marking. Non-finite verbs, like the infinitive *put* or the past participle *reintroduced* in (10), generally do not carry such marking.

(10)   Anthony and John were put in touch with George and Joy Adamson, who had reintroduced a female lion into the wild some years earlier.

There is a proliferation of auxiliaries in English. In (10) we have *had reintroduced* where *have* builds a perfect, and *were put in touch* where *be* builds a passive; (11) shows two further possibilities: *be* to build a progressive, and modal auxiliaries, like *could*, to express ability or possibility:

(11)   Christian was growing too big, and they could no longer keep him in the basement.

This proliferation of auxilaries means that even categories like tense and agreement – finiteness – are often no longer expressed on the lexical verb – *put* and *reintroduce* in (10), *grow* and *keep* in (11) – but on a separate form, the auxiliary.

There is a relationship between the lack of inflection on English

Table 1.2 Functional categories expressed as a bound morpheme or a free form

Lexical category	Functional category	Expressed by bound morpheme	Expressed by free form
V	Agreement	Latin: *videbunt* see.Fut.3.pl 'they will see'	PDE: **they** will see
N	Definiteness	Swedish: *landet* 'the land'	PDE: **the** land
V	Modality	Latin: *veniant* come.Pres.Subj.3.pl 'they may come'	PDE: they **may** come
N	Thematic role	Icelandic: *Ég gaf manninum bók* I gave man-the-Dative book 'I gave the man a book'	PDE: I gave a book **to** the man
N	Linking	Latin: *Senatus Populusque Romanus* lit. Senate People-and Roman	PDE: The Senate **and** the Roman People
A	Degrees of comparison	PDE: *greater, greatest*	PDE: **more** important, **most** important
V	Causation	Proto-Germanic: *satjan* 'set,' lit. 'cause to sit' *drankjan* 'drench', lit. 'cause to drink'	PDE: **make** him leave

verbs and the existence of pronouns and auxiliaries in English: English tends to express such grammatical, or functional, information in the syntax where other languages might express it as morphology. This domain of variation is not restricted to the verb. Some examples of other categories are presented in Table 1.2.

English used to express more information in the morphology a thousand years ago than it does today – it used to be a **synthetic** language, but has become increasingly **analytic**. If morphology is lost and functional information is no longer expressed by endings on verbs, nouns and adjectives, new forms may be recruited to take their place. These forms typically come from the existing lexicon, and are nouns, verbs or adjectives that acquire new, functional meanings. Their original lexical meanings are gradually lost (this process is called **bleaching**), they no longer have stress (stress is associated with lexical meaning: nouns, verbs and adjectives have stress, but grammatical items like conjunctions, articles and auxiliaries are, as a rule, unstressed) and their forms may become phonologically reduced, with their vowels often being pronounced as schwa [ə]. This recruitment process is called **grammaticalisation** or **grammaticisation**. The present-day English (PDE) examples in the rightmost column of Table 1.2 derive from lexical items that have undergone this process.

As the transformation from synthetic to analytic is a major part of how the syntax of English has changed, the history of English includes many examples of grammaticalisation. We will discuss some of them in Chapters 2, 3 and 4.

1.3.3 The expression of the semantic roles

Although the conceptual structure of actions expressed by verbs would not be expected to differ from one language to another – an eating action presupposes an animate entity that does the eating, and a substance that gets eaten – languages may differ in how many roles they require to be expressed, and how these are expressed.

We saw in (4)–(6) how some verbs can have their roles expressed by clauses rather than by NPs, which is how sentences can become very complex. The subclauses we saw in (6) were of two types: the ones containing a **finite** verb, and the ones only containing a **non-finite** verb; (12) repeats a fragment of (6), indicating finite and non-finite clauses:

(12) ... and [$_{\text{finite}}$ that they invariably make it the one sole object and ground [$_{\text{finite}}$ on which they cannot be trapped into the utterance of a syllable]]. [$_{\text{non-finite}}$ This being the curious concurrent experience of all mankind], [$_{\text{finite}}$ it is the cautious custom of this particular dinner [$_{\text{non-finite}}$ to place its business in the very front of the evening's engagements]] ...

Sometimes there is a choice between finite and non-finite expressions:

(13) a. [$_{\text{non-finite}}$ This being the curious concurrent experience of all mankind]

  b. [$_{\text{finite}}$ As this is the curious concurrent experience of all mankind]

And some non-clausal complements, like the PP in (14a), can also be expressed by a non-finite clause:

(14) a. They cannot be trapped [$_{\text{pp}}$ into the utterance of a syllable].

  b. They cannot be trapped [$_{\text{non-finite clause}}$ into uttering a syllable].

The history of English shows a number of developments in this area, which will be discussed in Chapter 5.

Many languages that have case systems show a clear functional motivation for which roles are allowed to be coded by nominative case and which are not. Some languages only allow proper AGENTS, i.e. actors fully in control of the action, to be encoded as nominative subjects; participants undergoing emotions, dreams, physical sensations (including seeing or hearing) that they have no control over have to be encoded by non-nominatives, usually a dative or a locative case. Old English nominative subjects used to show a similar restriction, with verbs like *like* and *loathe* not having nominative subjects but dative EXPERIENCERS:

(15)   Ne mæg nan man hine sylfne to cynge gedon ac ðæt folc hæfþ cyre
       not may no   man him self   to king   make but the people have choice
       to ceosenne ðone   to cyninge ðe   **him**   sylfum   licaþ
       to choose   that-one to king   that them-DAT selves-DAT like-3SG
       'no man can make himself king, but the people have the option of
       choosing as king who they themselves like' <ÆCHom I, 14.1, 212, 6>

Lician 'like' in (15) has an EXPERIENCER-argument in the dative, *him sylfum* 'they themselves', and note that there is no agreement between that EXPERIENCER and the verb: the form *licaþ* is third person singular and hence does not agree with the EXPERIENCER (the plural form would have been *liciaþ*), showing that the EXPERIENCER is not its subject. The EXPERIENCER-arguments of PDE *like* are subjects.

From Early Modern English onwards, English becomes very flexible as to what kind of arguments can be subjects:

(16)   a. **2004** saw the advent of direct funding from the Scottish
           Government for Scottish Mountain Rescue Teams. <www.
           cmrt.org.uk/chairman.htm>
       b. Like all the best screwball comedies, **this film** is seeping
           with wit and romance. <letterboxd.com/amberson/film/
           midnight-1939/>
       c. **André Deed's surreal Christmas comedy** . . . ends our
           programme of short films. <https://www.dur.ac.uk/mlac/
           italian/2011silentfilmfestival/week9/>
       d. **Matching hood** converts into collar (Sears & Roebuck
           catalogue; Hundt 2007: 161)

Subjects as in (16a–d) would cross-linguistically be more likely to be encoded by adverbials or by objects, as in (17):

(17) a. In 2004, direct funding from the Scottish Government for
          Scottish Mountain Rescue Teams started.
      b. Through his film seep wit and romance.
      c. With André Deed's surreal Christmas comedy, our
          programme of short films ends.
      d. You can convert the matching hood into a collar.

English has also developed a number of unusual passives in the same
period:

(18) a. On the evening of April 18, 1775, Paul Revere **was sent for**
          by Dr. Joseph Warren and instructed to ride to Lexington . . .
          <www.paulreverehouse.org/ride/real.html>
      b. He **was alleged** to be a thief.
      c. He **was given** a standing ovation/a clean bill of health/a six-
          month community order.

1.3.4 Word order variation

Rewriting the narrative in (3) into (4) to make it easier to read was done
by redistributing the information over main and subclauses, and by
introducing syntactic operations like the passive:

(19) a. They were put in touch with George and Joy Adamson.
      b. Christian was released into a national park in Kenya.

As a rule, English does not allow subjects and objects to be reordered;
objects can be fronted (**topicalisation**), but (20b) shows that the results
are not invariably felicitous:

(20) a. ?Them, visitors put in touch with George and Joy Adamson.
      b. ?Christian, Anthony and John released into a national park in
          Kenya.

Topicalisation apparently adds an emphasis to the moved constituent
that goes beyond ordering information. Clauses usually keep to the
basic order of Subject-Verb-Object (SVO) if no emphasis is intended.
Adverbials are more flexible:

(21) a. When Anthony and John lived in London in the sixties, they
          bought a lion cub in Harrods.
      b. Anthony and John bought a lion cub in Harrods in the sixties,
          when they lived in London.
      c. In the sixties, when they lived in London, Anthony and John
          bought a lion cub in Harrods.

Word order routines develop to facilitate production and processing. If there is any variation in word order, it is usually given a 'meaning', a function. We will make some suggestions of what these functions can be in the next section.

Even though the scope for word order varation is fairly limited, changes in word order can happen. English went from a basic Object-Verb (OV) order to Verb-Object (VO) order around 1200 (Chapter 6), and saw an important change in the position of finite verbs in the fifteenth century (Chapter 7).

1.4 Word order and meaning

1.4.1 Introduction

If word order relies on automated routines, and there is a lot of chunking, we would expect it to contribute relatively little to the meaning of a clause. There is some support for this in the observation that we can get the drift of the meaning of a text in a foreign language as long as every word is **glossed** by its counterpart in a language that we do know. Although the word order of Old English, the language spoken in England about a thousand years ago, differs from that of PDE in a number of important respects, substituting PDE words for Old English ones while retaining the original word order does not materially affect our understanding of the text. An example of such a 'transliteration' is (22).

(22)   To those words another king's councillor and alderman
       agreement gave, and into that discussion entered and thus spoke:
       such me seems, O king, this present life of men on earth to
       eternity, the time that to us unknown is: as if you at dinner sit
       with your aldermen and thanes in winter, and the fire lit and your
       hall warmed, and it rains and snows and storms outside; comes
       a sparrow and in a flash the house throughflies, comes through
       one door in, through another door goes out. Well, he, during the
       period that he inside is, not is touched by the storm of winter;
       but that is an eye's blink and a very small period, and he quickly
       from one winter into the winter after goes. So then man's life
       as a limited period appears; what there preceded, or what there
       follows, we not know.

This is a transliteration of the famous description of how King Edwin of Northumbria was persuaded to be converted to Christianity in 627 during the mission of St Paulinus, from an Old English translation of Bede's original Latin text. Although the result is very unlike a PDE text, it is perfectly possible to make out its meaning because we can still work out who is doing what: the roles that come with the individual verbs (*enter, sit, come, precede, follow*) can still be matched to their subjects and objects. The relative positions of subjects, objects and adverbials are by and large what we are used to: 'old' information, often in the form of pronouns, comes first, and objects and adverbials, which generally present 'new' information, follow afterwards. The main point of difference seems to be the position of the verbs.

Although word order contributes so little to the meaning of a text that it does not affect our overall understanding of a transliteration like (22), it is not true that word order does not make any contribution to meaning. But that contribution is not lexical meaning – meaning in the sense that individual words like *sparrow* and *winter* have meaning – but a meaning, or function, of a different kind.

1.4.2 Pragmatics and information structure

If the first position in a sentence is usually occupied by old information, speakers can manipulate hearers' expectations by starting with information that is completely new. Such changes may acquire a momentum of their own when adopted and systematised by subsequent generations of speakers. Imagine an interaction between two speakers, A and B, as in (23). B's answers start with the adverbial of place *in York*, and this is very much a minority pattern in a PDE sentence, for only about 5 per cent of such adverbials end up in this position; the vast majority are clause-final.

(23) A: How successful was St Pauline's mission?
　　　B: Well, **in York**, he was welcomed with open arms, but **in Whitby** the King refused to see him.

There is a sense of contrast generated by the combination of this syntactic function, the first position, and the speaker's intonation. Even a shorter answer as in (24) is enough to imply contrast, and to convey the information that St Pauline was welcomed with open arms *only* in York:

(24) B: Well, **in York** he was welcomed with open arms.

Whether this 'meaning' of contrast is an integral part of English syntax or not depends on our definition of syntax. If we consider syntax to be a system of hard and fast rules, indicating which orders are possible and which impossible in a language, the contrast in (24) cannot be said to be part of syntax, because it is not the case that every clause-initial adverbial is contrastive. It is just that non-contrastive ones are much less frequent than contrastive ones, particularly with adverbials of place. If we want to keep syntax free of such gradient phenomena, we could say that this tendency is not part of syntax but of usage, pragmatics, or information structure, as separate levels of linguistic description, in addition to those in Table 1.1. Any changes in this area would then, strictly speaking, be a case of historical pragmatics, or historical information structure, rather than historical syntax; they are so relevant to the study of historical syntax, and interact so closely with word order, however, that it would be unwise to exclude them. In Old English, clause-initial adverbials were much more frequent than in PDE, and much less likely to be contrastive. This difference in function is part of a wider phenomenon involving first-position constituents. Consider the first-position adverbials in Middle English (25), particularly the one in bold:

(25) a. In þis tyme was founde a gret summe of mony at Rome in a
         rotin wal (. . .).
     b. **With þis mony** þe pope ded renewe þe Capitol and þe
         Castell Aungel. [CMCAPCHR 3763–8]

Although these word orders are not impossible in PDE (*At that time was discovered a large sum of money in a rotten wall; With this money the Pope renovated the Capitol*), they would not be the first choice. The order in (25a), with its subject-verb inversion, although marked, is still used in PDE for long, new, information-rich subjects just like the one in (25a). However, (25b) feels somewhat odd; PDE tends to encode old information like *this money* as a subject rather than as an adverbial, which might mean using a passive, as in (26):

(26) This money was used by the pope to renew the Capitol.

Such shifts in pragmatic meanings and information structure are reflected in falling frequencies of first constituent adverbials containing old information like *with þis mony* in (25b) in the course of ME and eMod, so it makes sense to consider changes in pragmatics when studying word order.

1.4.3 Discourse markers

Another word order phenomenon that conveys a range of pragmatic meanings in PDE is **Left-Dislocation** as in (27), from a corpus of American English telephone conversations. The Left-Dislocated constituent is in bold:

(27) A: Both my husband and I work, and our children are sixth,
           fourth, and third grade. And the school years are wonderful,
           they're just wonderful.
      B: Uh-huh.
      A: **The kids**, they are real people, and they are interesting, and
      B: \<Laughter\>
      A: They, they have all their own activities and, um, I think as
           parents we really enjoy them in, in our personal situation. . .
           Our children have not yet decided to rebel \<laughter\>. (The
           Switchboard Corpus, 4123_1595_1530; TOPIC#349; DATE:
           9203109)

The NP *The kids* in (27) is outside the clause proper, and the subject
of that clause, *they*, refers back to these *kids*. (27) has the same lexical
meaning as its unmarked alternative *The kids are real* people, so what is
the contribution of Left-Dislocation? Using the more elaborate Left-
Dislocation in (27) helps to signal to the hearer that the conversation
switches from the school years to the kids – the speaker introduces a new
topic. This function is part of the toolbox that regulates interactions in
conversation. Other such 'procedural' functions are giving a speaker an
opportunity to talk (turn-taking, holding the floor); showing the speaker
that the hearer is still listening; expressing a certain attitude towards the
message, or indicating to the hearer how the message should be interpreted. Many of these functions can be performed non-verbally, but
also by little words like *well, so, oh, you know* or longer phrases like *D'you
know what I mean?* – long a source of frustration in linguistic descriptions,
and hence ignored as if consigned to 'a lunacy ward . . . where mindless
morphs stare vacantly with no purpose other than to be where they are'
(Bolinger 1977: ix). The study of such items opened up a new field in
historical pragmatics, that of the **discourse markers**.

   Note that Left-Dislocation as a ploy to introduce a new topic is
optional – it is one of a range of options a speaker has at his or her
disposal. This makes the historical study of discourse markers quite
challenging. If a particular lexical item, construction or word order
pattern has some discourse function at an earlier stage of the language,
the optionality of discourse markers means that any positive evidence
for the hypothesised function is likely to be offset by robust negative
evidence: contexts where you might have expected the item to show
up, and it does not. Making a persuasive case is difficult even for PDE,
a living language; Gregory and Michaelis (2001), to name an example,
hypothesised that Left-Dislocation in the Switchboard Corpus signals
that a new referent, or an earlier referent that was mentioned so long

ago in the discourse that it first needed to be 'reactivated', is going to be the topic of the next unit. This hypothesis needed evidence that the referent introduced by Left-Dislocation would be the topic in that unit, and the best evidence is 'topic persistence', i.e. that the new referent is taken up in the discourse and talked about. But there were many Left-Dislocations whose referent never made it as a persistent topic in the following discourse. The problem was, as they explained, that topics of conversations are a matter for negotiation between the speakers; a speaker may want to introduce a new topic by Left-Dislocation, but the topic will only persist if the other speaker cooperates and agrees to talk about it.

1.4.4 Discourse routines become syntax

Word orders that may once have been just one option out of a toolbox of many may become so strongly associated with a particular function that it is no longer optional. Direct questions and relative clauses, for instance, are expressed in English by certain fixed word order patterns, and clearly part of syntax rather than pragmatics. The string of words in (28) contains four entities – the young men, the lion cub, Harrods and the sixties – which can all be questioned by a process of fronting.

(28) The young men could buy a lion cub in Harrods in the sixties.

The direct questions formed from (28) are given in (29); the dashes indicate the position of the questioned elements in the corresponding **declarative** in (28):

(29) a. Who _____ could buy a lion cub in Harrods in the sixties?
      b. What could the young men buy _____ in Harrods in the sixties?
      c. Where could the young men buy a lion cub _____ in the sixties?
      d. When could the young men buy a lion cub in Harrods _____?

Question formation in PDE apparently follows these steps:

(i)   replace the entity-to-be-questioned by the appropriate question word (e.g. *who, what, where, when*)
(ii)   move it to the front of the clause
(iii) move the finite auxiliary to the second position of the clause

Question formation in English is an example of syntax as a system of automatic routines. The three steps can be applied to any declarative sentence, however long and complex, to turn it into a question

Table 1.3 Question formation, step (i)

	Subject	AUX	Verb	Object	Place adverbial	Time adverbial
a.	who	could	buy	a lion cub	in Harrods	in the sixties
b.	the young men	could	buy	what	in Harrods	in the sixties
c.	the young men	could	buy	a lion cub	where	in the sixties
d.	the young men	could	buy	a lion cub	in Harrods	when

Table 1.4 Question formation, step (ii)

	First position	Subject	AUX	Verb	Object	Place adverbial	Time adverbial
a.	who	gap	could	buy	a lion cub	in Harrods	in the sixties
b.	what	the young men	could	buy	gap	in Harrods	in the sixties
c.	where	the young men	could	buy	a lion cub	gap	in the sixties
d.	when	the young men	could	buy	a lion cub	in Harrods	gap

Table 1.5 Question formation, step (iii)

	First position	AUX_2	Subject	AUX_1	Verb	Object	Place adverbial	Time adverbial
a.	who	could	gap	gap	buy	a lion cub	in Harrods	in the sixties
b.	what	could	the young men	gap	buy	gap	in Harrods	in the sixties
c.	where	could	the young men	gap	buy	a lion cub	gap	in the sixties
d.	when	could	the young men	gap	buy	a lion cub	in Harrods	gap

– even if the entity-to-be-questioned belongs to another clause, a subclause that is embedded in the main clause. Here is a question from the game *Trivial Pursuit: Millennium Edition* (Parker). The answer in (30b) can be expanded to represent the corresponding declarative sentence in (30c):

(30) a. Question: What was the Mohole project intended to drill a hole through?

    b. Answer: The earth's crust.
    c. The Mohole project was intended to drill a hole through the earth's crust.

Note that the original position of the questioned constituent is the NP inside the PP *through [something]* that belongs to the embedded clause *to drill a hole through [something]*. Although it has been fronted to the first position of the main clause, the hearer or reader is still able to reconstruct its meaning in relation to the rest of the clause, i.e. recognise its original position.

1.5 Interpreting historical data

1.5.1 Introduction

With the advent of corpora of digitised texts, research into the syntax of an earlier stage of a language no longer means trawling through pages and pages of manuscripts (or, more likely, of edited texts), in search of that one construction. Data can be gathered much more efficiently. But the problems and pitfalls of how to interpret such historical findings are the same, the most important one being: was there was a historical change at all?

1.5.2 Sufficient data

The first consideration is whether there is enough text to make sure the construction that is being investigated has had a chance to surface. The size of the building blocks of the levels of linguistic description of Table 1.1 – phonology, morphology, syntax – become progressively larger (phonemes, morphemes, words) and this means that we need progressively more data to deduce the system of how the building blocks combine. The historic records of many early Germanic languages are sparse before the ninth century: short runic inscriptions on stone monuments, metal amulets and bone artefacts, and isolated names in Latin histories or annals. This may be just about enough to say something about phonology, and perhaps a very little about morphology. It is often not enough to say anything about syntax.

    When texts do become available, they tend to be interlinear glosses of Latin texts (a Germanic translation scrawled under or over each Latin word), where the word orders we find will tend to say something about the syntax of Latin rather than the syntax of early Germanic. The fourth-century Gothic Bible is a proper translation, not a gloss, but still follows the original Greek word order so closely that we cannot be certain that its syntax is Gothic. This is one of the reasons why Old English is so important: it is an early Germanic language of which we have a sizeable corpus of texts, not only containing translations but also authentic Old English, and the text corpus is large enough to allow syntactic investigations. But we still need to be aware what the context of the data is, especially in the case of crucial examples. This was one advantage of the old-style method of data-gathering in the pre-computer era: you were forced to see the example in context.

1.5.3 Genre and register

Poetry tends to have its own rules and its word order is constrained by all sorts of considerations of metre, alliteration and rhyme, which is why investigations into historical syntax usually restrict themselves to prose. But Old English prose may have rhythmic requirements of its own; (31) appears in Ælfric's *Life of St Martin*, written in Ælfric's rhythmic prose:

(31)   7   geseah þær   standan ane atelice sceade
        and saw   there   stand   a   terrible shade
        'and saw a terrible ghost standing there' <ÆLS (Martin) 356>

Punctuation marks in the manuscript demarcate verse lines, and this has been followed in the printing of Skeat's edition. Although not without precedent, the word order of (31), with the subject *ane atelice sceade* 'a horrible ghost' 'extraposed' to the end of the clause, is unusual. A more canonical word order would be (32):

(32)   7   geseah þær ane atelice sceade standan
        and saw there   a   terrible shade stand

But this disturbs the metre, and the alliterative pattern – *geseah standan sceade*.
    A similar case in (33):

(33)   7 an þing ic eow secge gyt to gewisse, þæt witod sceal **geweorðan**
        and one thing I you say yet as certainty that surely will become

        godspel **gecyþed** geond ealle woruld ær worulde ende. . .
        gospel proclaimed throughout all world before world's end

        'and one thing I will tell you as a certainty, that the gospel surely will be proclaimed throughout the entire world before the world's end' <WHom 2, 57>

The NP *godspel* 'gospel' is in an even more unusual position than *ane atelice sceade* 'a horrible ghost' in (31). More canonical orders would keep the two verbs *gecyped* and *geweorðan* together:

(34) þæt witod sceal godspel gecyþed geweorðan

Here, too, the word order may well be a conscious choice. Wulfstan, a contemporary of Ælfric, writes sermons that are meant to be read from the pulpit, and uses a wealth of rhetorical devices, including alliteration (*gewisse witod geweorðan*) and rhythm; and *geweorðan* may well be fronted here for those reasons, in spite of the fact that Old English syntax is known to front finite verbs, not non-finite verbs.

The first diachronic collection of texts that could be searched electronically, and which was later expanded and further enriched with morphological tagging and syntactic parsing, was the Helsinki Corpus. Although care was taken to include texts from a range of different genres, the Corpus is largely based on editions, and hence depended on which texts were published; which in turn depended on which texts had been selected for editing and which had not; as the selection is likely to have been based on cultural and literary rather than linguistic considerations, some genres are under-represented. It has been estimated that only 1 per cent of extant texts of medieval instructional and scientific writing (in the broadest possible sense) has been edited and published.

Going back to the editions that the computerised corpora are based on can be helpful, although even then problems remain, particularly with many earlier editions, where editors have tacitly expanded abbreviations and even 'restored' texts where portions were missing, or where the syntax did not match the editor's ideas of what Old English syntax should be. Many such editorial interventions have made it into the tagged and parsed computerised corpora.

1.5.4 Spoken versus written texts

A caveat that is related to the register and genre problem is the fact that written conventions may develop that differ from the spoken language. Consider Figure 1.1, based on data from computerised corpora. The graph shows Left-Dislocated NPs, i.e. the construction in (27) that we discussed above. (27) is found in a corpus of conversations, and was argued to have a special function in regulating the interaction between hearer and speaker. As time goes on, and higher proportions of the population become literate, with a corresponding rise in the

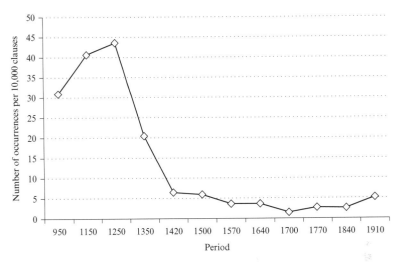

Figure 1.1 Left-Dislocated NPs in the Helsinki Corpora (Los and Komen 2012: 896)

availability of books, both handwritten and printed (Caxton set up his printing press in Westminster in 1476), the spoken and the written language start to grow apart. Many written texts were at first meant to be read aloud, to an audience; but they are increasingly written for readers rather than hearers, and this has an impact on particularly those features that are about regulating speaker/hearer interaction. Some of the decline in Left-Dislocated NPs in Figure 1.1 may be due to the fact that stylistic conventions for written texts discourage the use of Left-Dislocation, and that it survives in spoken language only. The decline in frequency could then be due to this phenomenon, rather than to a syntactic change.

A similar problem is posed by ME instances such as (35):

(35) This prison caused me nat for to crye, (Chaucer, *Canterbury Tales*, Knight's Tale l.1095; Robinson 1957)
This prison did not cause me to cry out
'It was not this prison that caused me to cry out'

Note that the PDE translation has to use a cleft here, where the original could apparently convey the focus now encoded by the cleft without having to resort to a special construction. Clefts show a rise in the history of English (see Figure 1.2).

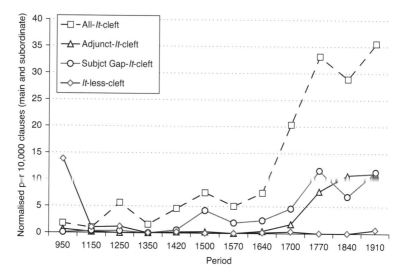

Figure 1.2 *It*-clefts in the Helsinki Corpora (Los and Komen 2012: 888)

Again, we have to ask ourselves whether the rise we see in clefts – particularly the stressed-focus *it*-cleft used in the PDE translation of (35) – is caused by new conventions for written texts that are different from the spoken language, or is a genuine language change. It is usually a good idea to investigate a PDE corpus, or consult Biber et al. (1999).

1.5.5 Dating texts

Texts come to us in physical manuscripts, sometimes in a number of different copies, sometimes in only a single copy. In many cases, the copies are much later than the estimated date of composition, and this information is not always easy to come by, especially when working with the computerised corpora. A copy made in the ME period (*c.* 1100–1500) of a text composed in the Old English period (*c.* 700–1100) may be influenced by the copyist's own language. Similar considerations hold for dialects. It is important to remember that the texts we have do not represent an unbroken record of a single variety of English. The Old English texts are mainly in the West-Saxon dialect, while much of the Early Middle English texts are from other areas, and this needs to be taken into account, particularly when we find frequency differences between Old English and Middle English.

1.5.6 *The problem of negative evidence*

One of the advantages of synchronic research is that researchers have access to native speakers' intuitions about what is grammatical or acceptable in their language. Diachronic researchers cannot rely on native speaker intuitions to help them out but have to work with the texts that happened to have survived. The data are 'usage-based', which has obvious advantages, but also poses some challenges. One is the problem of negative evidence. If a certain construction is not found in the data, does this mean that the construction was impossible, and hence that the data are evidence of a syntactic change, or is this absence in earlier texts an artefact of corpus size, genre, or usage?

The Old English text corpus is large enough to allow at times categorical statements of the type *only direct objects can passivise* (cf. Russom 1982) or *nothing can intervene between 'to' and its infinitive* (cf. Fischer 1996). These two phenomena are further confirmed by evidence from related, living languages. On balance, the probability is that the fact that indirect objects subsequently allow passivisation, as in (18c), here repeated as (36), or that *to*-infinitives may be split, as in (37), represents genuine examples of syntactic change.

(36)   He **was given** a standing ovation/a clean bill of health/a six-month community order.

(37)   To **boldly** go where no man has gone before.

But structures that are attested in PDE but not in Old English or Middle English texts cannot always be argued to be evidence of a change. Mittwoch (1990:107–8) discusses the difficulties of assessing the status of negation in certain infinitival constructions. Native speakers of PDE may construct 'laboratory' examples like (38):

(38)   John sees Mary not leave.

Mittwoch says that such examples are at best 'borderline, denizens of some limbo region between the grammatical and the deviant' and adds that, in five years of looking out for real-life utterances of such sentences, she never encountered a single example, 'not even one meant ironically' (Mittwoch 1990: 108). The reason is that infinitival constructions of the type of (38) in the complement of perception verbs, like *see* or *hear*, always express events, and can be expected to be affirmative rather than negative for that reason: *Mary leaving* is an event, whereas *Mary not leaving* is not an event. This means that we should not expect to find (38) in a usage-corpus, whether it is a corpus of PDE or a corpus of earlier English, even though it is grammatical. If a structure is not attested in a historical corpus, it is sometimes worthwhile to check a PDE corpus first, before claiming that the structure was apparently impossible at an earlier stage of the language.

1.6 Summary of points

- The main levels of linguistic description are phonology, morphology and syntax. Other levels are pragmatics and information structure, including discourse structure.
- As historical stages of a single language represent distinct 'lects' (dialects, varieties) in their own right, the same spread of variation that is found in synchronic languages is found in the diachrony of a single language.
- English is particularly interesting for the study of historical syntax because of the size and time-depth of surviving historical texts, and the range of genres they represent.
- Prose texts are particularly suitable for investigations into historical syntax because considerations of rhyme or metre do not play as large a role as they do in poetry.
- The advent of computerised corpora of historical texts has revolutionised research into syntactic change, but also has problems of its own. It is generally a good idea to check any data that are 'outliers', i.e. constructions or word orders that are very rare.
- There are three main areas of syntactic variation:
  - whether functional information is expressed in the syntax or in the morphology;
  - how semantic roles are expressed;
  - word order variation.

Exercises

1. SYNTACTIC OPERATIONS: RECONSTRUCTING DECLARATIVES. We had one example-question from the game *Trivial Pursuit: Millennium Edition* (Parker) in (30). More are given in (a–f) below. Make up possible answers and reconstruct the declarative counterparts of these questions as was done for (30a) in (30b).

   a. What did the Buddha predict a house with a light would never attract?
   b. What was the press adapted by Gutenberg for printing originally made to squeeze?

c. What did Hong Kong have 26 of when there were only 25 European families living there?

d. What did Percival Lowell predict the existence of long before anyone ever saw it?

e. What invention did Lord Kitchener dismiss as 'Too vulnerable to artillery'?

f. What were first added to watches in 1670?

For the correct answers turn to page 266.

2. SYNTACTIC OPERATIONS: CONSTRUCTING RELATIVE CLAUSES. A declarative clause like (28), here repeated as (i), 'generated' the questions in (29a–c), here given as (ii):

(i) The young men had bought a lion cub in Harrods in the sixties.

The dashes indicate the position of the questioned elements in the corresponding declarative in (i):

(ii) a. Who _____ had bought a lion cub in Harrods in the sixties?
   b. What had the young men bought _____ in Harrods in the sixties?
   c. Where had the young men bought a lion cub _____ in the sixties?

a. Now use these questions to create the relative clauses that complete the sentences below. The first one has been done for you, with _____ indicating a gap, and the brackets indicating that the relative clause (REL) is part of an NP:

   i [_{NP}The young men [_{REL}who _____ had bought a lion cub in Harrods in the sixties]] were called Anthony and John.
   ii .... was called Christian.
   iii .... was called Harrods.

b. What are the steps needed to form these relative clauses from the declarative clause of (i)?

3. SYNTACTIC TERMINOLOGY AND SYNTACTIC ANALYSIS. The text about the lion Christian in (4), although an improvement on (3), still lacks some features that we expect from narratives, such as an orientation-part that gives the reader/hearer some background of the protagonists and the situation, and, particularly, a clear sense of a *central reportable event* (Labov 1972) – the reason the story is worth telling in the first place.

a. Go to <www.youtube.com> and find the video of the reunion by typing in *Christian the lion reunion*. With the video in mind, decide what its central reportable event could be and revise and expand (4) accordingly, to make it into a proper story.

b. Analyse the changes you have made to the original text. Which of your changes are purely lexical (i.e. substituting one word for another) and which are changes in the syntax? Describe the syntactic changes. Be as specific as possible. Consider for instance the following points:

i. The original text in (4) uses few adjectives (examples are *adult, female, national*). Did you add any?

ii. Did you add any sentences? Do they contain any subclauses, and if yes, what is their syntactic function (subject, object, adverbial, relative clause)?

4. GRAMMATICALISATION.

a. Check the etymologies of PDE *they, the, may, to, and*, and *more* in the Oxford English Dictionary Online (the *OED*). Could they be cases of grammaticalisation?

b. Consider the case of the PDE verb *make* in Table 1.1. Would you classify it as an auxiliary or a lexical verb? Why?

5. GRAMMATICALISATION AND LOSS OF CASE. Although Gothic is a cousin rather than an ancestor of English, it is the earliest Germanic language to survive in a sizeable body of texts (fourth century AD). Consider the Gothic sentence given in (i), and its literal translation ('gloss'). DAT in the gloss stands for dative case.

(i) sa afar mis gagganda swinþōza mis ist (Gothic Bible, Mt 3.11; Streitberg 1965)
he after me coming mightier me-DAT is

This is an Old English translation of the same passage:

(ii) Se þe æfter me towerd ys he ys strengra þonne ic that-one who after me coming is he is stronger than I
<Mt (WSCp) 3.11>

a. Construct a PDE translation of (i) on the basis of the glosses of both (i) and (ii).

b. How did you translate Gothic *mis* in your PDE translation, and how is it translated in Old English?

c. The Gothic texts we have are very literal translations of the Greek Bible, so we cannot be certain whether (i) reflects 'genuine'

Gothic syntax. Gothic is a cousin rather than an ancestor of Old English. For the purpose of this exercise, we will ignore these issues and assume that Gothic represents a shared ancestor, so that (i), (ii) and your PDE translation represent a chain of changes. Describe these changes. Which of the examples of Table 1.1 does this change resemble?

6. CORPUSLINGUISTICS. Consider the following problem:
   There is a set of nouns in PDE that have preserved 'irregular' plurals marked by vowel change rather than -s:

   man – men
   foot – feet
   louse – lice
   mouse – mice
   goose – geese

   This group was much larger at earlier periods. Irregular forms usually survive because they are frequent. But an investigation of the Helsinki Corpus of Old English texts does not bear this out: *geese, lice* and *mice*, in particular, are not frequent at all, far less frequent than another pair that has nevertheless not made it into PDE:

   boc – bec
   'book' – 'books'

   Do these corpus findings mean we have to revise the claim that frequency is the most important factor for survival? Why/why not? You can check what types of text make up the Helsinki Corpus in the *Corpus Resource Database* <http://www.helsinki.fi/varieng/CoRD/>.

7. IMPERSONAL VERBS. Consider this Old English sentence with *licode* 'liked'(third singular):

   (i) he licode   þam ælmightigan Gode <GD 1 (C) 10.85.35>

   (a) *He* 'he' is a nominative, *þam ælmightigan Gode* 'the almighty God' is a dative. Look *like* up in the *Oxford English Dictionary* and suggest a PDE translation for this sentence.

Further reading

For surveys of the world's languages, see <http://www.ethnologue.com> (Lewis 2009), Ladefoged and Maddieson (1996). For a discussion about the linguistic levels in Table 1.1, see Stankiewicz (1991). A solid general work on historical linguistics is Hock ([1986] 1991); a textbook is Campbell (2004). The annual surveys of the *Year's Work in English Studies* (OUP) include a chapter on diachronic work in the field of English morphology and syntax. See also *Oxford Bibliographies Online* (OUP) <http://www.oxfordbibliographies.com/>. Textbooks on the history of English are Baugh and Cable (2002), Fennel (2001), van Gelderen (2006), Horobin (2010), and McIntyre (2009). A textbook on diachronic English linguistics is Görlach (1997) and Moessner (2003). For Middle English, see Burnley (1983). For Old English syntax, a valuable resource is Mitchell (1985). For a history of English syntax, see Traugott (1972) and the syntax sections in the various volumes of *CHEL* and its single-volume spin-off (Hogg and Denison 2006). Denison (1993) is an excellent sourcebook and includes a section on using secondary sources, with important caveats. For the syntax of early English, see Fischer et al. (2000). Even 'chunked' phrases like *ladies and gentlemen* and *black and white* (from Dickens' speech) apparently follow a system: see Cooper and Ross (1975) and Pinker and Birdsong (1979). For a discussion of pragmatic functions see Halliday (1973). For impersonal verbs in English, see again Denison (1993) and his references. For the dark side of lion-and-human relationships, see Attenborough (2011: 214–15).

2 Nominal categories: The loss of nominal morphology

2.1 Introduction

We noted in Chapter 1 that languages, or historical stages of a single language, differ in their syntax along three main parameters: (1) whether grammatical information is expressed by bound morphemes (in the morphology) or by free words (in the syntax); (2) how semantic roles are expressed; and (3) their word order. Both the present chapter and Chapters 3 and 4 focus on the first parameter: the relationship between morphology, particularly inflectional morphology, and syntax. The present chapter focuses on nominal morphology, i.e. morphology that appears on nouns, while Chapters 3 and 4 focus on verbal morphology. In both the nominal and verbal domain, the story of English is a story of losses in the morphology, and gains in the syntax, as items are recruited from the lexicon to express grammatical information.

Nouns prototypically refer to entities. Important categories for nouns are **number** (how many entities are there), **gender**, and **case** (what is the relationship between the entity and other elements in the clause). Number and gender, and **person**, are called *phi*-features. *Phi*-features are involved in agreement relations, as in subject-verb agreement (*I walk-ø* versus *he walk-s*), and in morphologically-rich languages, like Old English, the *phi*-features number and gender are visible on all the elements of the nominal group: determiners, adjectives and the noun itself. Person is visible in pronouns and on the verb, in subject-verb agreement. The remaining nominal category is case. In a case language, every noun is marked for case, and that case will be visible on the other elements inside the noun phrase (NP) as well. Case systems probably arise as a way to mark semantic roles like AGENT, PATIENT, RECIPIENT, EXPERIENCER, which interact with syntactic functions like subject, direct object and indirect object in interesting ways.

After case was lost, the relationship of the NP to the rest of the clause came to be signalled by word order (in the case of subject and object)

31

and by grammaticalised lexical items (prepositions), i.e. change in two of the three parameters of syntactic variation

2.2 Derivation and inflection

Morphology broadly divides into two subtypes: **derivational** and **inflectional** morphology. Derivational morphology, like -*ship* and -*hood*, builds new lexical items, warranting a separate entry in a dictionary. We would expect *friend* and *friendship*, and *child* and *childhood*, to be listed as separate lemmas. Unlike derivational morphology, inflectional morphology does not create new lemmas. The -*s* of the third person singular of a verb in the present tense in PDE (*he walk-s*), or the -*ed* of the past tense (*he walked*), are subsumed in the lemma of the verb *walk*. Unlike derivation, inflection attaches to an entire category (all lexical verbs in PDE have -*s* in the third person singular of a verb in the present tense) rather than to a subset of a category. Derivational -*ity*, for instance, only attaches to stems with a French or Latin origin (*familiar-ity*) and derivational -*ness* only attaches to native stems (*red-ness, heavi-ness*). Although the derivational affixes -*hood* and -*ship* both construct abstract nouns from other nouns (*child-hood, friend-ship*), they each have their own set of stems, so that we do not get *friendhood* or *childship*. Because there usually is more than one affix to do a particular job — create abstract nouns from concrete nouns, or nouns from adjectives, or adjectives from nouns — there tends to be some competition between derivational suffixes, which is why the sets of stems that go with any particular affix may wax or wane over time. Building a noun from the adjective *glad* is achieved by adding -*ness* in PDE, but by adding -*ship* in Old English. Finally, derivation, unlike inflection, may change the category of the stem: derivational -*ness* and -*ity* create nouns from adjectives, but inflectional -*s* attaching to a verb *walk* will result in another verb *walks*, and the plural -*s* after a noun *boy* will result in another noun *boys*.

2.3 Inherent versus contextual inflection

Within inflectional morphology, a distinction can be made between **inherent** and **contextual** inflection.

Inherent inflection depends on information from the socio-physical world, i.e. the world of physical and social relationships, rather than on information from syntax or morphology; the plural -*s* in *boys* depends on the number of boys that are involved: one, or more. Another example of inherent inflection is comparative and superlative marking on adjectives and adverbs (*great – greater – greatest*).

Contextual inflection requires syntax-internal information: the *-s* of the third person singular in *walks* depends on the person and number of the subject of *walk*: *the boy walk-s*, but *the boys walk-ø*. Other examples are case-endings on nouns: nouns can only receive the correct case if we know their syntactic function (subject, direct object, indirect object, etc.). This is contextual inflection.

Inherent inflection tends to be preserved in PDE, but was subject to extensive streamlining and levelling. Contextual inflection, case, was lost on nouns, and only preserved on pronouns, although in a simplified way as a basic opposition between subject forms and other forms.

2.4 Number

The expression of the morphological category 'number' in PDE is a straightforward affair: the distinction between singular and plural nouns is signalled by an *-s* ending on the plural:

(1)   book (sg) – books (pl)

Some nouns have special plural forms, either because they represent relic plural forms of an earlier stage, like *mouse/mice, man/men, foot/feet*, and the like, or because both the singular and the plural forms of a noun have been borrowed from another language as a package, like *criterion – criteria*. The *-s* plural is the **productive** plural in PDE: new nouns that enter the language as a rule have plural forms in *-s*.

The productive -s plural is the outcome of centuries of streamlining. Proto-Germanic had inherited a system of noun classes or declensions from its parent Proto-Indo-European. Each of these noun classes – and there were about a dozen – had their own sets of endings, not only for number (the singular/plural distinction) but also for the six cases. Table 2.1 presents some sample Proto-Germanic paradigms (from Ringe 2006: 280); all are reconstructed forms, with forms where the reconstruction is uncertain indicated with a question mark.

The classes are named after the vowels or consonants before the case endings, so we have a-stems, ja-stems, i-stems, o-stems, etc. These names are usually retained in Old English grammars, although the vowel or consonant that gave rise to them have often disappeared by the time we reach Old English. Table 2.2 shows these same declensions for Old English.

The instrumental has disappeared as a recognisably separate case as it merged with the dative in Old English, most endings are reduced, and the nominative and accusative endings are no longer distinct. The source of the singular/plural vowel alternations in *mouse/mice* (and *man/men, foot/*

Table 2.1 Sample Proto-Germanic paradigms

	day (m.)	army (m.)	guest (m.)	name (n.)	gift (f.)
singular					
Nom.	dagaz	harjaz	gastiz	namō̄	gebō
Acc.	dagą	harją	gastį	namō̄	gebǫ
Gen.	dagas	harjas	gastīz	naminiz	gebōz
Dat.	dagai	harjai	gastī	namini	gebōi (?)
Inst.	dagō	harjō	gastī	?	gebō
plural					
Nom.	dagō̄z	harjō̄z	gastīz	namnō	gebōz
Acc.	daganz	harjanz	gastinz	namnō	gebǒz
Gen.	dagǭ	harjǭ	gastijǭ	namnǭ	gebǭ
Dat.	dagamaz	harjamaz	gastimaz	namnamaz?	gebōmaz
Inst.	dagamiz	harjamiz	gastimiz	namnamiz?	gebōmiz

Table 2.2 Sample Old English paradigms

	day (m.)	mouse (f.)	guest (m.)	name (n.)	gift (f.)
singular					
Nom.	dæg	mūs	giest	nama	giefu
Acc.	dæg	mūs	giest	nama	giefe
Gen.	dæges	mȳs	giestes	naman	giefe
Dat.	dæge	mȳs	gieste	naman	giefe
plural					
Nom.	dagas	mȳs	giestas	naman	giefa
Acc.	dagas	mȳs	giestas	naman	giefa
Gen.	daga	mūsa	giesta	namena	giefa, giefena
Dat.	dagum	mūsum	giestum	namum	giefum

feet etc.) now becomes clear: backs vowels followed by an -i- in the next syllable have become front vowels (*umlaut*). This has changed the vowel -a- to -e- in *gastiz* throughout the entire paradigm, as all its endings contained -i- (as it is an -i-stem), but has affected *mūs* only in the dative singular and nominative plural, as it was those forms that had endings containing an -i-. As nominative and accusative fell together in Old English, the accusative plural of *mūs* also became *mȳs*. The vowel alternation is not yet a plural marker in Old English, as the dative singular was also *mȳs*; but with the loss of case in Early Middle English, the *mūs – mīs* (after unrounding of ȳ to ī) forms are associated with the singular/plural contrast. The orthography of PDE *mouse/mice* is the result of French-inspired re-spellings in Middle English, while the PDE pronunciation is due to the Great Vowel Shift, which diphthongised long u and i.

In some languages, the category number is not restricted to the opposition singular versus plural but may include a dual (two, a pair) or a paucal (a few). Old English has remnants of a dual, with special dual pronouns for first and second person plural: *wit* 'we two', *git* 'you two'. This third category of number marking was lost.

How important is number? There are many languages that only mark plurals on nouns if it is relevant to the communication and cannot be deduced from the context. The selection of a plural marker in those languages is not automatic but resembles the selection process of a lexical item. Some languages use different verbs for a single individual going somewhere and for a group going somewhere; for a single person sitting and a group of people sitting together; for a single person holding forth, and a group conversing; or for a single killing, and a massacre (Mithun 1989: 268). In other languages, like English, number is a syntactic category, which means there is no choice: every countable noun needs to be marked for number, and only mass nouns (*milk, paper*) are exempt. The pay-off is that it is an automatic routine (syntax) rather than a lexical choice that needs some extra effort to construct, but the downside is that every noun will have to have it, whether it is relevant to the situational context or not.

In the case of English plurals, what happened was not so much wholesale loss of an entire category but further streamlining, an extension of a process of simplifying endings that was taking place already in Old English. In some cases the streamlining process 'restored' a plural ending where it had previously been lost. Neuter nouns took -*u* as a plural ending for the nominative and accusative, as in *scip* 'ship'– *scipu* 'ships'. Neuter nouns that had long stems – a long vowel, or a short vowel followed by two consonants – had lost that final -*u* in a natural process of phonological erosion.

(2) Prehistoric OE: OE: ME:
     hūs 'house' – pl. *hūsu*   *hūs* 'house' – pl. *hūs*   *house* – pl. *houses*
     word 'word' – pl. *wordu*   *word* 'word' – pl. *word*   *word* – pl. *words*
     þing 'thing'- pl. *þingu*   *þing* 'thing'- pl. *þing*   *thing* – pl. *things*

The streamlining process resulted in these words being marked for plural again.

Streamlining is resisted by items that are very frequent, like the umlauted plurals *mouse/mice, man/men, foot/feet*. An interesting case is the word *cow*, Old English *cū*:

(3) singular   plural
     cū   OE: *cȳ* (umlaut, OE)

| cow | ME: *kine* (OE *cȳ* + productive plural suffix -*n*) |
| cow | eModE: *cows* (*cow* + productive plural suffix -*s*) |

Cow was repeatedly subject to streamlining: first the umlauted plural form acquired the suffix -(*e*)*n*; this ending derives from the -*an* plurals of the -n stems like *nama* in Table 2.2, and became quite productive in Middle English, extending to nouns of other declensions. Note that *kine* contained two plural markings: umlaut, and -n. Other examples of double plurals are *children* (*cild*+ru+n) and *brethren* (*brother*+umlaut+*en*). In turn, *kine* was outcompeted by *cow*+s.

The competition between (ø)n and (ø)s as the productive plural ending was ultimately 'won' by -(*e*)*s*. Such an outcome, with only a single productive plural suffix, is not inevitable. A similar state of affairs in Middle Dutch, involving the same -*en* and -*s* endings from the same origins, reached some sort of equilibrium in Modern Dutch. Dutch favours trochaic plurals (stressed syllable–unstressed syllable), and this is where, it has been claimed, the two endings have each found their domain: -*en* attaches to single-syllable nouns, adding an extra syllable, and turning them into trochees, the 'ideal' plurals: *paal* 'pole' becomes *palen* 'poles'. The -*s* ending, very conveniently, does not add an extra syllable, keeping 'ideal' plurals 'ideal': *foto* 'photo' becomes *foto's* 'photos' (Booij 2002).

2.5 Gender

PDE has **natural gender**. As a rule, *his* and *her* refer to animate entities, especially to human entities, whereas all inanimate entities are *it*. How animate but non-human entities are referred to varies; a sparrow cadging crumbs from picknickers is more likely to be referred to as *it*, whereas a sparrow feeding her nestlings in *Spring Watch* will probably be referred to by the commentators as *she*. Whatever the system that is followed, the rules for referring back to entities in the discourse depend on features that can be deduced from the nature of these entities themselves: *he*/*his*/*him* for single male entities, *she*/*her*/*her* for single female entities, and the rest is either *it*/*its*/*it* for the singular or *they*/*their*/*them* for the plural. Old English had **grammatical gender**, masculine, feminine and neuter; a sparrow in Old English is referred to as a *he* (OE *hē*), not because it is a male individual but because *spearwa* is a masculine noun in Old English. Pronouns referring back to nouns usually show grammatical gender, but with exceptions for human beings: a child (OE *cild*, neuter) may be referred to as *it* (OE *hit*), but the neuter noun *wīf* 'woman' and the masculine noun *wifmann* 'woman' will tend to be referred to as *she* (OE *hēo*).

In compound nouns, like *handgeweorc* 'handiwork', it is always the final element that determines the gender of the compound; *hand* is feminine, but *geweorc* was neuter, so the compound is neuter, too; this is not an Old English quirk but a more general phenomenon, known in morphology as the Right-Hand Head Rule: the item on the right in compounds is the head. This makes sense if you think of PDE compounds like *postman* and *greenhouse*: a postman is a kind of man, a greenhouse is a kind of house.

The Right-Hand Head Rule also holds for derivational morphology: *cild* 'child' is neuter, but *cildhad* 'childhood' is masculine. As derivational morphology is often the second element of a noun + noun compound that was lost from the language as a free form but survives in compounds, the fact that the derivational element determines the gender of the word is not surprising. The suffix *-had* derives from a masculine noun with the meaning 'manner, quality', and is found as a free form *haidus* in Gothic. The origin of other suffixes are lost in time, but have probably similar histories, as they also show the Right-Hand Head Rule: Old English *ung/-ing* builds nouns from verbs (*endung* 'ending' from *endian* 'end', *feding* 'feeding' from *fedan* 'feed'), and these nouns are always feminine.

The loss of gender is first attested in the north; the interlinear gloss added to the Lindisfarne Gospels in the tenth century shows a number of misassignments – it assigns masculine gender to the feminine noun *endung* 'ending', for instance. Grammatical gender is completely gone from the language by the middle of the fourteenth century, when it is lost from Kentish, the dialect that kept it longest (Mustanoja 1960: 43–54).

2.6 Case

The loss of inflectional morphology on nouns also meant the loss of case. Case is usually expressed by an ending on the head noun of an NP. There are several cases, and their use depends on the syntactic function of that NP in the clause. Every NP has to have case in case-languages, which means that every possible NP function has to be catered for. This does not mean that syntactic functions in case-languages are always unambiguously marked by case-endings; case is just one of the resources available. Word order and pragmatic context are other resources, also in case-languages. But the loss of case can nevertheless be expected to have an impact on how syntactic functions are marked.

Table 2.3 presents the bare bones of the Old English case system using PDE examples, even though PDE is not a case-language. It is just that using PDE words makes it easier to see how a case-system works.

Table 2.3 Cases and syntactic functions in Old English

Case	Used for	NP in brackets; head-noun underlined
Nom.	Subject	[<u>Beowulf</u>]$_{NP}$ was Ecgtheow's son
	Subject complement	Beowulf was [Ecgtheow's <u>son</u>]$_{NP}$
Gen.	Possession	Beowulf was [<u>Ecgtheow's</u>]$_{NP}$ son
	Complement of certain prepositions, like *during*	During [the <u>night</u>]$_{NP}$, Grendel attacked the sleeping men
Dat.	Indirect object	Queen Wealhþeow gave [<u>Beowulf</u>]$_{NP}$ gold and horses as a reward for his brave deeds
	Complement of certain prepositions, here *to*	The next night, Grendel's mother made her way to [the great hall]$_{NP}$
Acc.	Direct object	Queen Wealhþeow gave Beowulf [<u>gold</u> and <u>horses</u>]$_{NP}$ as a reward for his brave deeds
	Complement of certain prepositions, here *for*	Queen Wealhþeow gave Beowulf gold and horses as a reward for [his brave <u>deeds</u>]$_{NP}$

If we show the case-marking on all the N-heads of these NPs in a short narrative, following the system outlined in Table 2.3, this is the result:

(4) Beowulf-NOM was Ecgtheow's-GEN son-NOM. During the night-GEN, Grendel-NOM attacked the sleeping men-ACC. Queen Wealhþeow-NOM gave Beowulf-DAT gold-ACC and horses-ACC as a reward-DAT for his brave deeds-ACC. The next night-GEN, Grendel's-GEN mother-NOM made her way-ACC to the great hall-DAT.

Once the head noun of an NP has been identified as requiring a certain case on the basis of its syntactic function, any determiners or adjectives in that NP have to agree with that case. These elements play an important role in maintaining the case-system in Old English after case-marking on nouns had started to erode. The paradigms in Table 2.2 show that Old English nouns no longer have distinct endings for nominative and accusative case, many feminine nouns have the same form in the singular for the genitive, the dative and the accusative, etc. This falling-together of forms is known as **syncretism**. There are signs that endings had eroded so severely that the few distinct endings that remained, like *-es* for the genitive singular of masculine and neuter nouns, and *-ena* for the genitive plural of the *nama*-class, the so-called 'weak declension' were extended to nouns from declensions that did not

Table 2.4 The demonstrative pronoun/definite article in Old English

		Masculine	Feminine	Neuter
Singular	Nom.	se	seo	þæt
	Acc.	þone	þa	þæt
	Gen.	þæs	þære	þæs
	Dat.	þæm/þam	þære	þæm/þam
Plural	Nom.	þa		
	Acc.	þa		
	Gen.	þara		
	Dat.	þæm/þam		

have them originally: Old English *giest* would have been expected to end up with a genitive singular *gieste*, as final -z was lost, a form which would have been identical to the dative singular. Instead, we find *giestes*. *Giefu* would have ended up with a genitive plural *giefa*, and this form is found; but alongside it we find *giefena* – which restores a distinct form for the genitive plural, as the form *giefa* for the genitive plural is identical to the nominative and accusative plural. In spite of these functionally motivated extensions, case on nouns is no longer very distinctive. But case in the NP was not a matter of case on nouns only – adjectives, and particularly the demonstrative pronoun, contributed to the expression of case because they agreed with the noun head in number, gender and case.

The demonstrative pronoun *that*, which doubles as a definite article in Old English, has very distinctive forms in Old English for number, case and gender, as shown in Table 2.4.

We will use example (5) to illustrate how the expression of case in the NP worked.

(5) Þæt is forhwi   se   gooda   læce   selle þam   halum
     that is why   the-NOM good-NOM doctor-NOM gives the-DAT healthy-DAT
     men   seftne   drenc   & swetne
     man-DAT mild-ACC   draught-ACC & sweet-ACC <Bo 39.132.6>
     'That is why the good doctor gives the healthy man a mild and sweet draught'

In (5), the indirect object *þam halum men* 'the healthy man' has dative case, but the form of its head noun *men* is not specific for the dative singular; the form *men* could also be a nominative or accusative in the plural. The ending on the adjective *halum* 'healthy' can be either a dative singular or a dative plural, as can the definite article *þam*. What we see, then, is that the combined information of the constituent parts of the NP *þam halum men* points unambiguously at a dative singular.

The head noun *drenc* of the direct object NP *seftne drenc & swetne* 'a mild and sweet draught' [lit. 'a mild draught and a sweet'] is also not very informative as to case: it can be nominative or accusative. Its number is clear, however: it can only be a singular. The *-ne* ending on the adjectives *seftne* 'mild' and *swetne* 'sweet' is an unambiguous sign that the NP is an accusative masculine singular, though – no other adjectival or nominal ending has this form, and it is also visible on the article *þone* in Table 2.4. The accusative matches the syntactic function of this NP, which is direct object.

PDE no longer has case-endings – not on nouns, adjectives nor articles. The indirect object *þe healþy man* in PDE is either marked by a preposition *to* as in (6a) or by the position of the NP (before the direct object), as in (6b):

(6)   a. He gave a palatable draught to *the healthy man*
       b. He gave *the healthy man* a palatable draught

These are two strategies that may compensate for the loss of case morphology: a lexical form grammaticalises and expresses the syntactic function of indirect object, like *to* in (6a), or the syntactic function is signalled by word order, as in (6b). See also Table 1.2 in Chapter 1.

With the demise of the case-system, there does not appear to be any replacement for the nominative and accusative case in the form of a grammaticalised lexical item; the syntactic functions subject and direct object now seem to be signalled by word order. The recruitment of prepositions to express syntactic relations is limited to the other cases. This is what we would expect on the basis of what we find in other languages: cross-linguistically, such recruitment is vanishingly rare for nominatives; for accusatives, examples of preposition-marking can be found, but such marking never seems to grammaticalise fully, i.e. it will tend to mark only a subset of all direct objects, for instance only objects that are animate (Siewierska 1999; de Swart 2007). As the functions of subject and object are generally regarded as different in kind from other functions, a difference that is often described in terms of core versus peripheral, or structural versus inherent case, this is not unexpected.

The dative case was not only used to mark indirect objects in Old English, i.e. NPs with the role of RECIPIENT, or NPs that are complements of certain prepositions, like *to* in Table 2.4, but also of NPs that have the role of EXPERIENCER, an animate entity that experiences something – a vision, as in (7), or an emotion, like liking or disliking someone, as in (8). The relevant dative NPs are given in bold:

(7) **Me** þuhte   þæt we bundon   sceauas on   æcere
     me seemed that we bound   sheaves in   field
     'It seemed to me that we were binding up sheaves in a field'
     <Gen (Ker) 37.7a>

(8) Wel **me** licode þæt þu   ær   sædes
     well me likes   that you earlier said
     'I liked well what you said before'
     <Bo 35.98.23> (Möhlig-Falke 2012: 126)

Adjectives with meanings like 'pleasing' or 'displeasing' may also have
dative EXPERIENCERS, as in (9), from a very Early Middle English text;
the dative NP is in bold:

(9) se arcebiscop Turstein of Eoferwic wearð þurh   þone papan wið þone
     the archbishop Turstein of York   was   through the   pope   with the

     cyng acordad.   & hider to lande com.   & his biscoprices onfeng.
     king reconciled and hither to land   came and his bishopric   received

     þeah hit þam   arcebiscop of Cantwarabyrig swyðe ungewille   wære.
     though it the-DAT archbishop of Canterbury   very   displeasing was
     <ChronE 1120.17>

     'Turstein, archbishop of York, was reconciled with the king by the Pope
     and arrived in this country and was installed in his bishopric although it
     was displeasing to the archbishop of Canterbury'

The PDE translations of (7)–(9) show that such dative NPs are
expressed by subjects (as in (8)) or by PPs (often with *to*, as in (7) and
(9)) today.

   Adverbials in Old English may also appear as case-marked NPs, and
they typically require a preposition in PDE. An example is (10) (relevant NP in bold):

(10) He nolde   beon cyning, & **his agnum   willan**   he com to
      he not-wanted be   king   and his own-DAT will-DAT he came to
      rode gealgan <CP 3.33.19>
      cross gallows
      'He did not want to be king, and of his own free will, he went to the
      cross'

Many of these NPs are probably historically locative or instrumental
cases; these cases came to be identical in form to the dative in Old English.
   PDE, then, has found two alternative ways of expressing the dative: by
using prepositions or by word order. Subjects, marked by a nominative

in Old English, and direct objects, typically marked by an accusative in Old English, are only marked by word order in PDE. This means that the morphology has become simpler (no more case-endings to learn), but the syntax could be argued to have become more complicated: instead of just a noun, we now have a preposition and a noun, which means that the ordering of preposition and noun needs to be specified by a rule of some sort. The preposition adds another syntactic layer to the NP, which is now sitting inside a prepositional phrase, a PP. To visualise this, we can use tree structures as in (11):

(11)

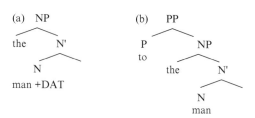

Tree structures are useful for syntax because they show two types of information: (1) the linear order of the words, which is the order of the 'leaves' of the tree as we walk the tree from left to right; and (2) the hierarchy of the various constituents, which is the order of the 'nodes' of the tree as we walk the tree from top to bottom: an NP-node is contained within a larger node, a PP.

2.7 The grammaticalisation of prepositions

2.7.1 To

We saw in the previous section that a case can be made that the preposition *to* in examples (6a), (7) and (9) is taking over some of the grammatical functions of the dative case, when inflectional morphology is lost. When a lexical item is recruited from the lexicon to express a grammatical function, it undergoes a process of grammaticalisation. Function words have less stress than lexical words, so a grammaticalising lexical item will not have as much stress, and hence tends to develop a phonologically-reduced form: the vowel may reduce to *schwa* [ə]. The item may be reduced so much that it can no longer be used as a separate word, a 'free form', but becomes a **clitic**, a form that is still recognisable as a word but is always found attached to another word (an example would be Latin *-que* 'and' in Table 1.2), or even a **bound** form, i.e. an

Table 2.5 The grammaticalisation of *afoot*

	on foot > *afoot*
Prosody	stress is reduced
Phonology	[on] > [ə]: final *-n* is lost, vowel is reduced
Morphology	*on* is a free word, *a-* a bound morpheme
Syntax	*on foot* is a phrase (a PP), *afoot* is a head (an adverb)
Lexicon	*on* has a concrete spatial meaning, *a-* has a very abstract, almost aspectual meaning ('in progress'); *afoot* no longer refers to people being on their feet, i.e. active, but to things being in operation: *the game is afoot*

affix, like the *-s* in *he walks*. This means a change in its morphological status. The reduction may affect the syntactic status of the entire constituent, which may be reduced, too, from a **phrase** to a **head**. A form like *afoot* illustrates all these developments (as shown in Table 2.5):

(12)   They take coach, which costs ninepence, or they may go **afoot**, which costs nothing (*OED*, 1762 *Cit. W.* cxxii. (1837) 474)

If prepositions grammaticalise to compensate for the loss of inflectional morphology like case-endings, those prepositions can be expected to lose some of their lexical meaning. This does not mean that *on* stopped being a lexical preposition after it grammaticalised into *a-* in *afoot*; the preposition *on* and the affix *a-* exist side by side. This phenomenon in grammaticalisation is called **layering**. Other examples are the noun *back* co-existing with the adverb *back*, and the lexical verb *have* 'possess' co-existing with the auxiliary *have* that builds a perfect tense, as in *he has walked*.

Grammaticalisation not only applies to lexical items becoming functional items, but also to functional items becoming even more functional. PDE prepositions can be ranked on a scale, with *in, from* or *during* representing the more lexical end, with clear spatial and/or temporal meanings, while some uses of *to* and *of* represent the more functional end. But *during* is itself a grammaticalisation of a present participle of a now defunct verb *dure* 'endure' (see *OED*).

To in (6a) marks the RECIPIENT of the giving-action, rather than primarily the spatial notion of direction; but it may continue to be used with that earlier, primary meaning elsewhere (layering again). Even in its grammaticalised version in (6a) it can still be said to involve the spatial notion of direction, albeit in a very abstract way: the draught travels from the doctor to the man. *To* could already mark the RECIPIENT of a verbal message in Old English: some verbs of saying, like *cweþan* 'say' had *to* (as in PDE *I said to John*) rather than an NP in the dative.

Another example of layering is the existence of *to* as a marker of non-finiteness in PDE, as in *I want to go home*. This *to* grammaticalised much earlier from the same preposition, and has developed into an element that is even less lexical than *to* in (6a). Its directional meaning lent itself well to expressing direction-in-time in addition to direction-in-space, and it was this aspect of its meaning that started this particular grammaticalisation path. We will discuss non-finite *to* in Chapter 5. One way of schematising the various layers of grammaticalisation is given in (13):

(13)

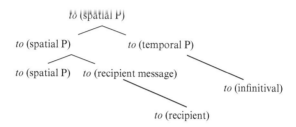

Note that (13) is meant to be an example rather than a definitive analysis; see for instance Cuyckens and Verspoor (1998) for an alternative. The connection between temporal *to* and infinitival *to* will be fleshed out in Chapter 5.

2.7.2 Of

The preposition *of* has also developed abstract meanings:

> From its original sense [of 'away,' 'away from'], *of* was naturally used in the expression of the notions of removal, separation, privation, deriva-tion, origin or source, starting-point, spring of action, cause, agent, instru-ment, material, and other senses, which involve the notion of 'taking, coming, arising, or resulting from' (*OED, of*)

Layering has resulted in two separate lexical items in PDE, a functional *of* and a lexical *off*, the former phonologically reduced, the latter less so. *Of* evolved into an alternative for the genitive case and expresses much the same relation as the -*s* ending in PDE: compare *John's sister* versus *the sister of John*. The two expressions have each found a niche of their own, with a number of formal and semantic factors determining the selection of one variant over the other (Rosenbach 2002).

The -*s* ending in PDE possessives like *John's sister* resembles the -*es* genitive singular form of some masculine and neuter noun classes in

Old English, but a closer look reveals that it is no longer a case-ending. It attaches to NPs rather than to N-heads, witness (14):

(14) [The king$_N$ of Elfland]$_{NP}$'s daughter$_N$ (Title of 1924 novel by Lord Dunsany)

In Old English, the genitive case ending would have attached to *king*, not to *Elfland*, and the NP *the King of Elfland* would either have been split up ('discontinuous'), with its postmodification *of Elfland* appearing after the N-head (*daughter*) of the larger NP, as in (15a), or would have followed the N-head *daughter* in its entirety, as in (15b).

(15) a. The king$_N$-GEN daughter$_N$-NOM of Elfland
      b. The daughter$_N$-NOM the-GEN king$_N$-GEN of Elfland

The genitive in Old English was not only used for possession, but also to mark arguments of **nominalisations**. Nominalisations are verb-stems that are turned into nouns by a derivational affix. As nominalizations contain verbal stems, they have semantic roles associated with them. These roles cannot be expressed as subjects or direct objects in the usual way, because those are the preserve of verbs, and nominalisations are nouns. This does not just hold for nominalisation in PDE but for languages generally; semantic roles of nominalisations in case-languages will not be expressed by accusative NPs but by NPs in, e.g., the genitive; in PDE, they are expressed by PPs, particularly PPs with the preposition *of*. Compare the words in bold in (16):

(16) The Government wants to stamp out the **drinking** of alcohol on streets. Allowing pubs and clubs to stay open later into the night has been claimed to have contributed to a **surge** in binge drinking and alcohol-fuelled violence. The Government's review of the **liberalisation** of the licensing laws will appear within a few weeks. Existing laws already brought down the **sale** of alcohol to minors. Chief constables have also given up their **opposition** to later drinking hours, despite concern that trouble in town and city centres now appears to have been shifted to the early hours of the morning.

The nouns in bold in (16) are all followed by a prepositional phrase that contains an argument expressing a semantic role of the nominalised verb:

(17) a. the drinking$_N$ **of** alcohol – they drink$_V$ alcohol
      b. a surge$_N$ **in** binge drinking – binge drinking surged$_V$

   c. the liberalisation_N **of** the licensing laws – they liberalised_V the licensing laws

   d. the sale_N **of** alcohol to minors – they sold_V alcohol to minors

   e. the Chief Constable's opposition_N **to** later drinking hours – the Chief Constable opposed_V later drinking hours

In (17), too, there is overlap with the -*s* genitive in PDE, in that one of the arguments of *oppose* is expressed by an -*s* genitive in (17e). Such roles 'inherited' from the verb could be marked by the genitive in Old English nominalisations:

(18)   manega ðæs   folces   menn gelyfdon on þone Hælend,
            many   of-the people's men   believed in the   Saviour
            þurh   ðæs   deadan   mannes   ærist
            through the-GEN dead-GEN man-GEN resurrection
            'many men of the people believed in the Saviour because of the resurrection of the dead man/the dead man's resurrection'
            <ÆCHom I, 14.1, 206.18>

Prepositions marking such 'inherited' arguments retain very little lexical, spatial content and are probably at the most grammaticalised end of the grammaticalisation cline of PDE prepositions.

   The layering of *of*/*off* can be schematised as in (19):

(19)

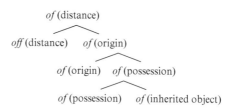

2.8 The expression of definiteness

Nouns are often marked for definiteness or indefiniteness, as a signal to the hearer that they should or should not be able to identify the referent of the noun. In PDE, possessive and demonstrative pronouns are a guide to identifiability, but in their absence definiteness-marking is achieved by the articles *the* and *a*(*n*), respectively.

   Languages vary as to whether they express definiteness/indefiniteness in the morpho-syntax or not. Such morpho-syntactic marking can be achieved by means of articles as in PDE, or by case, with, e.g., accusative objects marking definite NPs and genitive objects marking indefinite NPs. In some languages, definiteness-marking is not entrenched in the morpho-syntax, but is a by-product of using possessive pronouns, like *my* or *his*, or demonstrative pronouns, and only expressed when relevant to the situation. As with number (section 2.4, p. 35), the upside of incorporating definiteness-marking in the morpho-syntax is that it is an automatic routine, but the downside is that each and every noun phrase needs to be marked for definiteness once it is part of a language's morpho-syntax, whether definiteness is relevant in the situational context or not.

PDE *the* is a grammaticalised form of *that*, which has split off from the demonstrative – another case of layering. The Old English way to mark definiteness approaches that of PDE, and uses the demonstrative paradigm of *se* 'that' (see Table 2.4). Definiteness-marking is probably already part of the morpho-syntax. Although we must be careful not to interpret the language of poetry as a straightforward guide to an earlier stage of the language, the fact that the use of the demonstrative as a definiteness marker is more restricted there could be a clue to the early development of *se*. In *Beowulf*, *se* 'that' may signal that a referent, though new to the discourse (and hence unidentifiable), is going to play an important role later on – as if the speaker wants to signal to the hearer: 'Take a note of this one, he is going to be important.' Here is the very first mention of Grendel:

(20) Ða *se ellengæst*   earfoðlice þrage   geþolode, se   þe in
      then SE powerful-demon hard   grievance bore   that-one who in
      þystrum bad <Beo 86>
      darkness abode
      'Then *that powerful demon*, a prowler through the dark, nursed a hard grievance'

This technique is still found in PDE discourse:

(21) It was on the Chester road, in Birmingham. I saw *this* car with the keys in the ignition. (*OED*, s.v. *this*, 1976 *Drive* Nov.–Dec. 24/1; Breban 2012: 285)

(22) Martha gave him *that* enigmatic smile and said, 'I think it is time for supper.' (Cobuild Corpus; Breban 2012: 283)

Indefinite determiners, e.g. *a, some*, convey that the hearer is not expected to recover the precise identity of the referent. At most, the hearer recognises the referent as an instantiation of a generic type. The indefinite article *an* developed from the numeral *one* because *one* allows the speaker to single out a single individual from a set (Rissanen 1967). The grammaticalisation of Old English *an* 'one' into a marker of indefiniteness lags behind the development of *the* in the history of English: NPs without an identifiable referent are generally unmarked. When we do find *an*, it is often marking more than just unidentifiability. In (23), it serves as a presentative marker, denoting first mentions of referents that are going to play an important role in the discourse, just as *se* had done earlier:

(23)   ða   læg þær **an** micel ea   up in on þæt land.   þa   cirdon hie   up in
       Then lay there a   great river up in on   that land   then turned they up in

       on ða ea,   for þæm hie   ne dorston forþ bi þære ea   siglan for unfriþe,
       on the river for that   they not dared   forth by the river   sail   for hostility

       for þæm ðæt land wæs eall gebun   on oþre healfe þære   eas.
       for that the land was all   inhabited on other half   of-the river
       <Or 1, 1.14.18> (Breban 2012: 274)

       'There lay a great river up in that land; they then turned up into that river, because they did not dare sail past the river, because of the hostility, for the country on the other side of the river was inhabited.'

If this interpretation is correct, this means that 'procedural' signs to the hearer, of the type 'prick up your ears', are the source of both the definite and the indefinite article in English.

2.9 Loss of morphology and word order change

The two parameters along which languages, or historical stages of a single language, may differ in their syntax – their word order, and whether grammatical information is expressed by bound morphemes (in the morphology) or by free words (in the syntax) – have long been argued to be related. If morphological case is lost, there are fewer clues for the hearer to determine the syntactic function of an NP, and hearers have to rely on other clues to find out who does what to whom: the context, the roles of the verb, whether NPs are animate or inanimate (as inanimate NPs are less likely to be AGENTS of the action). In PDE, powerful clues are provided by word order: in an NP-V-NP sequence, SVO is the most likely interpretation. The development of a more fixed word order in Middle English has been linked to the loss of case at least since 1894 (by the linguist Otto Jespersen), and a similar relationship between case and word order has been argued to explain the greater flexibility of word order in a case-language like German, compared to PDE (Hawkins 1986). Detailed studies of Middle English texts exhibiting different degrees of morphological loss have so far failed to show a direct correlation between loss of case and changes in word order (Allen 2006); and Dutch, though as case-less as PDE, has German-like flexibility in its word order.[1] The most we can say is that deflexion promoted the fixing of certain word orders already dominant for pragmatic reasons. Subjects are prototypically AGENTS, and hence animate, and old information; direct objects are prototypically PATIENTS, inanimate, and new information. Loss of case does not immediately and automatically lead to less flexible word orders, but there is some functional overlap in that both case and word order may provide clues as to the syntactic function of an NP.

2.10 Modelling morpho-syntactic variation of case and prepositions

We saw earlier that the tree structures in (11) combine two types of information in one image: the linear order of the words as they leave our mouths, and the hierarchical order which tells us how the constituents relate to each other: (11b), for instance, shows an NP contained in a larger constituent, a PP. We will use tree structures to model the development of English from a synthetic to an analytic language.

The template we use for our trees is a very simple structure as in (24), which shows the basic structure of an NP. The NP has, at its core, a lexical head, N. Lexical heads automatically build up ('project') a position for a **complement**, and a position for a **specifier**.

(24)

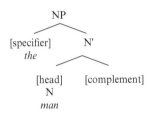

The phrases (nodes in a tree ending in P, e.g. NP, PP) are constituents. The lexical category of a phrase is determined by the word class of its head: a noun heads an NP, a verb heads a VP, a preposition heads a PP, an adjective heads an AP. Typical specifier material for N would be determiners, like *any, the* or *all*, or possessive pronouns like *his* or *her*, the complement-position is earmarked for constituents that are structurally required by the head, i.e. the head would not be complete without them. If the head N happens to be a nominalisation of a verb, like *opposition* in

(17e), the participant roles of that verb can surface in the internal positions that come with the NP: its 'inherited' object (*to later drinking hours*) is a reasonable candidate to fill the complement position, and the 'inherited' subject, *the Chief Constable*, with its possessive -*s*, is a reasonable candidate for the determiner position, the specifier:

(25)

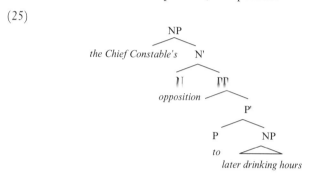

The triangle or coat-hanger symbol for the NP *later drinking hours* inside the PP *to later drinking hours* is an abbreviation device to show that there is more structure to this NP (it will also contain a N'-node and a N-head), but that this structure is not relevant at present.

N(oun), V(erb), A(djective) and P(reposition) are lexical heads (although some prepositions are more lexical than others) and build lexical phrases, NP, VP, PP and AP, on the same model as (24). If we regard N, V, P and A as variations of the theme of 'head', we can see heads as variables – Xs – and refer to phrases as XPs. In fact, (24) is an instance of a more abstract template, the X'('X-bar')-schema:

(26)

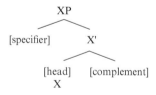

Our concern in this chapter is not only how to model lexical information, but specifically how to model functional information. The X'-template allows both lexical and functional categories to be modelled in very similar ways. If we want to abstract away from the formal difference between free forms and morphemes, and concentrate on the informational content of the functional category they express, we can refer to the expression of a functional category as a **gram**. The dative case and the preposition *to* are both grams. The notion of gram in the grammaticalisation literature is modelled in the template by positioning grams that express the same functional information in the same heads. If we want to express our intuitive impression that some PDE prepositions express information analytically that was expressed synthetically in Old English, one way to do this is to construct a functional XP on top of the NP, which can model the functional overlap between the dative ending in (5) and the preposition *to* in (6a). Let's call the functional category 'RECIPIENT', or R for short, just to illustrate the principle (a more mainstream label K, for Case, is less useful for our present purposes because it has an inbuilt bias that the gram we are investigating is a bound morpheme).[2] The R-head projects a Recipient Phrase, RP, along the lines of the X'-template in (26).

In the morphologically-complex structure (27a), a suffix is positioned (**merged**) in the functional head R. As a bound morpheme, it cannot stand on its own, and hence cannot remain in that position but has to attract another head, here the lexical head N, to attach itself to ('movement'). In the syntactically-complex structure (27b), a free form, a preposition, is merged in that same head R, but as it is a free form, there is no additional movement.

(27)

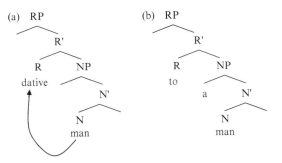

Note that this modelling subsumes both inflectional morphology and syntax in order to bring out the functional 'overlap' between them – it should not be taken to mean that morphology does not exist as a separate level of linguistic description or that *all* prepositions are functional and expressed as R-heads in an RP.

The modelling of a gram as in (27a–b) shows up the relationship between losses in the inflectional domain and syntactic change: if the gram 'Recipient' loses its designated marking in the morphology, in time another element may develop to mark it. The most common route is that such an element is recruited from the lexicon as a free form, and needs to have its place specified in the word order of the resulting phrase. This is how two of the three parameters of syntactic variation discussed in Chapter 1, word order and morpho-syntactic expression of a gram, are connected.

2.11 Why is morphology lost?

Morphological endings are vulnerable to two things: processes of phonological erosion and language contact situations. Phonological erosion is a natural phenomenon in language change; living organisms have a natural drive to preserve their energy, and tensing up the many muscles required in articulation costs effort. If speakers can get away with less forceful and precise articulation, they will do so. This tendency towards ease of effort at the production end of language is kept in bounds by the needs of hearers at the perception end: hearers can deal with lots of break-ups in the signal – phonological features that have gone missing because the speaker has neglected to make a full closure of the oral cavity or has mistimed voicing can be tacitly 'filled in' by the hearer, helped by the syntactic expectations of what the word might be, the pragmatic expectations of what is a relevant utterance in the given context, facial expressions, gestures, etc. Hearers are in fact extremely good at this and it is one of the factors that causes headaches for scientists working on speech recognition programs: 'While we understand the insults hurled at us by the inarticulate drunk, no automatic speech recogniser will achieve the same feat for many years to come' (Gussenhoven 2011: 7).

In Germanic, stress became fixed on the first lexical syllable, which may have made the syllables at the end of a word, furthest away from the stressed syllable, vulnerable to phonological erosion. As syllables at the end of words typically encode morphological information, morphology was vulnerable after the stress change.

A second factor in the loss of morphology is language or dialect contact. There have been many language contact situations in the history of English: with Celtic when the Anglo-Saxons first came to Britain, with Old Norse when Vikings settled in England in large numbers, with Old French after the Norman Conquest, with Latin in the Old English period when the English were christianised, and in the Early Modern English period, when there was extensive borrowing from Latin for scientific and other concepts. The contact with Old Norse in the ninth and tenth centuries is of particular interest, as Old

Norse was a North Germanic language and hence shared much of its vocabulary with Old English, but had different inflectional endings; this may have led to such confusion that the inflections were discarded altogether.

English lost its system of grammatical gender on nouns (three genders), retaining only natural gender in its personal pronouns; it also lost its case system, and much of its verbal inflection. Although such deflexion is also evident in the history of the other Germanic languages, English appears to have come off worst: no verbal categories like subjunctive, very little person/number marking on the verb (only the distinction between *I/you-singular/we/you-plural/they walk-Ø* versus *he/she/it walk-s*, and then only in the present tense), no marking on infinitives (although some infinitives are marked as such by a grammaticalised preposition, *to*, instead). The only West Germanic languages that come close to such an extreme level of deflexion are Afrikaans and Dutch, languages whose history has also been marked by language contact, which may be significant. Gender is particularly vulnerable in a language contact situation as it is best memorised, or, better, internalised, at a very young age, and this is only possible if the child is exposed to massive amounts of input of the gendered language at the right age. This offers some suggestive circumstantial evidence for the notion that language contact, particularly contact with Old Norse, is at the heart of the deflexion in English.

2.12 Which morphology is lost?

The distinction between inherent and contextual inflection described in section 2.3 may account for which type of inflection survives in times of loss, in some form or other, and which does not; inherent inflection expresses language-external information, information from the socio-physical world, which means it is more 'meaningful' and hence less likely to be lost; and if it does happen to be lost, speakers are more likely to find a new expression for it.

The situation of gender is interesting here. It is inherent inflection (it does not reflect relations in the socio-physical world), and does not appear to communicate anything meaningful to the hearer; it is a baroque bit of linguistic ornamentation that arose and survived in the absence of large-scale language contact; its loss has been hailed as 'the elimination of that troublesome feature of language, grammatical gender' (Baugh and Cable 2002: 154). Its loss was not entirely without consequences, however, as a gendered system helps the hearer keep track of referents in a discourse. Consider (28a–b), often used in psycholinguistic studies about what kind of systems hearers follow to decode the referents, the antecedents, of pronouns:

(28) a. John borrowed a bike from Mike. He _____
      b. John passed the comic to Mike. He _____
      c. John hugged Mike. He _____
      d. John helped Mike. He _____

Subjects in such studies are asked to complete the sentence, and the point of the investigation is to see whether they are more likely to identify John or Mike as the antecedent of *he*. If they go for *John*, they are continuing the topic of the previous clause ('topic continuity'); if they go for *Mike*, they are switching topics ('topic shift'). PDE speakers are heavily dependent on their internalised 'social scenarios' that prompt expectations of which coherence relation is most likely. Any hint of the focus being on interpersonal relations, as in (28c), or on character traits of the protagonists, as in (28d), will tend to lead to the expectation that the new clause will give an explanation of John's motivations, and John will be selected (topic continuity). If such hints are absent, subjects will tend to go for Mike (topic shift). Unlike PDE, German has a dedicated system to force topic switch: a gendered demonstrative paradigm as in Table 2.4 that can be used as independent pronouns to refer to people. If the personal pronoun *er* 'he' is used in the German equivalents of (28a–d) both John and Mike are potential antecedents; but if the masculine demonstrative *der* 'that (one)' is used, it can only be Mike. It follows that the joke in (29) is impossible to translate in idiomatic German (or Dutch):

(29) Columbo: No, my wife is not here. She had to go to Chicago to look after her mother. **She** had a fall and broke her hip.

     Woman at party: Oh, your wife broke her hip? How terrible!

     Columbo: No, her mother.
     (*Columbo*, series 10.1, episode *No time to die*)

The most natural translation of *she* in bold would be a demonstrative, feminine *die*, which would pinpoint the new referent, her mother, rather than the old referent, Columbo's wife. Old English seems to use its two pronoun systems in much the same way. The loss of a gendered demonstrative paradigm to refer to people as well as things must have placed a higher processing burden on English speakers, who can no longer rely on morphological cues to track referents like John and Mike.

2.13 Summary of points

- This chapter focused on the loss of nominal morphology, i.e. morphology in the noun phrase.
- Old English nouns were gendered, and marked for case and number, although there was already some falling together of endings at this early stage.
- The inflection that survived in the NP is mainly inherent inflection, the sort of inflection that has semantic consequences: plural forms are used because plurality is a notion in the socio-physical world.
- Some of the information lost when case was lost was restored by the use of prepositions. This is an instance of one of the three main parameters of syntactic variation, i.e. whether functional information is expressed in the morphology (case) or in the syntax (preposition).
- This can be modelled in a tree structure with a simple template (X-bar) of heads and phrases, in which the morphological and the syntactic expression of a 'gram' are both associated with a particular functional head.
- The prepositions that were recruited from the lexicon to express information that was earlier expressed by morphology underwent a process of grammaticalisation: loss of lexical meaning (bleaching) and phonetic reduction.
- The demonstrative pronoun *that* grammaticalised into a definiteness marker, the definite article *the*, and the numeral *ān* 'one' developed into the indefinite article *a(n)*. One of the prime functions of the articles is to mark identifiability.

Exercises

1. CASE, GENDER, NUMBER AND SYNTACTIC FUNCTION. Each of the PDE sentences below has one or more determiners (articles/demonstratives) missing. If you were going to use the correct Old English determiner, which would you need to fill the gaps? Use Table 2.4.

   a. _____king bought _____horse (assume that *king* is masculine and *horse* is neuter)
   b. _____horse was brown (assume that *horse* is neuter)
   c. The king gave _____queen _____ horse (assume that *queen* is feminine)
   d. _____queen saw _____horses

2. Case, gender, number in Old English. The same exercise, but now with real Old English. Also, provide a PDE translation on the basis of the literal word-by-word translation, the **gloss**.
   Note 1: (m) = masculine, (f) = feminine, (n) = neuter. *Note 2*: the preposition *to* 'to' takes a dative complement.

   a. þa   ongann _____ apostol (m) hi   ealle læran _____ deopan lare (f)
      then began   the   apostle   them all teach   the   deep   doctrine
      be   drihtnes tocyme to _____ worulde (f)
      about lord's coming to the   world

   b. and hu he to _____ heofenum (m) astah   on heora   ealra gesihðe
      and how he to the   heavens   ascended in of-them all   sights
      (i.e. while they were all looking on)

   c. and him siððan   sende _____ soðan frofer (m) _____ halgan gastes (m).
      and them afterwards sent   the   true comfort   of-the Holy   Ghost.

Text: From Ælfric's *Catholic Homilies*, <ÆCHom II, 18 170.27>

3. Case and syntactic function.
   a. Provide a PDE translation of the following Old English text on the basis of the gloss.
   b. Consider the NPs that are marked for case in the gloss. Give the reason for every case, i.e. why the NP is found with that particular case. Note any nouns that do not show the case you would expect on the basis of Table 2.3.
   c. Comment on how the syntactic function of these nouns is expressed by PDE.

   Legend:
   NOM = nominative
   ACC = accusative
   DAT = dative
   GEN = genitive

   Text:
   & þa   gelamp   hit, þæt sum ealdorman wæs Daria gehaten,
   and then happened it,   that some lord-NOM   was Daria called,

   se   wæs mid   here cumende of   Gotena   þeode
   that-NOM (i.e. Daria) was with (an) army coming from the Gothic-GEN people-DAT

   on þa ylcan stowe   þæs   halgan weres[1]
   at the same place-DAT of-the holy   man-GEN

---

[1] Libertinus, Prior of the Abbey of Funda and the hero of this story

& þa wearð se ylca Godes þeow   adune aworpen
and then became that same God-GEN servant-NOM down thrown

of   his horse fram þæs ylcan ealdormannes mannum.
from his horse by   that same lord-GEN   men-DAT.

&   he þa se Godes   man   wæs lustlice   þone lyre
and he then that God-GEN man-NOM was unconcernedly the   loss-ACC

þæs horses   þoliende & eac þa swipan   þe he on his handa hæfde,
that horse-NOM suffering and also the whip-ACC   that he on his hand   had

þa   he þam reafiendum mannum brohte þus cweðende:
that-one-ACC   he the plundering men-DAT   brought thus saying:

nimað nu þas swipan,   þæt ge magan þis hors   mid mynegian . . .
take   now this whip-ACC which you may this horse-ACC with drive

Text: From the Old English translation of *Gregory's Dialogues*, <GD (1) C 2.14–18>

4. LOSS OF CASE AND WORD ORDER. In PDE, powerful clues are provided by word order: in an NP-V-NP sequence, SVO is the most
likely interpretation.

   a. For every clause in the text below (main clauses and subclauses),
   determine whether they conform to SVO order or not. Note
   that prepositional objects, like *into tears* in *She burst into tears*, and
   subject complements, like *lost* in *She is lost* count as objects in
   terms of basic SVO word order.

   b. 'The most we can say is that deflexion promoted the fixing of
   certain word orders already dominant for pragmatic reasons'
   (section 2.9). Such pragmatic reasons might be the universal tendency (1) to begin a clause with 'given' information and end it
   with new information ('the point' of the clause) or (2) for AGENTS
   (subjects) to be animate and PATIENTS (objects) to be inanimate.
   Does the text below support these statements? Tabulate for each
   clause whether it starts off with (relatively) given information and
   ends with new information, and whether its subject is animate and
   its object inanimate.

Text:
   'She burst into tears as she alluded to it, and for a few minutes could
   not speak another word. Darcy, in wretched suspense, could only say
   something indistinctly of his concern, and observe her in compas-
   sionate silence. At length she spoke again. 'I have just had a letter

from Jane, with such dreadful news. It cannot be concealed from any one. My youngest sister has left all her friends – has eloped; – has thrown herself into the power of – of Mr. Wickham. They are gone off together from Brighton. *You* know him too well to doubt the rest. She has no money, no connexions, nothing that can tempt him to – she is lost for ever.' (Jane Austen, *Pride and Prejudice*, chapter 46).

6. DEFINITENESS MARKING. Many languages use genitive objects to mark unidentifiable NPs, and accusative objects to mark identifiable NPs. Why would marking objects generally be enough (i.e. why can languages get away with not marking the subject for identifiability)?

7. X'('X-BAR') TREE STRUCTURES. The general 'template' for X' tree structures is:

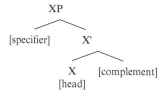

How would the following italicised phrases (NP, AP, VP, PP) fit into this structure?

a. The little boy was *terrified of dogs.*
b. That guy *in the tuxedo* is my cousin.
c. *My daughter sold her apartment.*

Further reading

The term grammaticalisation is due to Meillet (1903). The textbook on grammaticalisation is Hopper and Traugott (2003). For a study testing a direct link between the loss of case and the development of a more fixed word order, see Allen (2006). For the link between accusative case and definiteness, see Hopper and Thompson (1980). The history of impersonal verbs in English is investigated by Möhlig-Falke (2012). For the internal structure of the NP in Old English and later developments, see Denison (2006) and Allen (2012). For language contact see Thomason and Kaufman (1988) and Thomason (2001). A study of a recent case of language contact and loss of inflectional morphology is Kusters (2003). Language contact can also lead to greater complexity (Trudgill 2011). For the idea of the contact situation of Old English and Old Norse as the source for the loss of inflection, see Poussa (1982) and Danchev (1988);

see also McWhorter (2002). For formal syntax and X'-theory, see the introduction by Radford (2004). For the notion *gram*, see Bybee et al. (1994). An analysis of case in terms of a KP is found in, for example, Bittner and Hale (1996). For the history of the definite article in English, see McColl Millar (2000) and Breban (2012). For more about the sentence completion tasks of (28a–d), see Majid et al. (2007) and Kehler et al. (2008).

Notes

1. With one possibly telling difference: like PDE, Dutch insists on the indirect object being expressed by a PP if it follows rather than precedes the direct object (exactly like the 'dative alternation' in (6a and b) above), but in German both orders are possible when the indirect object is expressed by an NP rather than by a PP.
2. The label C had already been bagged by the functional category *Complementiser* when structures like (27) were first mooted in the literature. This CP (Complementiser Phrase) is discussed in Chapter 4, 7 and 8.

3 Verbal categories: The rise of the auxiliaries *have* and *be*

3.1 Introduction

The previous chapter looked at losses in the inflectional domain and how some of these losses were compensated for by the rise of new uses of existing forms. These forms, recruited from the lexicon, gradually acquire grammatical functions that may in time come to express the same functional information as the lost inflection. We saw in the previous chapter some examples of the grammaticalisation of prepositions, the demonstrative *se* 'that' and the numeral *ān* 'one' to fulfil functions in the nominal domain. The present chapter looks at the rise of auxiliaries: *be*+past participle and *have*+past participle for the perfect, *be*+present participle for the progressive, and *be*+past participle for the passive. Such combinations of auxiliaries and lexical verbs, in contrast with single verb forms with inflection, are referred to as a **periphrastic** expression, a **periphrasis**. *Have* 'to possess' and the copula *be* continued to be used as lexical verbs side by side with the grammaticalised auxiliaries *have* and *be*, another example of **layering**.

As with the prepositions *to* and *of* taking over some of the functions of cases in the nominal domain, it is possible to argue that the new auxiliaries took over functions that were earlier expressed in the morphology, by different forms of the verbs. This does not mean that the auxiliaries were a straightforward one-to-one replacement of tense and aspect markings that had been lost. Some categories had no morphological expression in Old English or in Proto-Germanic and yet ended up with a syntactic one in PDE. The future tense, for instance, was not expressed by a specific inflection in Old English or in Proto-Germanic, yet PDE ended up with a system in which the future is generally marked by *will* or by the newer periphrasis *be going to*. Even if the new periphrases with *have* and *be* to express the perfect, progressive and passive can be argued to restore aspectual distinctions that were lost at an earlier stage, there is a large time gap between the loss of morphological expressions of aspectual categories (in Proto-Indo-European) and the rise of the new periphrases (in Old and Middle English). The Proto-Indo-European aspectual systems were conflated in Germanic to form the simple past tense, and Germanic verbal morphology was reduced to a present/past contrast only (Lass 1990: 84–7). The Germanic languages went on to develop a number of alternative expressions for some of these aspectual distinctions, like prefixes or particles, or verbs with meanings like 'begin', 'stop', 'continue'.

Be (and *weorðan* 'become', extinct in PDE) as auxiliaries of the passive developed very early, and were in place by Old English times. *Be* and *have*+past participles as periphrastic expressions of the perfect appear to have developed from two different constructions, with *have* ousting *be* as perfect auxiliary in a process that took several centuries to complete.

Apart from *have* and *be*, PDE has a number of other auxiliaries, like *will/would, shall/should, can/could*. These modal auxiliaries will be discussed in the next chapter.

3.2 Modality, tense, and aspect (TMA)

Verbs have lexical meaning, which consists of information about the nature of the action and the participants that this action requires, i.e. the semantic roles. When a verb is used in an actual utterance, other information tends to be added that is not lexical but says something about the viewpoint from which the action should be regarded, as in progress or as completed (aspect), the likelihood of it taking place (modality) and when it takes place (tense). An example is (1):

(1)	they	would	have	been	looking	down.
	3pl	M(finite)	T(inf)	A(part$_{past}$)	V(part$_{pres}$)	particle

In (1), the verb is a phrasal verb, *look down*, which calls for at least one participant, an AGENT, which in (1) is the subject *they*. It is the only lexical verb, or main verb, in the sentence; the other verbs are all auxiliaries. *Would* expresses modality (possibility, likelihood) and requires the following verb to be an infinitive; in this case, this infinitive is itself an auxiliary and adds past tense. The auxiliary, *have*, requires the following verb to be a past participle; in (1), this past participle is itself an auxiliary and adds aspect. This auxiliary, *be*, requires the following verb to be a present participle.

As with inherent nominal inflection discussed in section 2.2 in the previous chapter, some TMA categories express language-external information from the socio-physical world, the world of physical and social relationships, and are 'meaningful' and hence less likely to be lost; of the verbal categories, tense is probably most easily identified as depending on such information, as it positions the event described by the verb on a timeline from the vantage point of the time of speaking, the present. Aspect and modality also require language-external information, although not of a straightforwardly socio-physical kind, as they represent choices by the speaker; by using a progressive, the speaker invites the hearer to regard the action of the verb as ongoing, not completed; and by using a modal, the speaker gives his or her opinion of the likelihood of the event.

Discussions of aspect often use the notions imperfective (ongoing, not completed) and perfective (completed). As 'perfect' or 'perfect tense' is traditionally used to describe the *have*+past participle periphrasis, this is a source of confusion. Matters are not made any easier by the fact that the 'perfect tense' that is constructed with the auxiliary *have* – and earlier with *be* – often expresses aspect rather than tense, as we will see below. We will go with the traditional terminology 'perfect tense' to describe the *have* (and, in earlier times, *be*) periphrasis. As perfective aspect often requires an event to be viewed from the outside, holistically, as a completed, self-contained event in the past, it has a natural connection with the past tense, which explains why the forms of the past tense in Germanic can be traced back to forms for perfective aspect in Proto-Indo-European. The point to remember is that the terms *perfect* and *perfective* do not refer to the same thing.

As a reminder that TMA can be expressed in the morphology, (2) presents a possible translation of PDE (1) in Latin. The form in (2) is a single verb. Latin does not require pronominal subjects as the inflection on the verb is informative enough to show that the subject must be a third person plural. The various morphemes are fused and not straightforwardly analysable into individual morphemes, and the morpheme boundaries provided in the gloss are an approximation:

(2)　　de-　　spic-　　iere-　nt
　　　　prefix　V　　ATM-3pl
　　　　'They may have been looking down'

Examples (1) and (2) can be regarded as exemplifying extremes of **analytic** and **synthetic** expressions of verbal categories, reminding us of the first of our three parameters of syntactic variation – that one and the same gram can be expressed as morphology in one language, or language stage, and as syntax in another.

3.3 Lexical and grammatical aspect

'One of the great innovations characterizing Germanic is the destruction of the Indo-European aspect system' (Lass 1990: 83). This aspect system appears to have been a three-way opposition traditionally referred to by the labels *present, aorist* and *perfect*. Each verb had a present stem, an aorist stem and a perfect stem, each of which had their own sets of morphemes expressing modality and agreement, and other verbal categories like **voice** (active/passive). Present stems marked imperfective aspect, aorist marked perfective aspect, and perfect marked resultant state, i.e. states resulting from actions, a relationship much like *break* (action)/*broken* (state) in PDE. This aspectual system morphed into a simplified tense-system in Germanic. For quite some time, Germanic did not have grammaticalised expressions for aspect. In what follows I will discuss lexical versus grammatical aspect at some length, and some of the ways in which they interact. We will build on this information not only in the remainder of this chapter, but also in Chapter 5, where it plays a role in verb complementation, and in Chapter 8, where speakers trying to create a sense of suspense in a narrative almost invariably use linguistic expressions of duration.

Prototypically, verbs express actions, although some verbs, like *sleep*, are such 'low energy' actions that they hardly seem to merit the term. Lexical aspect is about characteristics inherent in the action of the verb that have to do with time. Some actions have **duration**, i.e. they take time to run their course, while others are **punctual** and are over in an instant. It is easy to see that actions that have duration are compatible with expressions that focus on the beginning of the action. This makes *He began to run* more felicitous than *He began to win*. Some actions contain a natural end point (they are **telic**) while others do not (they are **atelic**), and this makes them felicitous or infelicitous with certain expressions of time, like *for an hour* (only compatible with atelicity) or *in an hour* (only compatible with telicity):

(3)   a. He searched for his keys for an hour/*in an hour   atelic
       b. He found his keys in three minutes/*for three minutes   telic

These expressions can be used as diagnostics to test whether the verbal action is telic or not.

Another opposition that is relevant to aspect is whether the action of a verb constitutes a change of state or not. *Know* does not inherently refer to a change of state, and is a **stative** verb, but *break* refers to a change of state, and is **dynamic**. The simple present tense (i.e. without the *-ing* progressive) is only used in PDE with dynamic verbs when

Table 3.1 Vendler's categories, telicity, duration and dynamicity; see also Smith (1997: 20)

	Telic: V in an hour	Durative: V for an hour	Dynamic: *V-ing*
State	No	Yes	No
Activity	No	Yes	Yes
Accomplishment	Yes	Yes	Yes
Achievement	Yes	No	Yes
Semelfactive	No	No	Yes

they refer to a habitual situation (*He plays golf*), a universal unchanging truth (*Life doesn't always play fair*) or a planned future action (*United play Real Madrid in Old Trafford tonight*); when the present tense refers to a dynamic action happening right now, the progressive is obligatory in PDE, and this is sometimes used as a test for dynamicity. But note that some verbs are difficult to construe with a progressive not because they are statives, but because they have no duration, like *recognise*.

Telicity does not correlate with punctuality: actions may have a natural end point and still have duration. A classification that has been found useful is the one proposed by Vendler (1957): verbs can express **states** (*know*), **activities** (*break*), **accomplishments** (*knit a sweater*) or **achievements** (*recognise*). Activities can be durative or punctual, and some scholars distinguish between these two groups by reserving the label activity for durative activities (*run*) and the label **semelfactive** for punctual activities (*hit*).

These categories interact with telicity, duration and dynamicity as shown in Table 3.1.

Vendler's examples include direct objects or other arguments of the verb (*build a house*), which means that his categories refer to events or states-of-affairs rather than to single verbs and they are compositional, i.e. the result of a combination of expressions rather than inherent in the meaning of the verb alone, as it is clear that this inherent meaning can be manipulated by adding direct objects or adverbials. It is one of the reasons why the phenomenon of aspect is so complex. An atelic activity like cycling becomes a telic accomplishment by the addition of a GOAL:

(4)   I cycled to the shops this morning.

Knit and *run* are inherently atelic activities, but may acquire end points with the addition of a direct object like *a sweater*, or a distance like *a mile*.

(5)   She ran a mile in ten minutes

(6)   He knitted a sweater in a week.

This is why we take into account not just the verb but the entire VP, the **situation type**; lexical aspect, then, can also be labelled **situation aspect** (Smith 1983). *Knitting a sweater* and *running a mile* are accomplishment situation types. Punctual verbs acquire duration when they can be conceived of as a series of events, and such multiple achievements can be evoked by plural subjects or objects; if this is the case, the result is an accomplishment situation type, and expressions that require duration become possible, like the verb *begin*:

(7)   a. *John began to arrive at the house – Guests began to arrive at the house
       b. *He began to win the race – He began to win races

An alternative to Vendler's classification is to distinguish **processes, transitions** and **states**, which involves teasing apart complex events. Cycling is a process, a single event, which would become a transition, a complex event, by the addition of an adverbial like *to the shops*. Other transitions – changes of state – are also compositional, as their semantics necessarily include a state.

The fact that the end points of accomplishments may be achieved only after a considerable amount of time has passed – e.g. knitting a sweater – introduces some aspectual ambiguity: the presence of an end point could point to perfective aspect in which the event is viewed as completed, while the fact that the end point takes so long to achieve favours duration. This ambiguity is a potential breeding ground for change, as speakers might want to emphasise that the end point was not reached, i.e. when the knitting, running, or building is a background for some other event which interrupts it; more about such **time-frame uses** in section 3.6 below. Expressions that speakers use to emphasise the durative rather than completive point of view could develop into imperfective aspect.

The Vendler-situation types are inherent in the meanings of the verbs, and the meanings of their direct objects or adverbials, irrespective of tense or (grammatical) aspect, and this is why they can be referred to as **lexical aspect** or **situation aspect**. **Grammatical aspect** refers to options offered by the grammar to the speaker to present the situation to the hearer as, for instance, completed (perfective), not completed (imperfective), ongoing (progressive), or habitual. The following oppositions illustrate that PDE has developed these categories:

(8)   a. She plays golf. [habitual]
       b. She is playing golf. [progressive]

(9)   a. I have had lunch (and am therefore not hungry now)
          [resultant state perfect: past action has present relevance.
          Telic situation types only.]
      b. I have been abroad several times [perfect of experience;
          denotes a time span from a point in the past until the present
          day]
      c. We had lunch at the Olive Tree and then went to the
          museum [simple past: action completed in the past]

(10) a. She has played golf for years (and she still plays golf today)
          [continuative perfect: past action persists into the present]
      b. She played golf when she was young (but has since stopped
          playing) [simple past: action completed in the past]

Lexical and grammatical aspect interact. *She has won a competition* is an achievement situation type, and can only be a resultant state perfect, as this perfect does not set up an interval, and does not require a durative or iterative situation. But resultant state perfects need to be relevant to the matter in hand to be felicitous. A telic utterance like *I have spilled my coffee* is only felicitous if it explains why you are running to the kitchen to get a cloth, and not if the spillage has already been dealt with (cf. (9a)) (Moens and Steedman 1988: 19). So we would expect an utterance like *She has won a competition* to require a context which explains why someone is unusually euphoric, perspiring, generous, etc. But *She has been winning competitions for years* can be construed as setting up a time interval and hence as a continuative perfect because the plural object *competitions* evokes a series of victories. In (11), the use of the progressive with an achievement situation type – having one's name recognised – similarly forces a reading in which there are a series of recognition events, with many separate individuals recognising your name:

(11) Once your website is getting lots of hits and your business is
      booming, your articles are out there and your name **is being
      recognized**, you can capitalize on your success by developing
      a product of your own. <www.review-script.com/affiliates/
      articles/4450.php>

English gradually developed these oppositions between perfective/ imperfective/resultant states by means of periphrastic expressions. These developments involved the grammaticalisation of *have* and *be* into auxiliaries.

Have may express tense rather than aspect in non-finite contexts, as in the *to*-infinitive complement in (12), as non-finites have no past tense forms of their own:

(12) US scientists claim to have built the world's most accurate clock.

In the case of modal auxiliaries, pairs like *may/might, will/would, shall/should* originally reflected a present/past contrast, but do so no longer, as they have developed senses of their own. *Would, should* and *might* have come to convey not only distance-in-time but also distance-in-reality, i.e. more hypothetical situations or greater tentativeness than would have been expressed by *will, shall* or *may*, so here, too, *have* is drafted in to supply the past tense, as in (1) above, or (13a and b):

(13) a. You should warn him.
      b. You should have warned him.

The new aspect systems with *have* or *be* periphrases took a long time to develop in English. The next section will first look at other ways in which aspect could be expressed before these new periphrases arose, and then we will turn to the origin and development of the new *have* and *be* periphrases themselves.

3.4 Alternative expressions for aspect

3.4.1 Lexical items

If there is no grammatical expression for aspect, a lexical form can be used to mark viewpoint in cases where such marking is salient. In his Latin grammar, the Old English writer Ælfric uses explicit adverbs like *nu rihte* 'right now', or *fullice* 'fully, to completion' to express aspect in his Old English explanation of the Latin tense/aspect system; and *gefyrn* 'long ago' to indicate the past-before-the-past, i.e. the pluperfect. The relevant adverbs are given in bold:

(14) ac   swa ðeah   wise lareowas todældon þone *praeteritvm tempvs*,
      and yet   wise teachers divided   the preterite tense
      þæt is, ðone   forðgewitenan timan,   on þreo:
      that is the   past   time   in three
      on *praeteritvm   inperfectvm*,   þæt is unfulfremed forðgewiten,
      in preterite   imperfect   that is uncompleted past
      swilce þæt ðing beo ongunnen and ne beo fuldon: *stabam* ic stod.
      as   the thing is begun   and not is completed *stabam* I stood
      praeteritvm   perfectvm ys forðgewiten fulfremed: *steti* ic stod **fullice**.
      preterite   perfect   is past   completed *steti* I stood **fully**
      praeteritvm   plvsqvamperfectvm is forðgewiten mare þonne fulfremed,
      preterite   pluperfect   is past   more than   completed
      forðan ðe hit wæs gefyrn   gedon: *steteram* ic stod **gefyrn**.

because it was long ago done *steteram* I stood long ago
<ÆGram 124.1–7>
'and yet wise teachers divided the preterite tense, that is the past
time, in three: in *preterite imperfect*, that is uncompleted past, as the
thing has been begun and is not yet completed: *stabam* "I stood";
preterite perfect is past completed: *steti* "I stood fully"; *preterite
pluperfect* is past more than completed, because it was done long
ago: *steteram* "I stood long ago"'.

These adverbs are here used for the purposes of explanation, and are
not used systematically in Old English to express aspectual or tense distinctions; but the adverb *ær* 'earlier' is often used in Old English where
PDE would require a past perfect (an example is (18) below).

3.4.2 Prefixes and particles

Germanic developed a system early on to signal a change of state by a
prefix on the verb, with aspectual meanings as a 'side effect'. These prefixes were recruited mainly from prepositions, with functions much like
particles of phrasal verbs in PDE; compare PDE *eat* versus *eat up*, where
the particle *up* adds a sense of completion and, in combination with past
participles, resultant state (cf. *The window was bricked up*). A verb like *sleep*
is naturally durative, atelic (*he slept for an hour/ *in an hour*), and changes
of state need to be expressed when people go from waking into sleeping,
and from sleeping into waking. In the Gothic example in (15a), *slepiþ*
'sleeps', a present tense without a prefix, is the open-ended, imperfective state, while *anasaislep* in (15b), literally 'on-slept', signals the change
of state from waking to sleeping. This change of state is accomplished in
PDE by a copular construction with a dynamic copula (*fall* rather than
be), which also adds telicity, as being asleep is the end point of falling
asleep. In (15a), the past tense *swalt* of *sweltan* 'die' combines with a
prefix *ga-* to signal perfective aspect:

(15) a. ni **ga**-swalt   so mawi, ak slepiþ (The Gothic Bible, Mt 9:24)
        not GA-die-PAST-3sg the girl but sleeps
        'the girl has not died, but is sleeping.'
     b. þaruh   þan swe faridedun, **ana-saislep** (Gothic Bible, L 8:23; Streitberg 1965)
        there-and then so sail-PAST-3pl ANA-sleep-PAST-3sg
        'and when they were sailing thus, he fell asleep.'

The prefix *ge-* that is the **cognate** (related form) of Gothic *ga-* now marks
past participles in Dutch and German, as a grammaticalised resultant
state; it has become inflection, and is no longer used on finite forms (like

gaswalt in (15a)) to create aspectual oppositions in those languages. *Ge-* fizzles out in Middle English, where it appears as *i-* or *y-*, typically on past participles, suggesting a parallel development to Dutch and German *ge-* (an example is *ifolen* 'fallen' in (32)). In Old English, however, *ge-*, like Gothic *ga-*, is more 'protean' in its functions and very difficult to assign a single meaning. As a change-of-state element, it may indicate the initial change (like *ana-* indicated getting into a sleeping state in (15b)), as well as the terminal change (getting out of a state, like waking up). With verbs with positional meanings (of *sit, stay, stand*, etc.) it may even apply to the state in-between, in which case it tends to negate a presupposition that the sitting, staying or standing might end. This explains why Old English *gestandan* 'ge-stand' may mean any of these three things: stand up, remain standing, and cease to stand (Lindemann 1965: 67, 77).[1]

In later English, *forth*, a particle rather than a prefix, shows similar flexibility. It often means 'out', as in *come forth*, but there are some cases in which it has continuative meaning, as in (16) to (18), much like PDE *on*; (16) is Old English, (17) and (18) Middle English (from the Helsinki Corpus):

(16) Heald **forð** tela niwe sibbe. <Beo 948–9>
      keep forth truly new friendship
      'truly keep on this new friendship'

(17) ah þat ladliche   beast leafeð   & lest **forð** & þe of-þunchunge
      but that loathsome beast remains and lasts forth and the disgust
      þrof   longe þrefter
      thereof long thereafter
      (CMHALI; *Hali Meidenhad*, ed. Furnivall 1922: 34)
      'but that loathsome beast remains and lasts on; and the disgust at it long after'

(18) &   he læʒ **forð** alswa he ær   dude
      and he lay forth as   he before did
      (CMROOD; The History of the Holy Rood Tree, ed. Napier 1894: 32)
      'He continued to lie there as he had done before'

Some languages develop fully-fledged aspectual systems from such prefix or particle systems.

3.4.3 Positional verbs

Positional (or posture) verbs (*lie, sit, stand, stay*) are a frequent source of continuative or progressive aspect in many languages (Heine and Kuteva 2002), and this is also true of Old and Middle English. Van der Gaaf (1934: 81, 90) notes the following examples of the positional verb *lie*, which occurs in a number of different syntactic constructions (the positional verb and its complement in bold):

(19) ealle him wære gehefgode ða eagan of ðam menigfealdum biterlicum
     all   them were made-heavy the eyes by the manifold   bitter

    tearum ðe hi   þær aleton and on ðam sare   þam mycclan
    tears that they there shed and on that sorrow the great

    hi   ***lagon and slepon***
    they lay   and slept
    <ÆLS (Seven Sleepers) I,502,251>

    'of all of them the eyes had become heavy with the many bitter tears that they had shed there and in that great sorrow they lay and slept'

(20) Ða **læg** se earming his yrmðe **bemænende**. <ÆHom II 312>
     then lay the wretch his poverty bemoaning
     'The wretch lay bemoaning his poverty'
     Lat. quare... peruigil sederet

(21) And in my barm ther **lith to wepe**/Thi child and myn
     and in my bosom there lies to weep   thy child and mine
     (Gower, *Confessio Amantis* III 302; Macaulay 1899–1902)
     'and in my bosom there lies weeping thy child and mine [i.e. our child]'

(22) He **lay slepe** faste ibonde wiþ tweie raketeien stronge.
     he lay sleep fast bound with two   chains   strong
     (*MED*, South. Leg., Corp-C, 249/78)
     'he lay asleep bound fast with two strong chains'

The 'hendiadic' construction of (19) with *and*, and the present participle construction of (20) – but with *-ing* rather than *-ende* – are still found in PDE, as is (21); van der Gaaf quotes the example *Groups of guests stood to watch the arrivals*, from a 1916 novel (*Lady Connie*, by Mrs Humphrey Ward; van der Gaaf 1934: 93).

3.4.4 In *or* on

Another construction often found in the world's languages to express a progressive is that of a preposition, usually *on* or *in*, combined with a verb or a verbal noun. An example from Early Modern English with *in* is (23):

(23) and while it [=drawing up the document confirming Pepys' new appointment] was doing in one room, I was forced to keep Sir G. Carteret (who by chance met me there, ignorant of my

business) **in talk**, while it was a doing. (*The Diary of Samuel Pepys*, entry for Friday 13 July 1660, <http://www.pepysdiary.com/diary/1660/07/13/>)

PDE would probably have *I was forced to keep him talking* here. Note also the progressives *it was doing* and *it was a doing* in this entry, where PDE would have *it was being done*, for these passive progressives, see section 3.7 below.

An example in Middle English is an alternative to (22), *lay on slepe* 'lay on sleep', found in another manuscript of the text (van der Gaaf 1934: 88). The PDE adjective *asleep* derives from this PP. Another example of this construction is (24), also from van der Gaaf (ibid.: 98):

(24) the old year lies **a-dying** (Tennyson, *Death of the Old Year* 5; Tennyson 1842: 210)

3.4.5 Aspectualisers

Another way of creating aspectual oppositions is to use verbs with meanings of *begin*, *continue* and *stop*, and such verbs are sometimes referred to as **aspectualisers** for that reason. An Old English example is (25) with *beginnan* and *onginnan*, both meaning 'to begin'. Such verbs emphasise the beginning of an action or event rather than its completion:

(25) **Begann** ða   to secgenne þam sceaðan geleafan. and mid
      began   then to say   the ruffian faith and with
      boclicere lare   hine læran **ongann**; Hwæt ða se sceaða
      scriptural doctrine him teach began   lo   then the ruffian
      sona   gelyfde. on ðone lifigendan god. and tolysde ða benda
      at-once believed in   the living   god and released the bonds
      <ÆCHom II, 39.1 290.70–1>
      '[he] began then to explain faith to the ruffian and began to guide him with scriptural doctrine; Lo, then the ruffian at once believed in the living God and untied the bonds . . .'

The aspectual opposition is here between the simple past (*he explained faith*) and a periphrasis with *beginnan* 'begin' (*he began to explain faith*). The periphrasis with *begin*-verbs is useful for describing actions that are not brought to completion because they are interrupted by the main action. In other words, using a *begin*-verb sets up a time frame during which something else happens. Crucially, the action in the time frame must be presented as uncompleted, as ongoing, to allow the foregrounded event to interrupt it; an PDE example with *begin* is (26):

(26) He had just **begun** to describe where he worked and what he did
      when two students arrived with a cheery 'Hi'. He sympathised
      with their complaint about the lack of time between teaching
      sessions and the PD group, and then began again. (Chris Rose
      (2008), *The Personal Development Group: The Student's Guide*,
      London: Karnac)

Giving a description is an accomplishment, and we saw in section
3.3 that accomplishments have both duration and telicity, which may
prompt speakers to use an explicit expression to emphasise that the
action should not be viewed as completed. Leaving *begin* out in (26) – *he
had just described* – forces a reading that the description was completed,
as does using a simple past instead of a past perfect – *he just described* –,
after which the entry of the two students fails to be interpreted as an
interruption. The problem with using aspectualising *begin*-verbs in
Old English to mark imperfective aspect seems to have been that they
tended to lose the meaning of focusing on the beginning of an action,
possibly because their time frame use started to signal the imminence
of an important turn of events (note that *hwæt* 'Lo!' in (25) is a typical
marker of such events). The use of *begin* in (26), reinforced by *just*, similarly implies an imminent interrupting event. These discourse uses will
be discussed further in Chapter 8.

    Another aspectual opposition was created in the passive by the use of
either *beon* 'be' or *weorðan* 'become' as the passive auxiliary. These will
be discussed below (section 3.7).

3.5 The perfect

3.5.1 The development of the have+past participle perfect

The *have*+past participle perfects as in (9) and (10) seem to have developed out of a construction in which *have* was a lexical verb denoting
possession, and the participle was an adjective rather than a verb, giving
additional information about the object that was being possessed:

(27) Ic **hæbbe gebunden** þone feond þe hi   drehte.
      I have   bound   the enemy that them afflicted
      <ÆCHom I, 31 458.18; Traugott (1992: 191)>
      'I have bound the enemy that afflicted them'

There are two readings for (27): a perfect reading, as in PDE *I have bound
the enemy that afflicted them*, or a possessive reading, as in PDE *I have the
enemy that afflicted them in a bound condition*.

Although there is broad agreement that the *have*+participle construction is a fully grammaticalised perfect by Middle English, showing the aspectual oppositions in (9) and (10), there is no consensus about whether these oppositions were already present in Old English. Most scholars agree that the periphrasis has grammaticalised beyond the adjectival construction; this is shown most clearly by cases like (28), where the verb *gewician* 'encamp' is intransitive and hence without the direct object which would have been required by the adjectival construction:

(28) Þa   hie [. . .] þær to **gewicod hæfdon**. þa onget   se here þæt
      when they   there to encamped had   then realised the host that
      hie   ne   mehton þa scypu ut   brengan
      they not could   the ships out bring
      <ChronA 896.12 (Macleod 2012: 116)>
      'When they had encamped for this, then the army perceived that they
      could not bring the ships out'

It might be thought that the presence or absence of inflection could help to disambiguate the old and the new meanings, as the participle in the original construction, like any other adjective modifying a noun, could have been expected to agree with the object in case, number and gender, but this is not the case. Example (29) shows two conjoined participles, one with and one without inflection, suggesting that the inflection had become a meaningless relic by Late Old English, no longer a sign of the adjectival status of the participle (participles in bold):

(29) Fela Godes wundra   we   habbað **gehyred** and eac **gesewene**
      many God's wonders we   have   heard   and also seen-INFL
      'We have heard and also seen many of God's wonders'
      <ÆCHom I, 39 578.24, from Denison (1993: 347)>

There are examples of the reverse situation, too, in which the construction is clearly adjectival without the participle being inflected (Wischer 2004: 246).

Although there is a periphrasis for the present perfect and the past perfect (also known as the pluperfect), the simple past tense is still capable of expressing either in Old English. In (30), we have a past action that holds into the present, and would require a *have*-perfect in PDE, but what we see in this Old English example is the simple past; the relevant verb is in bold:

(30) Ic **heold** nu   nigon gear wið   ealle hynða þines fæder gestreon
      I held   now nine years against all   loss thy   father's property
      <ÆLS (Lucy) 41> (Macleod 2013: 1)>
      'I have now held your father's property nine years against all loss.'

The time-before-past, which requires a past perfect in PDE, is often expressed in Old English by the simple past tense and the adverb *ær* 'earlier, previously':

(31) He towearp   all þa bigong   þara deofolgelda,   þa   he **ær**   **beeode**
      he destroyed all the practice of-the devilworships that he earlier observed
      <Bede 2 6.114.31> (Macleod 2012: 212)>
      'He cast aside all the practice of devilworship that he had observed
      previously'

Macleod (2012: 160) has shown that there is considerable variation between texts in Old English, even within the same genre, as to how the division of labour between the simple past tense and the new *have*-perfect is worked out; and that there is no discernible diachronic trend over the course of the Old English period – the periphrasis is, if anything, becoming less rather than more frequent towards the Late Old English period (ibid.: 163).

3.5.2 *The development of the* be+past participle *perfect*

Many Germanic languages, including Old English, developed a second periphrastic perfect with the auxiliary *be*. The *have*-perfects derive from expressions with transitive verbs, like *bind* in example (27), in which the past participle has a passive meaning; 'the enemy' is in a bound condition, i.e. he has been bound (passive) by someone. *Be*-perfects derive from resultatives of intransitive verbs, particularly verbs denoting a change of state, including motion verbs. An example is (32) (Middle English), from the Helsinki Corpus:

(32)   as   ha   þreo **weren ifolen** onslepe (CMANCRIW 2,II.272.440)
      when   they   three were fallen asleep
      'When the three of them had fallen asleep'

The *be*-perfect is probably an extension of a construction with the copula *be*, which means that there is some overlap with the periphrastic passive, as both perfect and passive consist of a form of *be* and a past participle. In practice, the overlap is limited, as the past participle in a passive construction is always transitive and would form its perfect with *have* rather than *be*. The only set of verbs that are a potential source for ambiguity are verbs like PDE *begin*, which have two different argument structures: *someone begins something* (causative and transitive) and *something begins* (non-causative and intransitive). In theory, the construction of a form of *be* with a past participle in (33) could be the passive of the causative/transitive *begin* (PDE *the work was begun/had been begun*) or the perfect of the non-causative/intransitive *begin* (PDE *the work had begun*).

(33) And þæt weorc   **wæs begunnen** ongean godes willan
     and the work [the tower of Babel] was begun   against God's will
     a.   'and the work was begun against God's will'
     b.   'and the work had begun work against God's will'
     <ÆCHom I, 22 318.17>

It is clear that the *be*-perfect is no longer a resultative but a proper perfect already in Old English, as it occurs with past participles of verbs like *cuman* 'come' that cannot be interpreted as a resultant state that persists at the time of speaking, unlike past participles of verbs like *feallan* 'fall' – compare PDE *a fallen tree* versus **a come man*.

3.5.3 Competition between have- and be-perfects

The *have*-perfect ultimately ousted the *be*-perfect in the course of Early Modern English (Rydén and Brorström 1987; Kytö 1997). The point where *have* starts to get the upper hand has been identified as around 1750 (Kytö 1997: 32). *Be* continued to be used until about 1900.

We saw in section 3.5.1 that the *have*-periphrasis derives from a construction with a direct object, and in 3.5.2 that the *be*-periphrasis derives from a copular construction without an object, so that transitive verbs can be expected to occur with *have* and intransitive verbs to occur with *be*. The expansion of *have*, then, must have taken place in the domain of the intransitives. But which intransitives were affected first? Cross-linguistic findings, including findings from languages that are not related to Germanic, have shown that the variation that emerges from such competition is not random but follows a particular path, a hierarchy, according to the semantics of the verb. This is known as the *Auxiliary Selection Hierarchy* (Sorace 2000), presented in Figure 3.1 with prototypical examples of each type.

This hierarchy is supported by cross-linguistic variability as to the position of the cut-off point – if a language selects *have* for uncontrolled processes, it will also select *have* for controlled processes, etc. – and by auxiliary selection data from first and second language acquisition. With respect to the competition between *have* and *be* in the history of English, the Auxiliary Selection Hierarchy reflects the finding that the intransitives that denote actions – like *laugh* in (34) from Middle English – are found exclusively with *have* rather than *be*, also in Old English, whereas *be* is found with the other intransitives, the verbs of change-of-location and change-of-state from the earliest times, and also tends to linger

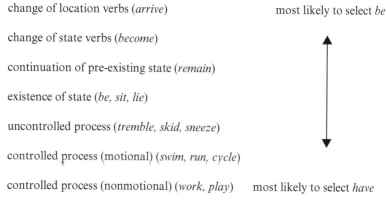

change of location verbs (*arrive*)   most likely to select *be*

change of state verbs (*become*)

continuation of pre-existing state (*remain*)

existence of state (*be, sit, lie*)

uncontrolled process (*tremble, skid, sneeze*)

controlled process (motional) (*swim, run, cycle*)

controlled process (nonmotional) (*work, play*)   most likely to select *have*

Figure 3.1 The Auxiliary Selection Hierarchy (Sorace 2000: 863)

longest with these verbs, when the other verb groups are starting to appear with *have*.

(34) Whan folk   **hadde laughen** at this nyce cas/   Of Absolon and hende Nicholas
      when people had   laughed at this foolish incident of Absolon and gentle Nicholas
      (Chaucer, *Canterbury Tales*, Reeve's Prol. l. 1–2; Robinson 1957: 55)
      'when the company had had a good laugh over this foolish
      business of Absolon and courteous Nicholas'

The last stronghold of *be* as the perfect auxiliary can be identified as the two most frequent change-of-location verbs, *come* and *go*, which continued to appear with *be* until about 1900, and in the case of *go*, up to PDE (*he is gone*).

Note that one-and-the-same verb can count both as a 'controlled process' in terms of the Auxiliary Selection Hierarchy and as a 'change-of-location verb'. This is particularly the case with manner-of-motion verbs like *swim, cycle, walk*: they are controlled processes, but become change-of-location verbs when an adverbial GOAL is added; in Dutch, they will appear with *have*-perfects as controlled processes and with *be*-perfects as change-of-location. The same phenomenon has been observed for *walk* in Chaucer (Middle English) – compare atelic (35) with *have* and telic (36) with *be*:

(35) 'Saw ye,' quod she, 'as ye   **han walked** wyde,
      saw you said she   as you have walked widely
      Any of my sustren walke you besyde [. . .]?'
      any of my sisters walk   you beside
      (Chaucer, *Legend of Good Women* 3, 978; Robinson 1957: 500)

'Did you, she said, while you were walking far and wide,
see any of my sisters walking beside you?'

(36)   Arcite unto the temple **walked is**/   of fierse Mars, to doon his sacrifise
Arcite unto the temple walked is   of fierce Mars to do   his sacrifice
'Arcite has walked to the temple of fierce Mars to make his offering'
(Chaucer, *Canterbury Tales*, Knight's Tale ll. 2368–9; Robinson 1957: 40)

There are only a few instances of this verb with a perfect in Chaucer,
and further research, with other verbs than just *walk*, is needed before
we can be certain that the difference between (35) and (36) is systematic.

The nature of the individual verb is not the only factor that drives the
selection of *have* rather than *be*. *Have* has been an alternative for all the
intransitive verbs, including the unaccusatives, in a number of syntactic
contexts that favour *have* ever since the two periphrases arose: the presence of modals, past perfects, progressive perfects (and iterative and
durative contexts in general), negatives and infinitives (e.g. Rydén and
Brorström 1987). Some of these past perfects and modal contexts share
the characteristic that they denote **counterfactuals**, i.e. 'closed' conditional clauses, like the following Middle English example:

(37)   And if þow **hadest come** betyme, he hade yhade þe   maistre
and if thou hadst   come in time   he had had   the mastery
[CMBRUT3 227.4102] (quoted in McFadden and Alexiadou 2013: 241)
'and if you had come in time, he would have prevailed'

Note that the condition – that the addressee should come in time – can
no longer be satisfied at the time of speaking and is the opposite of
what actually happened. Another counterfactual is the Middle English
example (38), with the modal *myton* 'might':

(38)   syþ   þei   myton liȝtly **haue come** to blysse
since they might easily have come to bliss
[CMWYCSER 303.1386] (quoted in McFadden and Alexiadou
2013: 241)
'since they might easily have come to bliss'

The remaining vector that determines the competition rates in the historical texts is genre; the selection of *be* rather than *have* is a feature of
poetry and of informal texts (Kytö 1997).

3.6 The development of the *be*+present participle progressives

The copula *be* also gave rise to another periphrasis, this time with a
present rather than a past participle: the English **progressive**. There

are instances in Old English that appear to prefigure the rise of a grammaticalised progressive, a periphrasis of the auxiliary *be* followed by a
present participle in -*ende* in Old English (e.g. (39)), -*ande* in Northern
Middle English, as in (40), and -*ing* as in Southern Middle English (41),
which became the dominant form:

(39) Wulfstan sæde þæt he gefore   of   Hæðum; þæt he wære on Truso
      Wulfstan said that he departed from Hedeby; that he was in Truso

      on syfan dagum and nihtum; þæt þæt scip **wæs** ealne weg **yrnende** under segle
      in seven days   and nights; that the ship was   all way running under sail.
      <Or 1.16.21>
      'Wulfstan said that he departed from Hedeby; that he was in Truso in seven
      days and nights; that the ship was running under sail all the way.'

(40) Where þe dragun **was wonande**
      where the dragon was living
      'where the dragon lived'
      (*Handlyng Synne* 1760; Furnivall 1901–3 (van Gelderen 2004: 205)).

(41) We han **ben waitynge** al this fourtenyght.
      'We have been waiting all this fortnight'
      (Chaucer, *Knight's Tale*, 929, example from Fischer 1992b: 256)

But where the progressive in PDE marks off ongoing situations from
habits and general truths, this was not the case in Old English, witness
(42), or Middle English, witness (43) – both are general truths rather
than temporary, ongoing situations:

(42) þæt   seo ea   **bið flowende** ofer eal Ægypta land
      so   that that river is   flowing over all Egyptians' land
      'so that this river floods all the Egyptians' land' <Or 1.11.17> (Traugott 1972: 90)

(43) But understond wel that evermo generaly the houre inequal of
      the day with the houre inequal of the night contenen 30 degrees
      of the bordure, which bordure **is** evermo **answeryng** to the
      degrees of the equinoxial. (Chaucer, *A Treatise on the Astrolabe*
      II.10, ed. Robinson 1957: 552)
      'But understand well that the unequal hour of the day with the
      unequal hour of the night always as a general principle comprise
      30 degrees of the rim, which rim always corresponds to the
      degrees of the equinoxial circle.'

These examples show that the *form* of the progressive, i.e. the *be*+present
participle construction, is already present in Old English, but not its
PDE function.

What is the function of the *be*+present participle periphrasis? The consensus about Old and Middle English *be*+present participle constructions appears to be that they are very common with verbs like *dwell* or *live* (as in (40)) and with expressions like *always* or *ever more* (as in (43); cf. also *al this fourtenyght* 'all this fortnight' in (41)). The key point appears to be duration: the construction serves to emphasise the length of time involved. Note the co-occurrence of the phrase *ealne weg* 'the whole way' in (39), in the report of Wulfstan's voyage. Sailing directions are an important part of this text, and the fact that it took the ship seven days and nights to reach Truso from Hedeby under full sail all the way emphasises the distance travelled.

The construction experiences something of a decline in Early Middle English but becomes more and more frequent from Late Middle English onwards, and used more and more systematically, so that it becomes easier to pinpoint a number of staging posts in its grammaticalisation process.

The first staging post is its increasing time-frame use; a Late Middle English example is (44):

(44) So the meanwhyle that thys knyght **was makynge** hym   redy
      so the meantime that this knight was making   himself ready
      to departe, there com into the courte the Lady of the Laake
      to depart there came into the court the Lady of the Lake
      [CMMALORY 48.1589]
      'So while this knight was making himself ready to depart, there
      came into the court the Lady of the Lake'

The second important modern function is the progressive proper that marks an action as going on right at this moment. The default interpretation of the present tense in Germanic was imperfective and ongoing, so no special marking for actions in the here and now had been required earlier, witness this Middle English example:

(45) What! how! what do ye, maister Nicholay?
      what how what do you master Nicholay
      (Chaucer, *Miller's Tale* 3437; van Gelderen 2004: 202)
      'What! how! what are you doing, master Nicholay?'

Note that PDE requires the progressive here. The periphrasis starts to be used for this function in the sixteenth century, but it is not until about 1800 that marking ongoingness in the here and now becomes obligatory.

The third staging post is a function that has been labelled *subjective* (e.g., Kranich 2008), as it expresses a subjective evaluation of a situation by the speaker. A PDE example is (46):

(46) I took seven games out of nine off the young squash pro this morning, but of course he **was being** gentle with me. (archerii\1950-99.bre\1963whit.j9, from Kranich 2008: 234)

If you compare this to the alternative without the progressive (*of course he was gentle with me*), the effect of the progressive appears to be to give the impression that being gentle is not a permanent characteristic of the young squash pro, in the opinion of the speaker (ibid.). One of the earliest examples of this subjective use is (47).

(47) You will be glad to hear . . . how diligent I have been, and **am being** (Keats 1819, *Letters* 137, p. 357, from Denison 1998: 146)

To understand what such an utterance is communicating, compare it to the simple present: *you will be glad to hear how diligent I have been, and still are*. This seems to be a case where using the progressive forces a dynamic reading, the idea of a potential change of state. We saw something similar with the *forth*-examples in (16) to (18) above; using a dynamic expression (*forth*) with a stative verb (like *keep, remain* and *lie*) tends to have the effect that the speaker stresses that a state will not change, as if s/he is battling against an assumption that it might end. Beowulf is in effect saying something like *do not break this new friendship, keep it going* in (16); the author of (17) is denying any notion people might have that the 'loathsome beast' (sexual desire) might die down of its own accord. In (47), Keats is denying any assumptions the reader might have that his state of *being diligent* might end.

Because the rise of the progressive periphrasis in its modern function is a much more recent change than the rise of the *have-* or *be*-perfects, it can be studied in far greater detail. We can see how individual eighteenth-century writers use the progressive in their private letters (Sairio 2006), and even seem to tailor their use to that of their correspondents (Kranich 2008: 174). We find clear differences in genre, as still today – fiction and drama show higher frequencies of the progressive than academic prose. Paradoxically, such detailed knowledge throws up new puzzles of its own. The first puzzle is that it becomes harder to decide whether any changes we see in these more recent centuries represent genuine diachronic changes or whether they are the consequence of the fact that higher rates of literacy and education led to the emergence of a written as opposed to a spoken style; if the progressive is taken to be a feature of colloquial, spoken styles, the increase we see in Figure 3.2 could be due to the fact that attitudes have changed with respect to which styles are suitable for which genres. Genres aimed at the general public, like news and sermons, increasingly come to be written in colloquial spoken styles rather than formal written styles in the course of Modern English, and this might explain the sharp rise in frequencies particularly in these styles (ibid.: 172–3).

Another factor that needs to be taken into account is the association of the time-frame function as in (44) with narrative styles, which might explain the greater frequencies in fiction or private letters. Then there is the association between ongoingness and the present tense; once that association has developed and instances like (45) start to require the progressive, the progressive can be expected to be more frequent in dialogues, as these tend to be about the here and now; its rise in frequency in fiction in the 1600–1900 period could be due to an overall increase in the proportion of dialogue passages in fiction (ibid.: 172), as part of the conventions developing for the modern novel. These and other considerations show that findings as in Figure 3.2 are the starting point rather than the end of an investigation.

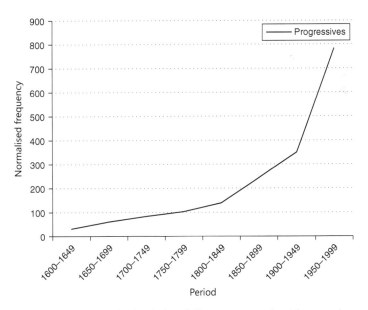

Figure 3.2 Progressives in the Archer-2 Corpus, normalised frequencies per 100,000 words, based on Kranich's data (2008: 171)

3.7 The passive

The passive is another verbal category that can be expressed in the syntax, by a periphrasis, or in the morphology, by an ending on the verb. Gothic has both: a morphological passive in the present tense, as in (48), and a periphrasis with *wairdan* 'become' (cf. (49a)) or *wisan* 'be' (cf. (49b)) everywhere else. The passive may well be the earliest of the verbal periphrases in Germanic.

(48)   jah þu,   barnilō, praúfḗtus háuhistins   **háitaza**
       and you child   prophet   highest-GEN call-PASS.PRES.IND.2sg
       (Luke 1:76; Wright ([1954] 1910: 191)
       'and thou, child, shalt be called the prophet of the Highest'
       Greek: καὶ σὺ δέ, παιδίον, προφήτης ὑψίστου κληθήσῃ

(49)   a. **gamarzidái**   **waúrþun**   in þamma
           offend-PAST.PART.NOM.MASC.PL   become-pret.3pl at that-DAT.MASC.SG
           (Mark 6:3; Wright ([1954] 1910: 191)
           'they were offended at him'
           Greek: ἐσκανδαλίζοντο ἐν αὐτῷ.
       b. jah **dáupiþs**   **was** fram Iōhannē
           and baptize- PAST.PART. NOM.MASC.SG   was by John
           (Mark 1:9; Wright ([1954] 1910: 191)
           'and he was baptized by John'
           Greek: καὶ ἐβαπτίσθη εἰς τὸν ἰορδάνην ὑπὸ ἰωάννου

The morphological passive has disappeared by the time of the earliest Old English, with the exception of the single relic form *hātte* 'is called' (Gothic *haitada*).

The verbs of the passive periphrasis in Old English use cognates of the Gothic verbs: *beon/wesan* 'be' (cf. Gothic *wisan* 'be') and *weorðan* 'become' (cf. Gothic *wairdan* 'become'). The cognates of *be* and *weorðan* have each found their own niche in Dutch and German, more or less along the lines of the difference between *be* and *get* in PDE, but the division of labour between them is not always clear in Old English (Mitchell 1985: §744ff; Kilpiö 1989). Aspect seems to be involved: *weorðan* appears to be used more often when there is a change of state, as in (50), while *beon* 'be' seems to be used with resultant states, as in (51):

(50)   Hi urnon on æfnunge ut of ðissere byrig, mid ðam ðe   ða
       they ran   in evening out of this   city   with that that the
       burhgata **belocene**   **wurdon**.
       gates   closed- past.part.nom.fem.pl became

'In the evening, they ran out of this city, at the time when the city gates were closed.' (<Josh: 2.5>, cited in Petré 2010: 63)

(51) Gehwa   wundrað hu   se hælend become into his apostolum
     Everybody wonders how the Saviour came to   his apostles
     &   **wæron** þeahhwæðere þa dura **belocene**.
     and were though   the gates closed- PAST.PART.NOM.FEM.PL
     'Everybody wonders how the Saviour came to his apostles, even
     though the doors were closed' (<ÆCHom I, 16: 308.27>, cited in
     Petré 2010: 62–3)

A change of state often does not have much duration, but it can be given duration in PDE by a progressive: 'just at the time when the gates were *being* closed' (50). In (51), it is the fact that the doors were in a closed state that is relevant, not the process of closing them.

There is a construction in which a *be*+present participle periphrasis is an active progressive form with passive meaning; it surfaces occasionally in Middle English, as in (52), and flourishes particularly in the seventeenth and eighteenth centuries (e.g., (53)):

(52) þai   crist till hething driue/ Sli   men quen þai   þam come to scriue,/
     they Christ to scorn drive such men when they them come to shrive

     þat þere er dedis doand neu,/þat þai   agh   sare   wit   resun reu
     that there are deeds doing again that they ought sorely with reason rue
     (Cursor Mundi (Vsp) 26810–13; Morris 1874–92 (Fischer 1992b))

     'they drive Christ to scorn, such people, that when they come to be shriven,
     deeds are being done again, which with reason they ought to rue deeply'

(53) Our Garden **is putting** in order, by a Man who. . . (1807, Jane
     Austen, *Letters*, Austen 1997: 119)

We find the same phenomenon with some of the *in*-progressives (cf. (23) above):

(54) While this gode   **was in gederyng** the grettes among,
     while this wealth was in gathering the greats among
     Antenor to the temple trayturly yode
     Antenor to the temple treacherously went
     (*MED, c.*1540(?a1400) *The Gest Hystoriale of the Destruction of Troy*)
     'while this money was being collected among the nobility,
     Antenor treacherously went to the temple'

From the latter half of the eighteenth century onwards, the passive meaning starts to be marked formally by the addition of the passive auxiliary *be*. Example (55) is the earliest unambiguous example found so far:

(55) That about three weeks ago, as she and her child **were being conveyed**, by a pass, to her parish (which she says is at Lidney, in Gloucestershire,) after coming part of the way, the officer set her at liberty (12–14 Nov 1761 *General Evening Post*, also 12–14 Nov 1761 *Whitehall Evening Post or London Intelligencer*, 12–17 Nov 1761 *London Evening Post*, and 16 Nov 1761 *Public Ledger*, [Burney] quoted in van Bergen (2013a))

3.8 Summary of points

- Tense and aspect are functional categories associated with the verb.
- Aspect allows the speaker to present a situation as not completed, ongoing, or completed.
- Tense and aspect categories interact with lexical (or situational) aspect of the verbs.
- Lexical or situational aspect can be described in terms of Vendler's categories of states, activities, accomplishments and achievements, and an additional category semelfactives.
- Periphrases with *have*+ and *be*+past participle developed as expressions of the perfect tense, with *have* ousting *be* in a long drawn-out process of competition.
- A periphrasis with *be*+present participle was available already in Old English to emphasise duration, and was grammaticalised into a syntactic expression of progressive aspect in Early Modern English.
- Periphrases with *be* and *weorðan* were available as a syntactic expression of the passive already in Old English, with *be* ousting *weorðan* in the course of Middle English.
- There were a number of alternatives available to express imperfective/perfective oppositions: verbal prefixes and particles, aspectualisers (*begin*), positional verbs (like *sit, stand* and *lie*), and constructions with prepositions such as *on* and *in*.
- The most recent development is the emergence of the progressive passive, towards the end of the eighteenth century.

Exercises

1. NO MARKING FOR ASPECT. Consider the following examples from the *OED* and comment on any simple verb forms that might require implicit aspectual marking by a *have*- or *be*-periphrasis in PDE.

a. But yesterday, the word of Cæsar might Haue stood against the World: Now lies he there, And none so poore to do him reuerence. (*a*1616 Shakespeare *Julius Caesar* (1623) iii. ii. 119)

b. We took a turn or two more, when, to my great Surprize, I saw him squirr away his Watch a considerable way into the Thames. (1711 E. Budgell, *Spectator*, no. 77.¶1)

c. There they reposed,..When from the slope side of a suburb hill,.. came a thrill Of trumpets. (1820, Keats *Lamia* II, in *Lamia & Other Poems* 28)

d. An inspector..tested the drain, when he found that the joints of the pipes were not properly cemented. (1893, *Law Times* **95** 62/2)

2. VERBAL PERIPHRASES.

  a. Analyse the verb strings in bold in the data below in terms of which verb selects which other verb, and name the periphrasis (or periphrases) involved.

  b. Comment on the function of the periphrasis, taking into account e.g. the period of the text, the situational aspect of the verb in question, or any other relevant information. The first one has been done for you.

(i) þa com se halga gast ofer him on fyres   hiwe, to ði
    then came the Holy Ghost over them in fireGEN shape to that [purpose]
    þæt hi **sceoldon beon byrnende** and caue   to godes willan
    that they should be   burning   and prompt to God's will
    (Old English; <ÆCHom II 44.30>)
    'then the Holy Ghost came over them in the shape of a flame so that they would be burning and ready for God's will'

Answer (a): *sceoldon* is the finite verb; it selects the infinitive *beon* (modal+infinitive periphrasis). The infinitive *beon* selects the present participle *byrnende* (*be*+present participle periphrasis). Possible answer for (b): although a verb like *burn* is dynamic and has duration, and hence is compatible with a progressive, *byrnende* is here more likely to be a present participle meaning 'in a burning condition' with *beon* as a copula. The fact that *byrnende* is conjoined with an adjective, *caf* (*caue*) 'prompt, ready' supports this interpretation.

(ii) þa he þærto **gefaren wæs**
    when he thereto gone   was
    'when he was arrived there'
    (Old English; <ChronC (894.52)>; Warner 1993: 97)

(iii) þa he þærto **gefaren hæfde**
    when he there to gone   had
    'when he had arrived there'

(Old English; *An Anglo-Saxon Chronicle from British Museum, Cotton MS.,
Tiberius B. IV* (ed. E. Classen and F.E. Harmer, Manchester University Press,
1926) 35.27 (894.59); Warner 1993: 97)

(iv)   &   in the same place þai   enterede Aurilambros, þe secunde ȝere of his
       and in the same place they interred Aurilambros the second year of his

regne, wiþ al þe   worship þat **myght bene longyng**   to soche a kyng,
reign with all the honour that might be   belonging to such a king,

of whos soule God haue mercy! (Middle English, *The Brut*, [CMBRUT 65])
of whose soul God have mercy

'and in the same place (i.e. Stonehenge) they interred Aurilambros, the
second year of his reign, with all the honour that should be due to such a
king, on whose soul God has mercy!'

(v)   Also in þat Ile   is the Mount Ethna þat men clepen Mount Gybell
       also on that island is the Mount Etna   that men call   Mount Gybell

&   the wlcanes   þat   **ben** eueremore **brennynge**.
and the vulcanoes that   are forever   burning
(Middle English, *Mandeville's Travels*, [CMMANDEV 36])

(vi)   Þer þat he hadde be   toforhand lyȝt   and nyce, he wax sad;
       there that he had   been earlier   frivolous and silly   he grew serious

þer he **hadde ibe   blaberynge and chaterynge**, he took hym to silence
there he had   been blabbing   and chatting   he took himself to silence
(Middle English, [CMAELR3, 31.148–57])

'Where he had earlier been frivolous and silly he grew serious; where he had
been given to idle chat before, he became silent'
Latin:
Successit   gravitas   levitati,   loquacitati   silentium.
succeeded seriousness light-heartedness, loquaciousness silence

(vii) þey founden an olde Cyte al wasted   &   forlete,   þat **nas**
       they found   an old   city all destroyed and abandoned that not-was

þer-in   nor man ne woman, ne   no thing **dwellynge**
therein nor man nor woman nor no thing dwelling
(Middle English, *The Brut*, [CMBRUT 8])

'They found an old city completely destroyed and abandoned in which
there was not a man, woman or other creature living'

(viii) These thingis **weren don** in Bethanye biȝende Jordan, whare Joon **was bap-
       tisyng**. (Middle English; John 1:28)

Latin:
haec in Bethania facta sunt trans Iordanen ubi erat Iohannes baptizans
these in Bethania done were over Jordan where was John baptizing

(ix) She (=Fortune) **hath** now **twynkled** ... first upon the with wikkid eye.
she   has now twinkled   first up on you with wicked eye
'she has now for the first time winked at you with a wicked eye'
(Middle English; *c.*1374; Chaucer's translation of Boethius De Consolatione
Philosophiae, Bk II, Pr 3; Robinson 1957: 332)

(x) On a day as þis creatur **was heryng** hir Messe, a ʒong man and a good prest
heldyng up þe Sacrament in hys handys ouyr hys hed, þe Sacrament schok
(Middle English, *Margery Kempe*, [CMKEMPE I, 47])

(xi) On a day long befor þis tyme, whyl thys creatur **was beryng** chylder & sche
was newly **delyueryd** of a chyld, owyr Lord Cryst Ihesu seyd to hir sche
xuld no mor chyldren **beryn** (Middle English, *Margery Kempe*, [CMKEMPE
I, 864])

(xii) a fellow whose uttermost upper grinder **is being torn out** by the roots by a
mutton-fisted barber. (1795, Robert Southey, *Life and Correspondence*, Vol I:
249; Mossé 1938, II: §263, quoted in Warner 1993: 63)

(xiii) We **are** now **having** a spell of wind and rain. (1808, Southey, *Life* III. 163,
OED, example from Warner 1995: 546)

(xiv) Like all other contestants, he hopes to make the highest jump, make the
longest freefall, and attain the highest altitude, although this achievement
will not **be recognized** as a record because he will not return to earth in
the balloon. (based on <www.balloonlife.com>, 2001, issue 10, accessed via
Webcorp)

(xv) 'Have you got a plaster handy?' says James. 'Carol went for a pee in some
primitive loo at a garage we stopped at and gashed her leg on a rusty pipe.'
Carol lifts her skirt to show a slick of dried blood across her calf. '**I'm being**
incredibly brave,' she says. [...] James, on his knees, wipes the wound.
Carol protests, laughing. '*Ouch!* James, you'**re being** absolutely brutal. Ow!'
(Penelope Lively (1996), *Heat Wave*, London, pp. 38–9)

3. THE *HAVE*-PERIPHRASIS. Identify all cases of the use of the perfect
tense in the following Middle English fragment. Say for each perfect
whether it conforms to any of the PDE usages in (9) and (10) above.
If there are any *be*-perfects, do they occur with the type of verbs that
you expect on the basis of what was said in sections 3.5.2 and 3.5.3?

And chantecleer tho seyde: Mercyful lord, my lord the kynge plese
it yow to here our complaynte, And abhorren the grete scathe that
reynart hath don to me and my children that hiere stonden. It was
so that in the begynnyng of appryl when the weder is fayr, as that I
was hardy and prowde, bycause of the grete lynage that I am comen

of and also hadde; For I had viij fayr sones and seuen fayr doughters whiche my wyf had hatched. and they were alle stronge and fatte and wente in a yerde whiche was walled round aboute, in whiche was a shadde where in were six grete dogges whiche had to tore[1] and plucked many a beestis skyn in suche wyse as[2] my chyldren were not aferd, on whom Reynart the theef had grete enuye by cause they were so sure that he cowde none gete of them. How wel oftymes hath this fel theef goon rounde aboute this wal and hath leyde[3] for vs in suche wyse that the dogges haue be sette on hym and haue hunted hym away. (Caxton, *The History of Reynard the Fox*, [CMREYNAR 11])

4. Example (55) is presented as 'the earliest unambiguous example' of the passive progressive, which implies that there are earlier examples that are ambiguous, or at least debatable. One such example is (i):

(i)   Also in what Coast or part of heauen, the Sunne, Moone, or any other starre is at any time being mounted aboue the Horizon (1597; Elsness 1994: 15, quoted in van Bergen 2013a)
     Why is (i) ambiguous? As a hint, consider (ii), from the same text:

(ii)   to shew the Altitude of the Sunne or Moone, or of any other starre fixed or wandring, being mounted at any time aboue the oblique Horizon (Helsinki Corpus; van Bergen 2013a)

Further reading

For the expression of aspect, tense and modality categories in language, see Bybee (1985) and Bybee et al. (1994). Callaway (1913: 200–3) has statistics of the Old English translation of various Latin verbal constructions. The classification of verbs into aspectual categories like activity, state, achievement and accomplishment is due to Vendler (1957). The Indo-European systems of verbal categories are set out in, e.g., Clarkson (2007). The development of aspect in English is discussed in Brinton (1988) and van Gelderen (2004). The development of the English progressive has been studied by Scheffer (1975), and more recently by Kranich ([2008] 2010); Killie (2008) presents a concise overview of the work done in this area, and of the various proposals about its emergence. The development of the English perfect is discussed in Carey (1994),

[1]   *to tore*: past tense of the verb *totear* 'tear to pieces'
[2]   *as* 'that'
[3]   *leyde* 'laid in wait'

Rissanen (1999), Wischer (2004), Lecki (2010), and Macleod (2012, 2013). The competition between *be* and *have* as perfect auxiliaries has been investigated in Mustanoja (1960), Traugott (1972), Rydén and Brorström (1987) and especially Kytö (1997). The distribution of *have* and *be* perfects with the verb *walk* has been noted by by Fridén (1948: 100) and Kerkhof (1966: 78). Toyota (2008) offers an account of the passive in English, including a very extensive bibliography. For the process of verbs developing into auxiliaries, see Kuteva (2001). For grammaticalisation in general, see Hopper and Traugott (2003) and Heine and Kuteva (2002, 2006).

Note

1. Note that these possibilities by no means account for all the uses of *ge-* in Old English, many of which are still uncharted territory. The situation is further complicated by the fact that *ge-*, in addition to the aspectual uses, is also a derivational prefix, building new lexical items: *ge-deorfan* 'perish' from a verb *deorfan* 'labour'.

4 Verbal categories: The rise of the modal auxiliaries

4.1 Introduction

The periphrases we discussed in the previous chapter developed from various syntactic constructions with *have* and *be* as full, lexical verbs, and present and past participles. There is another periphrasis that grammaticalises in English: the combination of a modal verb and an infinitive, as in (1) and (2) (modals in bold):

(1) The first lecture **will** take place on Tuesday 15 January.
(2) Students **should** attend a minimum of 75 per cent of the lectures.

The set of modal verbs has as its core members *will/would, shall/should, may/might, can/could* and *must*; these are sometimes called **central modals** because they are the most prototypical members and consistently show auxiliary behaviour in PDE. Apart from the central modals, there is a second set of expressions that have been called **emerging modals** (Krug 2000): *going to, have to, want to, got to.* These expressions share much of their meaning with members from the central group (*be going to, want to* with *will; have to, got to* with *must*) but not their syntactic behaviour; they take *to*-infinitives rather than 'bare' infinitives, for instance. Then there is a third set of verbs that oscillate between central and emerging modals: the **semi-modals** *need* (*to*), *dare* (*to*) and *ought to*.

The central modals originate from a construction in which a lexical verb took an infinitival clause as its complement. As every lexical verb builds a clause of its own, the resulting combination consists of two clauses (is **bi-clausal**), much like the periphrasis with PDE *begin* in (3):

(3) [main clause I began [subclause to see my friends in a new light.]]

Begin is a lexical verb and the nucleus of the entire clause; its complement is a *to*-infinitive, *to see*, which is also a lexical verb and the nucleus of a subclause, *to see my friends in a new light*. The central point of this chapter is that modal verbs started out as lexical verbs, with both the modal and the infinitive in its complement building clauses of their own, like *began* and *see* in (3); and that this situation changed when they grammaticalised into auxiliaries. The earlier structure of a sentence like (1), then, would have been along similar lines as PDE (3):

(4)   [main clause The first lecture will [subclause take place on Tuesday 15 January.]]

One of the effects of the grammaticalisation process is that a structure that was bi-clausal develops into a structure that is monoclausal. The modal loses lexical meaning and argument structure (**bleaching**) and the complement, the non-finite clause that follows it, loses some of its clausal structure.

4.2 The NICE-properties in PDE

4.2.1 Introduction

The characteristic that sets auxiliaries apart from lexical verbs in PDE is their special behaviour with respect to *negation, inversion* in interrogatives, *code* (ellipsis) and *emphasis*. The acronym NICE for these properties is due to Huddleston (1976: 333).

4.2.2 Negation

The negation *not* in PDE follows an auxiliary but cannot follow a lexical verb:

(5)   You should not lock your door.
(6)   *You locked not your door.

If there is no auxiliary in the clause, as in (7), *do* needs to be added to make the clause negative:

(7)   You did not lock your door.

Note that *do* does not add anything to the meaning of the clause; its sole function is to support the negative (which is why this phenomenon is called *do*-**support**).

4.2.3 Inversion

There is inversion of subject and auxiliary in questions, as in (8), and in sentences that start with a negative adverb or a negative constituent, as in (9) and (10) ('inverted' auxiliary in bold); this includes constituents that start with *only*:

(8)   **Was** it raining when he left?
(9)   Under no circumstances **should** you just come out and tell your boyfriend what happened.
(10) Only when he renounces his ambition **will** they think him fit to lead.

As with negation, *do* needs to come to the rescue if there is no auxiliary to 'invert':

(11) a.   *?**Locked** you your door?
      b.   **Did** you lock your door?
      c.   *Only when I had been in the room for five minutes **noticed** I that everyone was staring at me.
      d.   Only when I had been in the room for five minutes **did** I notice that everyone was staring at me.

There is also inversion in *wh*-questions, as we saw in section 1.4.4, where one of the steps in the question formation routine was moving the auxiliary to the left:

(12) a.   Who could buy a lion cub in Harrods in the sixties?
      b.   What could the young men buy in Harrods in the sixties?
      c.   Where could the young men buy a lion cub in the sixties?
      d.   When could the young men buy a lion cub in Harrods?

Both auxiliaries and lexical verbs have the NICE-properties negation and inversion in Old English, as well as Modern Dutch and German, its West Germanic cousins. English has innovated here; its lexical verbs have lost these properties, and they are now the preserve of auxiliaries, and *do*-support *do*.

4.2.4 Code (or ellipsis)

The complement of an auxiliary may be deleted when it can be reconstructed from the context, usually because it is identical to a complement in the immediately preceding discourse (relevant auxiliaries in bold):

(13) Paul **has** written to his grandmother, and I suppose Robert may **have** ~~written to his grandmother~~ too, even if Charlie **hasn't** ~~written to his grandmother~~ (Warner 1993: 5)

The form of the lexical verb in the deleted verb phrases (VPs) in (13) happens to be exactly the same as in the first occurrence (the past participle *written*), but this is not a requirement; in (14), the ellipted VP has an infinitive (*do*) where the first occurrence has a past participle (*done*). This means that inflection is irrelevant to ellipsis:

(14) I haven't done it but I will ~~do it~~ (ibid.: 50).

Particularly interesting are cases of partial ellipsis (or **pseudogapping**) like (15) where it is not the entire complement *drive him crazy* but only *drive crazy* that is ellipted:

(15) Probably drives him crazy to have her call him all the time. It would ~~drive~~ me ~~crazy~~. (ibid.: 6)

Of the NICE-properties, code is particularly interesting as it seems to have been a property of a small set of verbs only throughout the history of English – the verbs that developed into auxiliaries: *be*, *have*, *do*, and the modals. Full or partial ellipsis has not been attested with other verbs. Code is not a feature of Dutch or German verbs, whether lexical or auxiliary.

4.2.5 Emphasis

An auxiliary can be used for emphasis:

(16) A: Paul should have written to his grandmother to thank her for her present.
      B: But he DID write to her.

This type of emphasis is known as **polarity focus** or **verum focus**. What is emphasised is the truth of the proposition that Paul wrote to his grandmother, usually as a response to a denial.

4.3 Modelling the NICE-properties

4.3.1 Introducing the IP

The tree structures in (27a–b) in section 2.10 contained both lexical and functional categories. In (27a–b), we had a lexical head N building an NP, with a functional category (with the *ad hoc* label 'Recipient Phrase') on top. We can do the same for the lexical head V, which builds a VP, on top of which are functional projections, a 'shell' of functional information that is associated with verbs, like tense, aspect and modality. These categories will be subsumed in a single functional projection in this chapter: the Inflection Phrase or IP. IP is the projection where subject-verb agreement is mediated, so that the verb in V can appear with the correct finite inflection. This inflection requires information about tense, and about the number and person of the subject; this is why the subject moves from the VP, where it is generated, to Spec,IP. Finiteness, then, is made up of information about agreement and tense, and the I-head is its locus. As the modal auxiliaries are always finite in PDE, there is a natural link between modals and I.

With auxiliaries in I, the differences between the syntactic behaviour of auxiliaries and lexical verbs translates as a difference in position: auxiliaries end up in I, while lexical verbs remain in V. An additional difference between lexical verbs and auxiliaries in PDE in the position of adverbs and quantifiers, and the existence of contracted negatives (like *isn't, won't*), also follows from placing auxiliaries in this higher functional position.

4.3.2 Negation

The inflection phrase IP is associated with finiteness features like agreement and tense. IP mediates the agreement between the subject, in its specifier, and the finite verb, which must agree with the person and number of the subject of the clause: *the boy walk-s*, but *the boys walk-ø* (section 2.1). The triangle shapes underneath the NPs node signify that the internal structure of the NPs is irrelevant for our purposes:

(17)

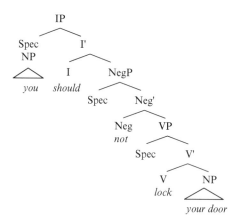

To express sentence negation, languages have the options of lexical expressions (a PDE example would be an adverb like *never*, or a quantifier like *no*) as well as morphosyntactic expressions, expressions like *not* that have grammaticalised to such an extent that they no longer behave like lexical items. In some languages, negation is an affix on the verb (and hence expressed morphologically), while in other languages it is a free form, usually with a specific position in the word order of the clause (and hence expressed in the syntax). PDE *not* is a free form, but it can also be a clitic in an auxiliary when it is contracted to *won't, shan't, haven't, wouldn't*, as we will discuss in more detail below.

The different behaviour of *not* (compared to lexical expressions like *never*) translates into a dedicated negation phrase NegP on top of VP, with *not* in the head Neg. The NICE-property negation can be accounted for in a tree structure like (17) by having the auxiliary positioned in I, rather than in V, the position of lexical verbs. If there is no auxiliary, the agreement and tense features in the I-head can be communicated to the V-head if that V-head is the next head down, and a verb like *lock* in *You lock-ø your door* or *You lock-ed your door* will appear with the correct inflection. But if the clause is negative, NegP will block the communication between I and V. This is not a problem when there is an auxiliary in I to carry the finiteness features, but if there is no auxiliary, the verb will fail to appear with the correct inflection and the clause cannot be constructed. In such cases, periphrastic *do* appears in I as a place-holder for the agreement and tense features, and the result is clauses like *You do not lock your door, He does not lock his door, You did not lock your door* – the finiteness features of tense and agreement are on *do*, and the V *lock* is in its 'bare' non-finite form.

4.3.3 Negative contraction

Placing the auxiliary in the I-head rather than in V accounts for another difference between auxiliaries and lexical verbs. Auxiliaries have a form with a contracted negative *-n't: isn't, aren't, weren't, haven't, hasn't, hadn't, won't, shouldn't*, etc., with some sociolectal variation in the acceptability of forms like *ain't, mayn't, mightn't, shan't*. Such contracted forms are not found with lexical verbs (**I known't*). Such contractions show that a reduced form of *not* attaches itself to the auxiliary as a **clitic**, a form whose morphological status hovers between a bound morpheme and a free word. In terms of a tree structure like (17), such **cliticisation** is possible with auxiliaries because they are in I, which allows *not* in Neg, as the next head down, to attach to it.

4.3.4 Inversion

The NICE-property inversion can similarly be accounted for in a tree structure like (17) by placing the auxiliary in I. Although the term 'inversion' suggests that subject and auxiliary swap places, we saw in the stepwise routines to create *wh*-questions in Tables 1.3–5 in Chapter 1 that the subject remains where it is; the auxiliary moves to a position to the left of the subject, and a *wh*-constituent moves to the very first position. In a tree structure like (18), we need two more slots to model questions, and these slots are provided by a CP layer on top of the IP. CP stands for complementiser phrase, and CP is, to all practical purposes, an alternative label for 'clause'. The auxiliary moves to the C-head from I:

(18)

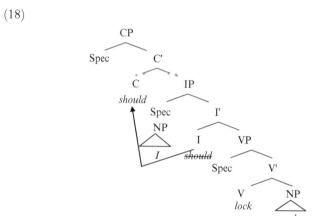

In a *yes/no* question like *Should I lock my door?*, it is enough to move the auxiliary. In a *wh*-question, there is the additional movement of the *wh*-consituent, which moves to the specifier of CP, which ensures that it is the first consituent of the clause; an example is (19):

(19)

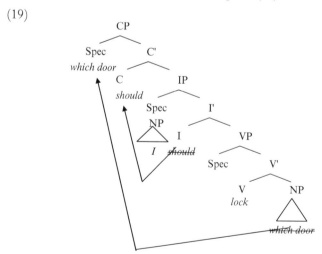

The label 'CP' requires some explanation. In a subclause, its head, C, is where the conjunction, the complementiser, would be accommodated; an example of such a conjunction in PDE is *that* in a sentence like *John told me that I should lock my door*. But why have a main clause labelled 'complementiser phrase', and why is a head seen to host two such very different elements: a conjunction like *that* in a subclause, but an auxiliary in a main clause? The way to look at this is to regard the CP as a projection that holds information about the *status* of the clause – main clause or subclause, a declarative clause or a question, etc. This information will be expressed by its head, C, either by an element whose main function is specifically to signal this function (like the complementiser *that*, which signals the start of a finite subclause) or by an element elsewhere in the clause that moves to fill C. Such an item will itself have to be a head, as it is a common observation that heads in such X'-trees are either filled by 'bespoke' elements like *that* or by other heads. In PDE, C will be filled by the next head down, I, as shown by the movement of *should* in (18) and (19). This movement is called **I-to-C movement**.

4.3.5 Code (or ellipsis)

If we position auxiliaries in I, we see that the NICE-property code translates as VP-ellipsis, although partial ellipsis is also possible, as we saw in (15). As IP is outside VP, positioning auxiliaries in I accounts for the observation in the literature that inflection is irrelevant to ellipsis; see example (14) above.

4.3.6 Adverb placement

The I position accounts for a further difference between auxiliaries and lexical verbs: the fact that adverbs and quantifiers (like *all, both* or *each*) follow an auxiliary but precede a lexical verb, as in (20a and b) and (21a and b) (adverb and quantifier in bold).

(20) a. He has **probably** locked his door.
     b. He **probably** locked his door.

(21) a. They have **all** locked their doors.
     b. They **all** locked their doors.

With auxiliaries in I and lexical verbs in V, and the adverb or quantifier in the VP, the ordering in (20 and 21) is what you would expect.

4.4 NICE-properties in historical perspective

4.4.1 Inversion: From V-to-I-to-C movement to I-to-C movement

In modern Dutch and German, finite verbs, lexical and auxiliary alike, regularly move to the second position in the clause, 'C' in tree structures like (19), not only in questions, as in PDE, but in main clauses generally. In those languages, the verb in C signals clause-typing: in main clauses, C is filled by the finite verb, and a constituent from the clause – subject, object or adverbial – has to move to the first position, Spec,CP. In subclauses, finite verbs do not move, and C is filled by a complementiser. The situation in Old English is not as clear-cut as this, although main clauses have higher rates of finite verbs in second position, and subclauses have higher rates of finite verbs in final position. An example of a finite lexical verb moving to C in Old English is (22) (moved verb in bold):

(22) a. þa   **gelædde** he hine to þæs   wyrtgeardes   gate
        then led   he him to the-GEN vegetable garden-GEN gate-DAT
        <GD (C) 3.25.13>
        'then he led him to the gate of the vegetable garden'

The corresponding tree structure is (23); note that the adverb þa 'then' comes from a position elsewhere in the clause but this movement is not shown here. The finite verb gelædde 'led' starts out in V but moves first to I to pick up its tense inflection and agree with the person (third) and number (singular) of the subject he in SpecIP and then moves to C. Note that (23) assumes underlying Object-Verb order, with the verb VP-final, rather than Verb-Object order as in PDE. The V–NP nodes of tree (18) have been flipped, so that we get NP–V. The headedness of the VP, and the IP, will be discussed in more detail in Chapters 6 and 7.

(23)

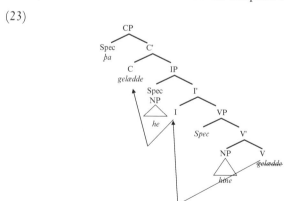

With interrogatives, movement of the finite verb to C is categorical in Old English, both for *wh*-questions as in (19) and for *yes/no* questions as in (24). The Old English example in (24) has the lexical verb *ongytest* 'understand' in C.

(24) ongytest   þu, Petrus, hu   swyðe seo eadmodnys þyhð & fremað,
      understand you Peter how much   the humility   avails and does
      þam   þe þa   godan   mægnu wyrcað?
      those-DAT that those good   miracles work
      <GD (C) 2.19.28>
      'Do you perceive, Peter, how much the virtue humility benefits and helps those who work those good miracles?'

V-to-I-to-C movement as a general grammatical rule declined in the fifteenth century, although the adverb *then* continued to trigger it well into the Early Modern English period. There is no falling-off for verb movement in direct questions, however, although V-to-I is lost with lexical verbs in the sixteenth century (as evidenced by the rise of *do*-support), and only I-to-C movement remains. Indirect questions (i.e. embedded, not main clause interrogatives), do not have finite verb movement, neither in PDE nor in Old English; see for example the *how*-clause that is the complement of the verb *ongytan* in example (24).

4.4.2 Negation

Sentence negation in Old English is achieved by a negator *ne* that cliticises onto the finite verb. If the finite verb moves, *ne* moves with it. We can assume the same structure as in (17), with *ne* in the head Neg instead of *not*. We saw that *not* may cliticise onto the auxiliary in I, but also occur as a free form; for Old English *ne*, cliticisation is obligatory, which translates as the verb having to move to Neg to pick up the negation. With a number of verbs there is also contraction, often when the verb starts with /w/: *ne is* 'not is'> *nis, ne wære* 'not were'> *nære, ne wille* 'not will'>*nylle, ne wite* 'not know'>*nyte, ne aht* >*naht* 'not ought', etc. (see Warner 1993: 151). Note that this list includes many verbs that are potential auxiliaries. An example of *nis* is given in (25).

(25) nis   se cnapa na   her
      not-is the boy   not here
      <Gen (Ker) 37.30b>
      'The boy is not here!'

There is a second negative element, *na*, in (25) whose function is to strengthen the negative meaning of the clause; *na* (also *na(wiht)* 'no creature', *naht/noht/not*) can at this stage be supposed to be in SpecNegP, and becomes the Neg head only later, after the decline of *ne* in Middle English.

A possible tree structure for (25) is presented in (26); note that (26) assumes underlying Object-Verb order, as in (23), with the verb VP-final, so that we get NP–V, or rather, in this particular case, XP–V (as *her* 'here' is not a noun). There is successive head movement: the finite verb picks up *ne* in Neg, after which the combination *ne+is* moves to I and to C. This movement would hold for lexical verbs and auxiliaries alike, until the rise of *do* support.

(26)

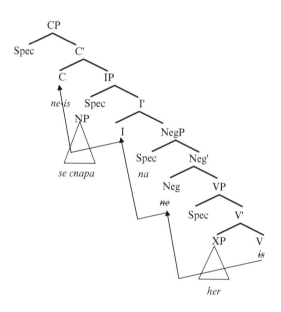

4.4.3 Code (or ellipsis)

This NICE-property, in which part or all of the VP is ellipted, appears to be attested with a number of verbs from Old English onwards. Two Old English examples are given in (27) and (28) (from Warner 1993: 112) (the relevant verbs are in bold):

(27)   deofol us wile ofslean gif he **mot**
        devil us will slay   if he can
        <ÆCHom I, 19 270.10>
        'the devil will kill us if he can'

(28) and gehwa   wende   þæt he þæs   cildes   fæder wære, ac he **næs**.
      and everyone thought that he that-GEN child-GEN father was   but he not-was
      <ÆCHom I, 13 196.12>
      'and everyone thought that he was that child's father, but he
      wasn't'

Examples of ellipsis with *if*-clauses as in (27) are also attested in the
other West Germanic languages, but not of the type in (28), nor the
Middle English examples of (29 to 30):

(29) a. Among vs he dwelleþ, And euer **haþ**..   and euer **schal**.
         among us he dwells   and ever has ... and ever shall.
      (*MED, c.*1390 *PPl.A(1)* (Vrn) 9.15)
      'Among us he lives, and always has, ... and always shall.'

(30) At hes comyng he undrestode ye were not there, and if ye **had**,
      my Lorde desired you to come. (*MED*, (1461) *Paston* 3.315)

The fact that Old English (28) and Middle English (29) and (30) show
post-auxiliary ellipsis (term due to Warner 1993) with everything after
the auxiliary being deleted indicates that auxiliaries acquired a special
status in English early on.

4.4.4 Emphasis

The NICE-property emphasis allows PDE to make a distinction
between verum focus, as in (31a), and contrastive focus, as in (31b) (both
examples from Warner 1993: 7):

(31) a. I *do* eat chocolates (in case you thought otherwise).
      b. I *eat* chocolates (I don't stuff them in my ears).

Before the rise of *do*-support which allowed this special use, (31b) would
have had to double as the expression for both verum focus and contrastive focus, as still in German and Dutch. The two types of focus only
show a difference in form in those languages if there is an auxiliary, as
in PDE (32a and b):

(32) a. But I *have* eaten the chocolates (in case you thought otherwise).
      b. But I have *eaten* the chocolates (I haven't stuffed them in my
         ears).

The close link of contrastive focus with code is clear from examples like
(29a) above, where the two auxiliaries contrastively emphasise the past
and the future (i.e. the tense of a clause). Code, then, has been a special
property of auxiliaries for many centuries, and the way code operates in

examples like (28) suggests that some of its aspects are English innovations, quite unlike code mechanisms in the other West Germanic languages.[1]

4.4.5 Adverb placement

We saw in section 4.3.6 that auxiliaries and lexical verbs in PDE are positioned differently with respect to quantifiers like *all, both* and *each*, and short adverbs like *never* or *always*. Earlier, there was no such difference; in (33), the adverb *alwayes* 'always' follows the lexical verb, whereas it would precede it in PDE (*always cries mercy*).

(33) This most precious bloud that he shed on the Crosse, cryeth
      alwayes mercye for sinners (John Fischer, *English Works* (1535),
      ed. J. B. Mayor, EETS ES 27 (1876), 412)

The date of this attestation places it right in the middle of an important development in the history of English: the rise of *do*-support.

4.4.6 Conclusions

In the tree structure modelling presented in this chapter, the NICE-properties negation and inversion, and the differences in adverb placement, translate as the V-head moving to functional heads to pick up functional information. The properties inversion and negation were not specific to auxiliaries, but common to all verbs. In this, the situation in Old English was quite similar to that in the other West Germanic languages. What has changed in the history of English is that lexical verbs are no longer moving – either because the V-head no longer moves, and only auxiliaries are able to move to C (in I-to-C movement), and act as hosts for the negative head (in Neg-to-I movement) because they start out in the I-head, or because only certain V-heads (i.e. auxiliaries) may move to the I-head. The rise of *do*-support, to be discussed in more detail in section 4.6, is the clearest sign that auxiliaries developed into a special category. Whether that means a special category within the class of verbs, or a category of items that are no longer verbs, needs to be decided on how verbal auxiliaries are. This will be discussed in the next section.

4.5 The verbal characteristics of auxiliaries

4.5.1 Introduction

We have translated the syntactic behaviour of auxiliaries and lexical verbs as a difference in position: lexical verbs in V, auxiliaries in I. The question is whether auxiliaries are in I from the beginning, or start out in V and move to I. Having them start out in V reflects an analysis in which they are a special category of verb – special in that they are the only verbs to move to I. Their special behaviour with respect to the NICE-properties is a consequence of this single property. Having them start out in I reflects an analysis in which they are 'bespoke' elements in I that are no longer analysed by speakers as verbs; such an analysis is more likely to fit the modal auxiliaries than *have* and *be*, as the modals have invariant forms in PDE, and no non-finite forms.

The question of whether auxiliaries are a special category of verbs or 'bespoke' elements in I hinges on the extent to which they exhibit typical signs of verbness like having inflections. A second characteristic of lexical verbs is that they have argument structure in the shape of semantic roles, like AGENT, PATIENT or EXPERIENCER, that are part of the lexical meaning of the verb.

4.5.2 Agreement and tense

Are auxiliaries in PDE still verbal enough to start out, or **merge**, in V, and allowed to move to I because they are a special class of V? Verbs have verbal inflections and show these inflections in a systematic way for the past tense and the past participle, -*s* for present tense third person singular versus zero-inflection for the other persons, and -*ing* for the present participle.

There is a clear distinction here between *have, do* and *be* on the one hand and the central modals on the other. *Have* shows the same inflections as lexical verbs, and its irregular simple past *had* and past participle *had* are unproblematic in view of the many irregular paradigms like *rise – rose – risen* or *keep – kept – kept* beside regular forms in -*ed*. *Do* has -*s* (*does*) and irregular past *did* and past participle *done*. *Be* is very irregular, as its paradigm is a combination of forms from several different verbs, but it does have clear present and past tenses, by which I mean that the present and the past tense have not developed distinct meanings.

The situation is somewhat different for the central modals. They lack non-finite forms (infinitives and participles). The lack of non-finite forms is of long standing; only finite forms have been attested for the forerunners of *dare, shall, should* and *must* in Old English, in spite of the fact that they are high-frequency verbs; *may* and *will* had lost them by Early Modern English, while *can*, the most lexical auxiliary of the set, retains non-finite forms in dialects, even in PDE. An Early Modern English example with a non-finite form of *may* is (34):

(34) yf we had **mought** conuenyently come togyther
      if we had might conveniently come together
      'if we had conveniently been allowed/able to come together'
      (1528 More, Worls (London, 1557) 107 H 6; The Complete
      Works of St. Thomas More, Vol. 6 (ed. Thomas M. C. Lawler,
      G. Marc'hadour and R. C. Marius, New Haven, Yale University
      Press, 1981) 26.20, Warner 1993: 200)

The central modals do not take third person singular -*s* either; there
is no agreement morphology. The reason is that these verbs were
already a special category in Old English, as **preterite-present verbs,**
a group of verbs whose past or perfect tenses had developed separate
meanings from the present tense. The Old English verb *witan* 'know'
derives from a perfect tense of a verb meaning 'see'; *witan* is cognate
with Latin *videre*, perfect *vidi* 'I have seen'. If you have seen something,
the implication is that you know it, hence the semantic shift. The
perfect paradigm had fewer inflections than the present tense, so that
we get *sceal/cann/āh/mōt* 'he shall/can/ought/must' in Old English,
with zero-endings instead of the expected -*e* for first person singular
or -(*e*)*þ* for third person singular. Importantly, these verbs did have -*t*
or -*st* for the second person singular *þu* 'thou': *þu scealt/canst/āhst/mōst*,
so that zero contrasted with -*t* or -*st* as a sign of finiteness. But this
contrast disappeared when singular *þu/thou* was supplanted by *you*, the
second person plural pronoun. When *you* was introduced as a singular
pronoun, it kept its plural, zero-inflection, rather than adopt the singular -*st* inflection of *thou*.

The preterite-present verbs used to have more members than just the
modals: *witan* 'know', *dugan* 'avail', *unnan* 'grant', *munan* 'remember', the
semi-modal *dearr* 'dare', the invariant form *uton* 'let's', and others. *Willan*
'will' did not belong to this group, but also had a deviant third person
singular, *wile*, an old subjunctive form.

Although the PDE modals are formally different from lexical
verbs because they lack inflectional endings and non-finite forms,
they do seem to have past tense forms, and these past tense forms
contain an echo of the productive past tense suffix -*ed*. They show the
expected present/past contrast in instances of direct versus reported
speech:

(35) a. She replied: 'I **will** meet you at the airport.'
      b. She replied that she **would** meet me at the airport.

We see here the usual adaptations made in reported speech: deictic
personal pronouns (*you* versus *me*) are adjusted to fit the situation, and

present tense modals turn into their past tense counterparts. This is an indication that modals still show a present/past contrast, like lexical verbs.

The present/past contrast of the modals can be argued to express more than distance-in-time; *might, should, could* and *would* have come to convey distance-in-reality, i.e. more hypothetical situations than would have been expressed by *will, shall* or *may*. However, such **modal remoteness** is a general characteristic of the past tense of any lexical verb (Huddleston and Pullum 2002: 148–51).

Unlike other lexical verbs, the present/past contrast with modals goes beyond modal remoteness in oppositions as in (36), where the difference between *can* and *could* is best decribed as a contrast in tentativeness or politeness:

(36) Can/could you pass the salt? (ibid.: 200)

The present/past contrast appears to be particularly weak with *shall/ should*, as *should* has come to be an expression of strong obligation ('ought to') that is not matched by *shall*. The modal *must* has no past tense counterpart at all; historically, it is itself a past tense, formed from a present tense *mote* which, as a preterite-present, is itself originally a perfect. *Mote* became obsolete in Middle English.

The result of this lack of inflected forms and the past tense forms acquiring independent meanings is that vital clues as to the originally verbal nature of the modals are obscured. Without inflections and little present/past contrast, speakers may analyse *shall/should* etc. as separate items rather than present and past forms of a single verb. What variation in form there is – weak forms (*'ll, 'd*, etc.) and negative contraction (*won't, wouldn't* etc.) – does not conform to what is found in lexical verbs, and hence does not provide any evidence for verbhood either. If central modals are perceived as **invariant** elements, more akin to 'bespoke' functional items like *that* or *the* than members of the category verb, this is likely to promote the analysis that they start out in I. The present/ past contrasts as still found in examples like (35) are perhaps the most robust cue left to help speakers analyse the central modals as (a special category of) verbs, starting out in V and then moving to I.

4.5.3 *Argument structure*

A second type of cue for verbhood is that lexical verbs have argument structure: semantic roles that come with the meaning of the verb. In (37), the verb *want* requires someone to do the wanting (the AGENT, or EXPERIENCER depending on how much you believe John to be in control of such an emotion), and something that he wants (in this case, *seeing you tomorrow*, a THEME). The verb *see* also requires two participants, and we have *you* as a PATIENT or THEME and *John*, again, as AGENT/EXPERIENCER.

(37) John wants to see you tomorrow.

If a PDE modal, like *will* in (38), is a lexical verb, we can expect it to have similar roles to *want*:

(38) John will see you tomorrow.

If *will* is not lexical enough to have semantic roles, *John* can only be the AGENT or EXPERIENCER of *see*, because that will be the only lexical verb in the clause. So how do we decide the status of *will* here? We could look at verbs that have no participant roles at all, like 'weather verbs'; a verb like *rain* in a sentence like (39a) is often analysed as not having any participants associated with it. Its subject, *it*, is required because finite English clauses must have subjects; *it* does not in fact refer to an entity. The fact that (39b) is not okay (unless as a creative, jocular invention that relies for its effect on the fact that using *want* adds participants, and hence evokes a mind-possessing entity) whereas (39c) with *will* is, could be taken as evidence that *will* does not have any argument structure – it does not evoke a participant, and *it* is as empty in (39c) as it is in (39a).

(39) a. It rains.
     b. *It wants to rain.
     c. It will rain.

Old and Middle English offer more scope for such diagnostic tests because of the existence of impersonal verbs. These verbs do not have the human participant in the nominative, usually because the participant is not a proper AGENT who is in control of the action but an EXPERIENCER; we saw examples in section 1.3.3. The verb *scamian* 'feel shame, be ashamed' may occur with the person who is ashamed in the accusative, and the cause of the shame in the genitive:

(40) Ðæs   us   ne scamaþ na, ac ðæs   us   scamaþ swyðe,
     that-GEN us-ACC not shames not but that-GEN us-ACC shames much

     ðæt we bote   aginnan swa. . . swa   bec   tæcan
     that we atonement begin   as   as   books teach
     <WHom 20.3 166> (see also Traugott 1992: 210)

     'and we are not at all ashamed of that, but we are ashamed of this: of beginning atonement in the way that. . . the books teach'

These verbs offer an interesting diagnostic test for the presence of argument structure with auxiliaries. What happens when we add a modal verb? Will such verbs still have non-nominative EXPERIENCERS, or will there be a nominative subject, as an argument of the modal verb? If the addition of an auxiliary does not change the case of these EXPERIENCER and CAUSE arguments, this means that the auxiliary has not brought its own participants with it, as its argument structure could have been expected to include a nominative subject. In (41), the presence of the modal *mæg* 'may' does not alter the accusative and genitive cases of the participants of *scamian*.

(41) Þon mæg hine   scamigan   þære   brædinge   his hlisan
      then may him-ACC be-ashamed the-GEN spreading-GEN his fame-GEN
      <Bo 46.5> (Denison 1993: 301)
      'then he may be ashamed of the extent of his fame'

Mæg 'may' does not appear to have come with its own participants in (41) – it is 'transparent' to the argument structure of *scamian*. This indicates that at least some modals may occur without an argument structure of their own, already in Old English, or, alternatively, that they have **defective** argument structure, and lack an argument, particularly an AGENT.

Arguments may be lost by shifts in meaning. *Shall* (OE *sceal*) originally meant 'owe, be under an obligation to' (cf. Old English *scyldig* 'guilty' and Gothic *skulds* 'obligatory'). Being under an obligation involves someone who imposes the obligation and someone on whom an obligation is imposed, so we have three arguments: an authority; a participant who carries out the act encoded by the infinitive, which we will call 'the operative'; and the content of the obligation, i.e. the infinitival clause. All three participants are present in (42a and b) with PDE *owe*:

(42) a. I owe it to you to pay this debt.
      b. I owe you this debt.

In so-called **deontic** modals, the authority-argument – *you* in (42) – is not overtly expressed, only the operative-argument. With deontic meanings like 'be obliged to' or 'be permitted to', the authority is still implicitly present. Old English (43a and b) are examples, with modals in bold; the authority in (43a) could be the speaker, or precepts laid down in law, or one's own moral standards, while in (43b) it is the holy man (addressed as 'father'):

(43) a. Ne nan man ne **sceal** elcian þæt he his synna gebete <ÆLS (As Wed) 164>
          not no   man not must delay that he his sins   atone
          'No one should delay atoning for their sins'

      b. ac þa   halgan nunfæmnan . . . hine bædon . . .: fæder, **mot** þes cniht þas niht
          but the holy   nuns   him asked   father may this boy this night
          mid þe wunian? þa . . . alyfde [he] þam cnihte, þæt he **moste** þa niht mid
          with you remain then allowed [he] the boy   that he might that night with
          him restan.<GDPref and 3 (C) 33.242.9–12>
          him rest
          'but the holy nuns asked him: Father, may this boy stay with you this night? He
          .. dien. . . allowed the boy to sleep with him that night'

When deontic modality shades into **epistemic** modality, which
expresses the subjective view of the speaker about the likelihood of
an event, there is no sense of an authority hovering in the background,
however nebulous. We can expect the single argument of epistemic
modals to be inanimate: 'something must be the case', expressing logical
deduction by the speaker rather than an obligation imposed by an
authority. In (44), the subject *hit* refers to the inanimate entity *þæt byne
land* 'the inhabited land' (modal in bold):

(44) and þæt byne   land is easteweard bradost and symle swa norðor
      and that inhabited land is eastwards broadest and always the more-northernly
      swa smælre. Eastewerd hit **mæg** bion syxtig mila   brade oþþe hwene brædre
      the narrower eastwards it may be   sixty   miles broad or   a-little broader
      <Or 1.15.25–6> (see Denison 1993: 299)
      'and that inhabited land is at its broadest in the east and it narrows steadily
      towards the northern end. At its eastern end it is probably be sixty miles broad or
      slightly over.'

If there was no subject at all, the evidence that we are dealing with
epistemic modality would be even clearer. As the requirement that
clauses must have overt subjects is not yet in place in Old English, such
examples can be found, like (45), with the impersonal verb *getimian*
'happen'.

(45) Nu **mæg** eaþe getimian, þæt eower   sum ahsige, hwi he ne mote wif
       nu may easily happen   that you-GEN.PL one asks   why he not may wife

      habban swaswa Aaron hæfde. <ÆLet 2 147> (see Denison 1993: 300)
      have   like   Aaron had

      'Now it may easily happen that one of you asks why he may not have a wife
      like Aaron had'

The development of epistemic meanings represents a further reduction in argument structure, as they can be argued to be more grammaticalised than deontic meanings. This conforms to the cross-linguistic finding that epistemic meanings tend to develop from deontic meanings rather than the other way around.

4.5.4 Concluding remarks

This section has outlined a number of characteristics that could be used to place auxiliaries on a scale from verb-like to auxiliary-like, at various points in their history. The scale reflects the degree to which auxiliaries have grammaticalised into functional rather than lexical items. It is quite likely that there will be major differences between individual auxiliaries here, with some auxiliaries showing advanced grammaticalisation early on. We will return to this point in section 4.7.

There are two phenomena that serve as watersheds here. One is the process in which the two infinitival complements – infinitives with and without *to* – were separated out into 'bare' infinitives being established as the typical complement of modals, and *to*-infinitives being established as the typical complement of lexical verbs; compare for instance (3) and (4) above. This point will be taken up in the next chapter.

The second phenomenon is the rise of *do*-support. Once *do*-support was established, I-to-C movement was restricted to the auxiliaries and to *do*-support *do*, also called periphrastic *do*, a clear sign that lexical verbs could no longer move to I.

4.6 The rise of *do*-support

A number of different origins have been proposed for periphrastic *do*, including language contact (see Denison 1993: 255–64). Two uses that may be relevant to the development of periphrastic *do* are its use as a substitute verb in ellipsis, as in (46), and as a causative as in (47), both from Old English:

(46) he ... het   þæt he wunode butan   worunge   on Godes þeowdome
      he   ordered that he live   without wandering in God's service

      þær on mynstre   a,   and he swa **dyde** eac siððan   of þam dæge
      there in monastery always and he so   did   also afterwards of that day
      <ÆLS (Maur) 96>

      'he ... ordered that he should always live without further wandering in God's service there in the monastery, and he did so, too, from that day onwards'

As a substitute verb, *do* appears in code (or ellipsis) contexts from very early on, often with *swa* 'so', as in (46).

As a causative, the verb is usually complemented by a finite clause in Old English. The infinitive in (47) is a rare example. Infinitives become more common from Middle English onwards.

(47) and treowa   he deð færlice   blowan   and eft   raðe   searian
      and trees-ACC   he does suddenly bloom-INF and again quickly wither-INF
      <HomU 34,109>
      'and he [God] makes the trees suddenly bloom and just as suddenly wither'

An interesting early example of *do* that seems to be purely periphrastic, with little lexical content of its own, is found in the thirteenth century, in rhyming verse from the southwest (Denison 1993: 264):

(48) toward þe stude þat þe sonne: In winter **does** a-rise
      towards the place that the sun in winter does arise
      (*c.*1300 SLeg. Patr. Purg. (Ld) 205.191; Horstmann 1887 (Denison 1993: 264))

Affirmative, non-emphatic declaratives as in (48) are exactly the environment that *do*-support does *not* occur in today. The rise and decline of *do* in this environment are visible in Figure 4.1 below. Today, *do* in declaratives expresses contrastive emphasis, including tense contrasts as in (49); for this type of emphasis with the other auxiliaries, see section 4.4.4 above. *Do* can also express emotive or exclamatory emphasis, as in (50) (Quirk et al. 1985: §§18.16, 1856; Denison 1993: 266).

(49) I did and do take great care of it.
(50) You do make a fuss of things.

Do has been attested reliably in this function from the fifteenth century onwards (Denison 1993: 266–7). Negative declaratives and interrogatives (questions) start to be found with *do* about a century later, but only in small numbers. The rise of *do*-support belongs to the first-half of the sixteenth century, as is evident from Ellegård's (1953) study on which Figure 4.1 is based.

Although the rise of *do*-support is more advanced in some environments (like questions) than in others, Kroch (1989) demonstrates that it proceeds in all its environments at the same rate ('the constant rate effect'). This makes it likely that we are dealing with a single underlying change. The steep rise of *do*-support in Figure 4.1 is striking: this is not a change that happened slowly, and incrementally, over many generations. Did a new generation of speakers adopt the new analysis – that

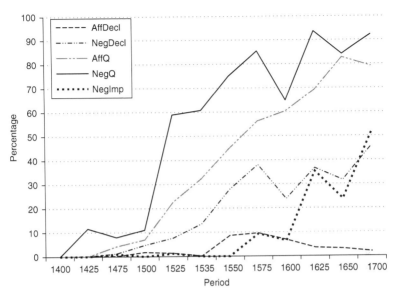

Figure 4.1 The rise of *do*-support, based on Ellegård (1953: 161, Table 7)

lexical verbs do not move to I – *en masse*, during acquisition? Was there a crucial change in their language input that tipped the scales? Had the slow erosion of verbal inflections on finite verbs reached a critical value, perhaps because of *thou* being replaced by *you*, with the loss of the distinct -(*e*)*st* inflection that we discussed in section 4.5.2? It was not just a new generation that changed its use of *do*, however – Warner (2004), investigating *do* in the works of individual sixteenth-century authors, concludes that individual authors changed the rate at which they used *do* within their lifetimes, e.g. long after the period of acquisition.

4.7 Ragged edges: *be, do, have, dare, need* and *ought to*

The rise of *do*-support was a watershed in the development of auxiliaries as a separate category. Within the class of auxiliaries exhibiting the NICE-properties, the modals are the least verb-like because of their lack of inflection and non-finite forms. *Be, do* and *have* are on the more verbal end of the scale because they have retained verb inflections, and they also have fully lexical counterparts: the copula *be*, full verb *do* and possessive *have* (**layering**, see Chapter 2). For *do*, there is a clear division between the auxiliary and its lexical counterpart: auxiliary *do* no longer has any non-finite forms, although it did earlier:

(51)   The parson wyth yow shall **do**   well sort my maister's evidenses
       the person with you shall do-INF well sort my master's evidences
       (?1456, *Paston Letters* 558.12; Denison 1993: 270)
       'The person with you will certainly sort my master's evidence for
       him'

Be is on the other end of the scale, as it has NICE-properties also as a
lexical verb (a copula); cf. *Is he ill? Isn't he ill? John is ill, and so is Susan.*
Have occupies a position between *do* and *be* in this in that it is moving
towards a complete split. Some varieties of PDE still have the lexical
verb showing NICE-properties, as in (52a), where the negation cliticises
onto the lexical verb *have*. Other varieties prefer (52b), where a new
lexical verb (*get*) rescues the situation: *have* can now be interpreted as
an auxiliary, and the mismatch between lexical verb-status and NICE-
properties in (52a) is resolved:

(52)   a. Have you any money? Haven't you any money?
       b. Have you got any money? Haven't you got any money?

Have is following in the footsteps of *do*, and of the semi-modals *dare*
and *need*, which also split into a lexical verb and an auxiliary. *Dare* (Old
English *dearr*) appears to be so bleached of lexical content that instances
like (53), in which *dearr* takes as its complement the verb *gedyrstlæ-*
can with a very similar meaning ('presume, dare, be bold') are quite
common:

(53)   Hwa dear nu   gedyrstlæcan, þæt he derige þam folce?
       who dare now dare   that he harm that people
       <ÆHomM 14, 306> (Beths 1999: 1081)
       'Who would now dare to be so bold as to harm those people?'

Dearr is a preterite-present verb in Old English and hence had fewer
inflections than lexical verbs from the beginning (see section 4.5.2).
The new lexical *dare* that develops in Middle English also develops a
fuller verbal paradigm (*dareth/dares, dared*). We find NICE-properties
and bare infinitive complements with auxiliary *dare*, and *do*-support and
to-infinitives with lexical *dare* (54a and b). Hybrids as in (54c) are not
uncommon.

(54)   a. (*OED*, 1870 E. Peacock *Ralf Skirlaugh* III. 218)   He did not
           dare to meet his uncle. Cf. *He dare not meet his uncle.*
       b. Dare he meet his uncle? *versus* Did he dare to meet his uncle?
       c. Did he dare meet his uncle? Dare he to meet his uncle? He
           did not dare meet his uncle.

Another interesting case is *ought to*, as in (55a), which has a deontic modal meaning (obligation) but appears with *to* rather than a bare infinitive. *Ought* is a grammaticalised past tense of the verb *owe*, Old English *agan*, a preterite-present verb. As a modal, its *to*-infinitival complement is unexpected. There is some hesitation in having *to* in NICE-contexts: in the question (55b) (the 'I' in NICE), *to* has been deleted; in the negative sentence in (55c) (the 'N' in NICE), we get *do*-support, as if *ought* is an infinitive of a lexical verb:

(55) a. You ought to think yourself lucky. . . to get a good position like that in these days. (*OED*, 1930 E. Waugh *Vile Bodies* ix. 150)

   b. Ought I feel ashamed of my ignorance? (*OED*, 1999 *Oxf. Times* 26 Mar. (Weekend Suppl.) 5/3)

   c. There is one voice among the altos that did not ought to be there. (*OED*, a1979 J. Grenfell *Turn back Clock* (1983) 122)

4.8 Modelling the grammaticalisation of the modals

When a lexical item grammaticalises into a functional item (or a functional item grammaticalises into an even more functional item), all levels of linguistic description may be affected, as with the grammaticalisation of *on* in *on foot* (>*afoot*) in section 2.7.1. The grammaticalisation of *will* from lexical verb to auxiliary shows similar effects (see Table 4.1).

   In section 2.7 the link between expressing functional information in the morphology, by a bound morpheme, and in the syntax, by a free word, was modelled by having the same functional head (with the working title of R for 'Recipient' in a 'Recipient Phrase') host an inflection at one stage, and a free form at a later stage – this is one of the parameters of syntactic variation discussed in Chapter 1. For the periphrases with *have* and *be* in Chapter 3, the inflections that may have expressed similar tense and aspect meanings had been long gone at the time the periphrases arose; in the case of the passive, Gothic still showed a morphological passive, side by side with a periphrasis. The morphological expression that might have filled the niche later occupied by the modals was the subjunctive.

   The subjunctive is a form of the finite verb that indicates that the action expressed is not a fact but a potentiality. Compare PDE (56a and b), from Duffley (1994: 234) (relevant verbs are in bold):

(56) a. John insists that Mary **knows** the answer   (indicative)
   b. John insists that Mary **know** the answer   (subjunctive)

Table 4.1 The grammaticalisation of *will*/*would*

	Lexical verb > auxiliary
Prosody	stress is reduced: *will* and *would* have weak forms, and clitic forms (*'ll*/*'d*)
Phonology	PDE has phonologically reduced forms [wəl, əl, l, wʊd, wəd, əd, d]
Morphology	*'ll*/*'d* are clitics that require a host (*he'll, he'd*)
Syntax	as a lexical verb, *will* is in V and has argument structure/semantic roles; as an auxiliary, it is in I and its argument structure is defective or absent
Lexicon	as a lexical verb, *will* has a volitional meaning ('want'); as an auxiliary, *will* is used to mark future tense while *would* marks epistemic modality

The form *knows* in the subclause in (56a) has the -s ending we expect for a third person singular subject like *Mary*. The form *know* without this ending in (56b) is a subjunctive. As the absence of an ending in (56b) contrasts with the -s in (56a), *know* in (56b) has a zero-ending rather than no ending. The contrast between a and b is that John takes Mary knowing the answer to be a fact in (56a), whereas in (56b) the implication is that Mary still does not know the answer; Mary knowing the answer is a potentiality or a possibility rather than a reality. For those languages that have a subjunctive mood, the 'normal' form, like *knows* in (56a), is known as the indicative mood.

The subjunctive mood in PDE is a fairly marginal phenomenon whose status is much debated (see Aarts 2012); note that (56b) sounds very formal, and is exclusively directive, i.e. it conveys an obligation (what people should do). In less formal contexts, we are more likely to find the modal *should* instead of the subjunctive:

(57) John insists that Mary should know the answer.

The subjunctive was alive and kicking in Old English. An example is (58):

(58) þu secst to witanne, hwilc his mod **wære**. . . <GD 1 (H) 5.44.29>
    you seek to know   which his mind were-SUBJ
    'you seek to know, what his mind might be'

Not surprisingly, typical environments for subjunctives both in Old English and in PDE include conditional clauses (*if I were rich*. . .), wishes (*God be with you*), and any action that is feared, promised, ordered, hoped, expected, or insisted upon by someone (as in 56b). Such subclauses could have modal verbs already in Old English, as in (59):

(59)   he him behet   þæt he cuman **moste**   mid him to ðam ecan wuldre
       he him promised that he come might-SUBJ with him to the eternal glory
       'he promised him that he would be allowed to enter into eternal glory
       with him' <ÆHom 20, 246>

Note that *moste* 'might' is itself likely to be in the subjunctive (even though indicative and subjunctive inflections are not formally distinct for third person singular in the past tense). Old English modals are not used as an alternative expression for the subjunctive; the modals are still used in their own right in Old English rather than as a substitute for eroded subjunctive endings (López Couso and Mendez Naya 1996). Modal verbs are primarily used for clearer and more concrete expression of the required nuance of volition, permission or obligation that the situation demands. This is the reason why the subclauses in the complement of some of these verbs of fearing, promising, ordering, hoping, expecting or insisting have far higher frequencies of modal verbs versus subjunctives than others; the wider the range of meanings such a verb allows, the greater the need for modals (Ogawa 1989). *Behatan* 'promise' in example (59), for instance, may express the speaker's promise that s/he will perform the action expressed by the subclause, but may also express a permission promised by the speaker. These interpretations affect the identity of the subject of the subclause. A modal verb may disambiguate these meanings, as shown in (60); the indices *i* show the intended referent of the pronominal subject of the subclause:

(60)   a. He$_i$ promised him that he$_i$ would enter into eternal glory with him
       b. He promised him$_i$ that he$_i$ might enter into eternal glory with him

If (59) had not had a modal verb, but only *cume*, the subjunctive form of *cuman* 'come', the hearer would have had to rely on the context only. The presence of the modal *moste* immediately disambiguates the intended meaning, and the reference of the pronoun. Modals started to be used primarily as expressions of irrealis in Middle English.

   To model this development, we start from the morphologically complex structure (61a). The subjunctive ending is merged in the functional head I. As a bound morpheme, it cannot stand on its own, and hence has to attract another head to be its host. This is the lexical head V, which moves to I for that purpose. In the syntactically complex structure (61b), a free form, a modal, is merged in that same head I, without requiring any additional movement. This is completely parallel to the modelling of dative case and a prepositional phrase with *to* in section 2.7.

(61)

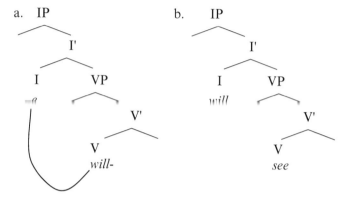

How these structures sit in the sentence is shown in (62a and b), for *will* in example (38):

(62)

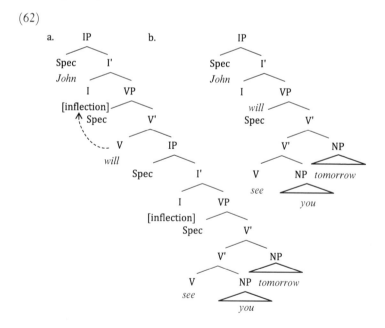

Will as a lexical verb in (62a) has more structure than *will* as an auxiliary in (62b): there are two lexical verbs, so two clauses, and two IPs, in

(62a), and one lexical verb, so one clause, in (62b). Positioning *will* in I in (61b–62b) reflects an interpretation in which it is no longer recognisable as a verb (an invariant form without argument structure), and where *John* and *you* are semantic roles of *see*. There is in fact a middle position between these two extremes in which *will* is still a verb that starts out in V and moves to I, as in (62a). Its movement is not required because of the presence of a subjunctive inflection in I (we would suppose the modal to be inflectionless at this middle stage) but because the *irrealis* information in I has to be expressed.

This kind of modelling leads to the insight that functional information can be expressed in three ways rather than just two: (1) a bound morpheme merged in the relevant functional head, which requires another head to move to that functional head (*merge* and *move*); (2) a free form moving to the relevant functional head (*move*); and (3) a 'bespoke' free form merged in the relevant functional head (*merge*) (Roberts and Roussou 2003).

4.9 Summary of points

- The auxiliaries in PDE shows different syntactic behaviour from the lexical verbs in negation, question formation, code/ellipsis and emphasis; these are the so-called NICE-properties.
- In X'-tree structures, the NICE-properties translate as properties of the I(nflection)-Head of the I(nflection) Phrase or IP, and the interaction between this I-head and other heads.
- I(nflection) contains information about tense and agreement, the two features that make a verb finite. The agreement feature depends on the person and number features of the subject of the clause, in Spec,IP.
- N in NICE for negation translates as I not being able to communicate its agreement-features to the lexical verb in V because there is an intervening head Neg(ation).
- I in NICE for inversion translates as I-to-C movement in questions.
- The loss of NICE-properties for lexical verbs, and the development of *do*-support, can be modelled as the loss of V-to-I movement.
- Highly grammaticalised auxiliaries can be argued to start out in I rather than V, while less grammaticalised auxiliaries can be argued to start out in V but move to I, an analysis which reflects their status as still verbal enough to be recognised as verbs, but distinct from lexical verbs in being able to move to I.
- The degree of grammaticalisation depends on what clues are available to speakers to decide whether a linguistic form is a verb.

Important clues are the presence of an inflectional paradigm and the evidence of argument structure.

- Unlike the modals, *have, be* and *do* have split into a lexical verb and an auxiliary, but the syntax of their respective lexical and auxiliary counterparts is not always neatly aligned with their status. The same goes for the semi-modals *dare, need* and *ought to*. In the case of *dare*, the lexical features – having inflections, non-finite forms and *do*-support – are a relatively recent development.
- The grammaticalisation of lexical verbs into auxiliaries was a long-drawn out process that was probably already underway in Old English; some modals have never been attested in non-finite form.
- The modals were part of a larger class of preterite-present verbs that had fewer inflections to start with. The loss of the second person singular inflection -(e)st (for *thou*) in the sixteenth century removed the only remaining finite inflection.
- Two developments were important watersheds for the development of modal auxiliaries: (1) lexical verbs ceased to take bare infinitives as their complement in Middle English, which meant that bare infinitives were increasingly associated with modals rather than with lexical verbs; (2) the rise of *do*-support, indicating that V-to-I movement was lost with lexical verbs. These two developments set modal auxiliaries apart as a special category.

Exercises

1. MEANINGS OF MODAL VERBS. Look up *can, may, must and need* in the *OED*. What are their original meanings? Construct from the meanings given in the *OED* how their meanings may have bleached into their present epistemic and deontic meanings. Give an example of each meaning, and note the argument structure of each example.

2. DEFECTIVE PARADIGMS. We saw in the previous chapter (section 3.4.1) that Ælfric's *Latin Grammar* can be very informative about Old English. Consider the following passage in which Ælfric discusses the conjugation of the Latin verb *licere* 'be allowed'. What do his Old English translations tell us about the Old English verb *mot* 'may'?

(i) a. licet mihi bibere: mot   ic drincan
                                MOT-1SG I drink-INF
   b. mihi licuit: ic moste
                               I MOT-past
   c. si nobis liceret: gyf we moston
                               if we MOT-PAST-1PL

d. *infinitivvm* licere: beon alyfed
be   allow-PAST.PART (from OE *aliefan* 'allow')
<ÆGram 207.1> (Warner 1993: 146)

3. INFLECTION. PDE speech errors: compare the actual utterance with the intended utterance and analyse what has gone wrong. Be as specific as possible:

(a) (i)   Actual utterance: He kinds a tend ta (Thompson 2005: 163)
Intended utterance: *He kind of tends to*
   (ii) Actual utterance: Rosa always date shranks (Cutler 1988: 221)
Intended utterance: *Rosa always dated shrinks*
   (iii) Actual utterance: He not seem happy now (Thompson 2005: 164)
Intended utterance: *He doesn't seem happy now*
   (iv) Actual utterance: Aren't you glad you not gent? (Cutler 1988: 221)
Intended utterance: *Aren't you glad you didn't go?*

4. THE SEMI-MODAL *DARE*. The preterite-present verb *dare* (OE *dearr*) split into an auxiliary and a lexical form in Early Modern English (see section 4.7). Consider the following examples, presented in chronological order (from Beths 1999: 1094–1099).

a.   Which are examples of *dare* as an auxiliary and which are of *dare* as a lexical verb? On what criteria do you base your judgements?
b.   Note any hybrids (such as (54c) in section 4.7).
c.   A phenomenon observed with the other modals is that the present and past tense forms fail to encode a present/past contrast and go on to develop separate meanings. Note any forms of the *durst* – the original past tense of *dare* – in these data that appear to have a non-past meaning.

   (i)   He a word ne sal   dur   speke.
He a word not shall dare   speak
(a1300 Cursor 22603 [Cott.]; Visser 1969: §1366)
'He will not dare to say a word.'
   (ii) (*MED, c.*1400 St. Anne [1] 1415)
Þai went be nyght, for þai ne dursted Be day.
   (iii) (*MED*, a1425 (a1400) RRose 809)
If I hadde durst, certeyn I wolde have karoled
   (iv) (1448 Shillingforth 53; Visser 1969: §1368)
Þe Mayer hath not dar do right lawe ne execucon.
   (v)   (*c.*1451 Bk. Noblesse 72; Visser 1969: §1366)
That none of youre officers roialle, . . . shalle darre . . . to take no bribe.

(vi)   (*MED*, a1500 Man yff thow 39–40)

          I dare wel say, To do the [=thee] to deth they had not durst.

(vii)   (1509 Barclay, *Shyp of Folys* I, 207; Visser 1969: §1368)

          They sholde not have durst the peoples vyce to blame.

(viii)   (*OED*, 1529 W. H. Turner Select. Rec. Oxf. 65)

          They have dared to break out so audaciously.

(ix)   (1533 J. Heywood *Mery Play*; Visser 1969: §1362)

          The kokold . . . for his lyfe daryth not loke hether ward.

(x)   (1587 Marlowe *Tamb.* 10; Crawford 1911)

          where the sun dares scarce appear for freezing meteors

(xi)   (1589 Marlowe *Dido* 1350; Crawford 1911)

          but dares to heap up sorrow to my heart

(xii)   (*OED*, 1580 Lyly *Euphues* 316)

          An English man .. [cannot] suffer .. to be dared by any.

(xiii)   (*OED*, c.1590 Greene *Fr. Bacon* iv.10)

          Lovely Eleonor, Who darde for Edwards sake cut through the seas.

(xiv)   (1591 Marlowe *Locrine* 1835; Crawford 1911)

          think'st thou to dare me, bold Thrasimachus?

(xv)   (1592 Kyd *Sol. & Pers.* 2056; Crawford [1906–10] 1967)

          and one that dares thee to the single combate

(xvi)   (1606 Shakes. *Anth. & Cleo.* III.xiii.25; Spevack 1969)

          I dare him therefore To lay his gay Comparisons apart.

(xvii)   (1611 Shakesp. *Cymb.* IV.i.24; Spevack 1969)

          the fellow dares not deceive me.

(xviii)   (1611 Shakesp. *Cymb.* III.iii.33; Spevack 1969)

          A prison for a debtor, that not dares To stride a limit.

(xix)   (1634 Milton *Comus* 577; Visser 1969: §1359)

          Longer I durst not stay.

(xx)   (*OED*, 1641 Burroughs *Sions Joy* 26)

          They dared not doe as others did.

(xxi)   (1644 Milton *Areopagitica* 150; Visser 1969: §1362)

          the printer dares not go beyond his licenc't copy.

(xxii)   (*OED*, 1650 Fuller *Pisgrah* I.145)

          They dared not to stay him.

(xxiii)   (1668 Dryden *Essay D. P.* 306; Visser 1969: §1360)

          as if they . . . did not dare to venture on the lines of a face.

5. a. Draw a tree structure of (xviii), in the simplified form of *he not dares to stride a limit*, and of (xxi). (Do not attempt to show the internal structures of any PPs or NPs – draw triangles instead, as in (17).) You might want to take the structure in (17), for PDE modals, as a model. Discuss any problems.

6. Go to the *OED* online <www.oed.com> and look up *not*, 'adv., n., and int.'

    a. In section A I.1, '1. Preceding a simple tense or form of a verb', you will find 21 examples of *not* preceding a lexical verb, ranging in date from 1299 to 2000.

    b. In section A 3, 'Following a full verb' you will find 19 examples of *not* following a lexical verb, ranging in date from ca. 1330 to 2000.

    c. In both these lists, the headings indicate that these orders are apparently no longer productive in PDE: 'Now usually (chiefly N. Amer.) with a subjunctive verb in a subordinate clause. Relatively common in 15th-cent. texts; subsequently often poet[ical]' (for section A I.1) and 'Now chiefly arch[aic] or literary and humorous' (for section A 3). What is the productive order? How would you analyse these two unproductive orders in terms of a tree structure such as (17)?

    d. Go though both lists, and mark any examples in which the older order is probably used as a deliberate archaism (for a literary, poetic or humorous effect). Do their dates tally with what you would expect?

    e. The *OED* warns that the speaker of this quotation is German:
        (i) (*OED*, 1816 Scott *Antiquary* II. ii. 48) My little secret..– you sall forgife me that I not tell that.
    What difference does this knowledge of the context of (i) make to our interpretation of it?

Further reading

For an account of the development of modal auxiliaries in English, see Lightfoot (1979), Planck (1984) and particularly Warner (1993). Verum focus is discussed in Höhle (1992) and Gutzmann and Castroviejo Miró (2011); and lexical expressions for epistemic modality in the history of English are investigated in Lenker (2000) (Old English *witodlice, soþlice* 'in truth') and Bromhead (2009) (Early Modern English *verily, surely, forsooth, by my troth*, etc.). For the development of *dare*, see Beths (1999); for the development of *need*, and other expressions of necessity, see Loureiro-Porto (2009). Duffley (1994) provides a detailed account of the different semantics of lexical and auxiliary *need* and *dare* in PDE. The present chapter has only briefly mentioned the invariant Old English auxiliary *uton* 'let's'; it is discussed in detail in van Bergen (2013b). The loss of the NICE-properties and the development of *do*-support was first described in terms of V-to-I movement by Roberts (1985). Getty (2000) has an interesting account of the grammaticalisation of Old English verbs by using stress in Old English poetry as a diagnostic. For modelling grammaticalisation in a generative framework, see Roberts and Roussou (1999, 2003) and Fuß (2005). Evidence for the development of *do*-support can be found in Ellegård (1953), and see Kroch (1989) and Warner (2004), (2006) for interpretations and further data. Face and politeness also have a bearing on modal meanings; see Brown and Levinson (1987) and Mills (2003). An interesting account of grammaticalisation cycles in negation in English can be found in van Kemenade (2000). For negation in Middle English and the loss of *ne*, see Ingham (2000) and Iyieri (2001).

Note

1. German and Dutch have developed modal adverbs (*doch*/*toch*, cognates of PDE *though*, and *wohl*/*wel*, cognates of PDE *well*) as an additional resource to express verum focus lexically. These particles include the negative adverb *nicht*/*niet* 'not' and the additive adverb *auch*/*ook* 'too', and form a coherent group, showing the same behaviour in code.

5 Complementation

5.1 Introduction

The previous chapters involved the grammaticalisation of various individual elements, prepositions, articles and auxiliary verbs, which exemplify the first of the three parameters of syntactic variation we set out in Chapter 1: the morphological or syntactic expression of functional information. The present chapter involves the second parameter, the expression of the semantic roles of the verb. The expression of these roles depend on the meaning of the verb. AGENTS will be NPs, LOCATIONS will be PPs (in a language like PDE) or NPs with particular cases (in a language like Finnish), so that the expression of the various roles of verbs like *come, go, roll* or *sit* are fairly predictable across languages. What is interesting from the perspective of variation and change is the complements of verbs that themselves contain a verb: complements that encode propositions (as with the verb *think*), events (as with the verb *see*), or actions and activities (as with the verb *persuade*). The embedded verb can be a V in a finite clause, as in (1), where the proposition is encoded by a finite subclause (in bold), or a V in a non-finite clause, i.e. an infinitive or a participle, like the *to*-infinitive in (2):

(1)   He thinks that stalking is a crime.
(2)   He considers stalking to be a crime.

Propositions are often pronouncements or claims that involve a copular relationship; (1) has a finite form of *to be*, while (2) has the non-finite form. There is also a verbless construction that expresses a copular relationship, and this, too, can be used to express the propositional complement of verbs like *think* and *consider*.

(3)   He considered stalking a crime.

See, or *hear*, as perception verbs, can be expected to be complemented by an NP (*see a comet, hear music*) but also by a constituent containing a

123

verb, as what can be seen or heard can be events. PDE has two non-finite expressions for events: a bare infinitive in what is called an accusative-and-infinitive construction or AcI,[1] and a present participle:

(4)   He heard a glass/glass/glasses smash in the beer garden.
(5)   He heard ?a glass/glass/glasses smashing in the beer garden.

Example (5) brings out an aspectual difference between the two complements. *Smash* is a punctual verb with very little duration (see section 3.3). Perception verbs force durativity, and hence are compatible with present participle complements, alongside the older AcI. When there is only one glass, the present participle becomes far less acceptable, and the bare infinitive is a better option. The plural *glasses* sets up a series of punctual events (iterativity) which gives the event duration; the mass noun *glass* leaves the quantity of glass unspecified, leaving room for the interpretation of multiple smashing events, and duration. The present participle apparently requires duration, while the bare infinitive is aspect-neutral.

A finite clause is possible with *see* or *hear*, as in (6)–(8), but the meaning of *see* with such a clause often seems to be more akin to *detect, find (out)* or *understand*, verbs of thinking and declaring that take propositions (*consider* in (2)–(3) also belongs to this group) – the finite clauses in (6)–(8) do not report events, but conclusions based on witnessing events:

(6)   I spend days and evenings with him and can see that he has severe depression.
(7)   If people see that you aren't excited or optimistic about their involvement, then they probably won't invest very much of themselves.
(8)   I saw that my life was a vast glowing empty page and I could do anything I wanted. (Kerouac 1959: 148)

Apart from (3), the examples so far are of clauses as complements (and even the construction in (3) is sometimes referred to as a small clause). Another complement that contains a V is a nominalisation, a V inside an N. In (9) we have a string of verbs originally referring to quenching a fire but metaphorically extended to quench various goings-on; the NPs are the result of internet searches and the *OED*:

(9)   a. put down – a mutiny/a rebellion/an uprising/the whisky trade
       b. quell – false reports/someone's fears/the opposition/a quarrel/an uprising
       c. stamp out – this cruel practice/drug use/a thousand other sufferings and evils/sex-selective abortion/drinking

The complements in (9) are NPs, but their head nouns contain stems of verbs. Such nominalisations are of particular interest in this chapter because they can be the origin of non-finite verbs.

Complementation patterns usually show broad trends, with verbs with similar meanings tending to take similar complements; and the association with certain groups of verbs lend some sort of meaning to the complements themselves, albeit a highly abstract one. Matching verbs to complements is a bi-directional process: the more verbs a complement appears with, the more general its meaning will become; and the more general its meaning becomes, the more verbs will appear with it. This chapter will chart the waxing and waning fortunes of the most recent innovations, the *to*-infinitival clause, the present participle clause, and the gerund.

5.2 Ragged edges: Usage and productivity

5.2.1 Introduction

The fact that there is a system does not mean that we can predict which complement an individual verb will take at any one time; there is a lexical component as well, in that a combination of verb+complement must be licensed, as it were, by use. We saw in section 4.7 that most PDE modals take bare infinitival complements, but *ought* takes a *to*-infinitive, and *dare* and *need* take both. A new complement, like the *to*-infinitive in Old English or the *ing*-gerund in Early Modern English, diffuses only gradually through any particular subset of verbs, and this process is bound to leave ragged edges. The verbs *set, make* and *cause* in (10) express causation: someone or something is causing some event. Their complements differ, however. Relevant verbs are in bold; relevant non-finite verbs are underlined; all from De Smet (2013: 5):

(10) a. The examples here should **set** you thinking. [*ing*-gerund]
      b. It **made** Euphrasia think. [bare infinitive]
      c. If there are any defects likely to **cause** the house to fall down around your ears, they are not the inspector's concern. [*to*-infinitive]

The period in which individual verbs were borrowed, or in which they acquired the meaning that made them good candidates for any of the clausal complements in (10), has a bearing on the complement they appear with in PDE. The reason is that the complements in (10) were not all as productive in any given period. It is this phenomenon that seems to underlie the mismatch in (10). We will describe the histories of each of these verbs below.

5.2.2 Set

The verb *set* originally means 'cause to sit', hence 'cause to be, put, place', said of inanimate things. Later meanings involve people: 'To place (a person) in an office, appoint to a certain function or to perform a certain duty' (*OED, set* V†46), and 'to allot or enjoin (a task)' (*OED, set* V55), first with a *to*-infinitive: *I shall not set him anything to do* (*OED* 1847). Even later is the meaning 'to set (a person) upon: to put in the way of doing or performing, cause to be occupied with (something): often with implication of urging or impelling' (*OED, set*, 114): *set a wheel on going* (later *a going* or just *going*). This is the causative meaning that makes examples possible like (11a and b), the forerunners of (10a):

(11) a. It was perhaps this that set..Jem on stealing my own silver goblet (*OED*, 1889 'F. Pigot' Strangest Journey 188)
   b. Which perhaps will set..You..a thinking. (*OED*, 1660 R. Boyle New Exper. Physico-mechanicall xvii. 129)

5.2.3 Make

Make in (10b) acquired its causative meaning much earlier. It was not the 'causative of choice' in Old English – that position was taken by *lætan* 'let' – and its meaning was probable closer to 'see to it, bring about' than to 'cause'. As such it appeared with a finite complement in Old English. Its causative meaning became more prominent in Middle English, and we find it with an AcI, as in (12), by analogy with *lætan* 'let':

(12) King willam..made hom bere him truage (*OED, c.*1325 (*c.*1300) Chron. Robert of Gloucester (Calig.) 7669)
   'King William made them pay him tribute'

We also find *make* with the *to*-infinitive, as in (13), which was the productive complement for **directives** – verbs with meanings like 'order, command'.

(13) Þe oþer leuedis..maked hir away to ride. (*OED, c.*1330 Sir Orfeo (Auch.) 329)
   'The other ladies made her ride away'

Ultimately, each complement found its own syntactic niche, with the bare infinitive for active, and the *to*-infinitive for passive *make*. The reason for this strange arrangement is that AcIs do not allow passives: *She saw John cross the road*, **John was seen cross the road*. There was no such restriction with the *to*-infinitive with directives (*She ordered John to cross the road, John was ordered to cross the road*). *Make* dropped the *to*-infinitive for the active, but kept it for the passive. This juxtaposition of an AcI in the active and a *to*-infinitive in the passive became a model for the perception verbs, which followed suit: *John was seen to cross the road.*

5.2.4 Cause

Cause, in (10c), is a late borrowing, from Latin, first attested in English in 1340 (*OED*) and appearing with the *to*-infinitive, which was the productive complement of directives at the time. The *to*-infinitive has remained its complement to the present day, although there was a brief window (*c.*1500–1650) where we find AcIs (with bare infinitives, in bold):

(14)   How durst thou..to be so bold To cawse hym **dy**? (*OED c.*1485 Digby Myst. (1882) iv. 543)

(15)   Take heed, you doe not cause the blessing **leaue** you. (*OED* 1612 B. Jonson Alchemist ii. iii. sig. D3v)

5.2.5 Conclusions

The ragged edges of the distribution of non-finite complements, then, are not as ragged as all that if we take into account the period the verbs entered the language, and which other verbs served as their model at the time. A complement in time may come to be associated with a coherent family of verbs that share a meaning component, and hence acquire a (very abstract) meaning of its own. Verbs may switch to that complement if their meaning fits it, as in the case of *cause* and *make*, which switched from the complement-of-choice for directives to what had become the productive complement-of-choice for causatives, but they may also remain associated with their earlier complement, as an effect of frequency and usage.

The situation of PDE *set, make* and *cause* in (10) can be clarified by the diagram in Figure 5.1 on the next page.

5.3 The rise of the *ing*-form

5.3.1 Introduction

The *ing*-form as complement – both present participles and gerunds – is of such a recent date that its progress can be charted in some detail. Our main source for this section is De Smet (2013), which in turn builds on earlier work (Fanego 1996a, b, c and 2004; Tajima 1985).

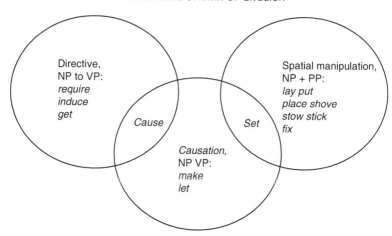

Figure 5.1 Directive, causation and spatial manipulation complements

As a first introduction, consider the PDE text below (*ing*-forms in bold):

(16) A third of **aspiring** first-time buyers have given up hope of
owning a property and spent what they had saved for a deposit
on holidays, cars and other luxuries, a survey has found. A
study of 2,000 under-35s found that, despite the Government's
Help to Buy scheme, large deposits are **ruining** their dreams of
getting onto the property ladder. Around 70 per cent of those
saving for a deposit have become so disillusioned that they have
abandoned the effort and spent the money on holidays, cars or
simply to cover bills. Results revealed many people now see
becoming a home owner as so unrealistic that they've decided
to splash money on temporary luxuries or intangible things,
further **reducing** their ability to buy property in the future.
Shared ownership has historically been there to help support
low-income families purchase part of their home, but is now
increasingly **being** seen as a way to get on to the property ladder
in London. Seven in 10 think it will be five years or more before
they can turn their dreams of **being** a home owner into reality. A
fifth of those **saving** deposits end up **abandoning** their attempts
and **spending** the money, while a similar number spent 'most of
it' and 31 per cent spent some of it rather than **leaving** it intact.
Just 30 per cent of those **trying** to save a deposit have managed
to leave their savings untouched. **Needing** money to cover day-
to-day bills was the biggest reason to dip into the deposit, while
a third spent it on a holiday. Reasons to abandon attempts to own

a home ranged from worries about job security to a long-term relationship **ending**. A third of the sample had explored their property-**buying** options and were disappointed by what was available in their price range. (*Telegraph*, 20 October 2013)

Some of the *ing*-forms are gerunds, while others are present participles. The present participles are found in various syntactic functions: (1) adjectival, premodifying nouns (*aspiring*); (2) expressing the progressive in periphrasis with *be* (*ruining, being seen*); (3) as a non-finite relative clause (*those saving, those trying to save*, cf. their finite counterparts *those who are saving, those who are trying to save*); (4) as a non-finite adverbial clause (*further reducing their ability to buy property in the future*, cf. its finite counterpart *while they further reduce their ability to buy property in the future*).

These participles are verbs: a clear diagnostic for verbhood is that they take objects (*reducing* has as its object *their ability to buy property in the future*). They are also extremely versatile; *buying*, used as an adjective to premodify the noun *options*, comes with its own object, *property*, as the leftmost-member of a compound *property-buying*, compare a similar construction with past participles like *laden* as in *an explosives-laden car*.

The *ing*-forms that appear in syntactic functions associated with NPs are gerunds. In (16) we have gerunds appearing: (1) as subject (*Needing money to cover day-to-day bills*), (2) as object (*becoming a home owner*) or (3) as complement to a preposition (*owning a property, getting onto the property ladder, leaving it intact*).

Present participles used to have the ending *-end(e)/-and(e)* in Old and Early Middle English (section 3.6), but this ending merged with the *-ing* ending of the gerund (earlier *-ung/-ing*). Deciding whether an *-ing*-clause in PDE is a gerund or a present participle is not always easy (see De Smet 2010).

5.3.2 Origin of gerunds

The *-ing* of the gerund derives from an Old English suffix (*-ung/-ing*) that formed **nominalisations**, i.e. nouns from verbal stems. Old English examples are given in (17)–(20):

(17) ðises   lifes   **gewilnung** gelæt þa unstæððian to manegum leahtrum
      this-GEN life-GEN longing-NOM leads the weak   to many   vices
      <ÆLS (Sebastian) 67>

      'The longing for this life leads the weak to many vices'

(18)   Him becom þa   on mod þurh   **mynegunge**   godes   þæt heo sceolde
       him came   then in mind through admonition-DAT God-GEN that he   should
       secan þa soðan lare . . . <ÆLS (Basil) 29>
       seek the true   doctrine
       'It then came into his mind through the admonition of God that he should seek
       the true doctrine'

(19)   Godes ængel . . . þæt cweartern   geopenade mid his handa   **hrepunge**.
       God's angel   that prison   opened   with his hand-GEN-PL touch-DAT
       <ÆLS (Julian and Basilissa) 233>
       'God's angel opened the prison with a touch of his hands'

(20)   Hi   wurdon þa   ealle þurh   þa wundra onbryrde, and on godes
       they became then all   through the miracles excited   and in God-GEN
       herungum hi   sylfe   gebysgodon <ÆLS (Sebastian) 148>
       praises-DAT they themselves busied
       'They then all became excited because of the miracles and busied
       themselves in God's praises'

Note that all these -*ung* forms are fully nominal. They show the case
expected for a noun: nominative in (17) because the NP containing
gewilnung is the subject of the clause, accusative in (18) because the NP
containing *mynegung* is complement of a preposition *þurh* 'through' that
governs the accusative, dative in (19) and (20) because the NPs containing
hrepung and *herung* are complement of the prepositions *mid* 'with' and *on*
'on, in' that govern the dative. Other typically 'nouny' features are gender
(all -*ung*/-*ing* nouns are feminine) and number (*herungum* in (20) is a plural
noun, 'praises'). Because these -*ung* forms contain verb stems, they involve
semantic roles: longing (*gewilnung*) evokes an EXPERIENCER who longs and
something s/he longs for; and an admonition (*mynegung*) evokes an AGENT
who admonishes, someone who is being admonished, and the action that
this someone is being admonished to do. But nouns, unlike verbs, do not
require their roles to be expressed. If they are expressed, they cannot
appear as straightforward subjects or objects, but have to appear either
as a genitive (in Old English) or as a PP, usually with *of*, as we saw in
section 2.7.2. Compare the PDE transliterations of the nominalisations in
(17)–(20) and their verbal counterparts in Table 5.1. The fact that such
'inherited' arguments of the verb stem are encoded by the genitive, or
by a PP, is not true of just Old English or PDE nominalisations, but of
nominalisations in many other languages.

    These -*ung*/-*ing* suffixes in Old English were standard-issue deriva-
tion: they did not attach to any verb stem but only to a subset (mostly
weak verbs of class I and II). PDE -*ing* attaches to any V.

Table 5.1 The expression of arguments 'inherited' from the verb

Nominalisation	Verbal counterpart
(17) this life's longing	He longs for this life
(18) God's admonition	God admonishes him
(19) a touch of his hands	His hands touch it
(20) God's praises	They praised God

5.3.3 From nominalisations to gerunds

What makes the PDE *ing*-gerund different from the normal run of nominalisations is the fact that -*ing* is no longer an ordinary derivational suffix. Adding a derivational suffix to a verb stem creates a noun, and a new lemma (see section 2.2 for the distinction between derivation and inflection). Derivational suffixes only attach to a subset of a category (like V), not to the entire set (every V), which means that there are usually several derivational suffixes that do the same job. PDE has the following derivational suffixes that create nouns from verbs: -*ation* (*consider* – *consideration*), -*ment* (*improve* – *improvement*), -*ure* (*depart* – *departure*), -*al* (*propose* – *proposal*), and less transparent suffixes such as *stand* – *stance, descend* – *descent, believe* – *belief, lose* – *loss, see* – *sight*; there are also nominalisations that have no derivational suffix (**zero-derivations**) like *fear* (v) – *fear* (n), *need* (v) – *need* (n), *increase* (v) – *increase* (n), and *walk* (v) – *walk* (n); and action nouns that appear to be formed from agentive nouns, like *theft* (from *thief*), *lechery* (from *lecher*) and *whoredom* (from *whore*). By contrast, -*ing* may attach to *any* verb stem. There are many verbs that do not have 'proper' nominalisations (*eat, drink, be, have, let, carry, sit*, and many others) – other than the one-size-fits-all *ing*-form.

The other difference is that PDE *ing*-gerunds, unlike nominalisations, which are always nouns, can be fully verbal and take proper direct objects and other complements, rather than the 'inherited' objects in the genitive or in the form of a PP that are the only possibility for expressing participants of the verb stem in the case of nominalisations. Some of the gerunds in (16) are listed in Table 5.2 with their finite counterparts, which shows that the gerunds are capable of taking any complement that the finite verb can take.

Other indications that these *ing*-forms are verbal are the fact that the modifiers that can be added to gerund clauses are typically verbal modifiers: adverbs (21a), tense (21b) and negation (21c) (Fanego 2004: 8):

(21) a. their dreams of [$_{\text{gerund clause}}$**quickly** getting onto the property ladder]

Table 5.2 The expression of arguments with gerunds and finite verbs

Syntactic function	Gerund	Finite counterpart
Direct object	Needing money	They need money
Direct object	Owning a property	They own a property
Subject complement	Becoming a home owner	They become home owners
Small clause subject	Leaving it intact	They leave it intact

b. the achievement of [_gerund clause_**having** become a home owner]
c. the relief of [_gerund clause_**not** having to ask one's parents for a deposit]

Another typically verbal operation is passivisation:

(22) the risk of [_gerund clause_**being** forced to sell their house]

The process of nominal to verbal took place in stages (Tajima 1985; Fanego 2004). The *ing*-nominalisation started to appear with adverbial modifiers (adverbs) around 1200. Direct objects followed around 1300. Tense and passives appeared in Late Middle English and Early Modern English.

Another important diagnostic for verbhood is how the subject of the gerund is expressed. Compare the variations of the PDE example (23) given in (24a–c):

(23) Research showed that one in ten potential buyers were actually put off by [_gerund clause_the owner being present during viewings]. (*Webcorp*, from <www.mwultd.co.uk/>)

(24) a. . . .by the owner's/his presence.
      b. . . .by the owner's/his being present.
      c. . . . by the owner/him being present.

Presence in (24a) is a noun, but contains the stem of a predicate (*be*) *present*; any 'inherited' arguments from that predicate may surface as a genitive (as the 'inherited' subject does here) or an *of*-phrase (as in *the presence of witnesses*), as we saw in the previous section. The gerund in (24b) expresses its subject as a genitive (an *of*-phrase is not possible), but is otherwise fully verbal: *being* is followed by a subject complement, completely analogous to the finite clause *he is present*. The gerund in (24c) expresses its subject as an object form, *him*. As *his*, as a determiner, is associated with nouns, the gerund construction can be argued to be less verbal in (24b) than in (24c). Constructions like (24c) appear on the scene well after (24b), which is consistent with a scenario of a progression from nominal to verbal.

Following De Smet (2013), we will refer to gerunds that have their own subjects, as in (24a–c), as non-bare gerunds, as opposed to the 'bare' gerund of (25), where we have just the gerund and its complement, and no overt subject; we infer that the subject of *being* is *the owner*, the subject of the higher verb *insist*. This is called **subject-control**:

(25)   The owner insisted on being present during the viewing of the property.

In PDE, gerunds tend to be either clearly nominal (with determiners, gerund subject expressed by possessive pronoun, premodification by adjectives, and 'inherited' objects in *of*-phrases) or verbal (no determiners, gerund subject expressed by object form as in (24c), proper direct objects or other verbal arguments, modified by adverbs rather than adjectives). But we find nominal/verbal 'hybrids' persisting throughout the Early Modern English period. In (26) and (27), we have a determiner *the*, but the gerund is followed by a complement that can only appear with verbs, not with nouns, as shown by the counterparts in italics with genuine nominalisation:

(26)   that all the distempers of our bodys, which must need be many while we live here, may be a means of [$_{\text{gerund clause}}$the cureing the great distempers of our soles]. [CEPRIV2, Masham 92]
       cf.: He cures$_V$ the distempers/*The cure$_N$ the distempers

(27)   This may be done, and also [$_{\text{gerund clause}}$the teaching of children to spell any syllable], before the child do know any letter on the booke [CEEDUC2A]
       cf.: He teaches$_V$ the children to spell any syllable/*The instruction$_N$ the children to spell any syllable

What this section shows is that English developed a gerund clause, with a verbal gerund at its core. The distribution of the gerund reflects its earlier nominal status, as it occupies the NP slot in PDE, appearing as subject, object and as complement to a preposition. As NPs and PPs can be also complements of verbs, we can expect gerunds to be complements of verbs too. The rise of the gerund as verb complement shows that the earliest model was not the NP but a more circumscribed entity, a noun of a particular form – a bare noun without any modifiers – and a particular meaning that corresponded to certain abstract nouns that appeared as complement to a small 'family' of verbs.

5.3.4 The rise and spread of the gerund as verb complement

5.3.4.1 Introduction

The first gerunds that appear as verb complements are bare gerunds as in (28). These early gerunds do not have any modifiers or complements, which makes it difficult to determine whether they are still nominal or already verbal:

(28) and halde þe   in chastite, and iuil langingis do away; luue **fasting**
      and hold yourself in chastitie and evil longings do away love fasting
      (*MED*, a1425 Ben.Rule(1) (Lnsd 378) 8/19; De Smet 2013: 162)
      'and keep yourself chaste, and get rid of evil desires; love fasting'

Unambiguously clausal gerunds as verb complement start to appear in reasonably frequent numbers in the sixteenth century.

Luue 'love' in (28) is one of the first verbs attested with a gerund complement. When we look at other complements of this verb, and the other early gerund-taking verbs, we find that they share another complement: the abstract noun. Typical examples of such nouns are provided by the list of vices in (29):

(29) Jake loves lechery, foul language, war, theft, whoredom and
      drunkenness.

The PDE example of a bare gerund in (25) forces subject control, but this is not what we find with these early bare gerunds. They are closer to the bare abstract nouns as in (29) in this respect, which do not have any determiners, and hence denote generic rather than specific acts, events or situations. The context in which bare abstract nouns as in (29) appear is usually sufficient to determine whether Jake loves committing these vices himself or whether he enjoys them in general, i.e. when committed by others. It is probably for the same reason that gerunds do not at first appear in a passive construction with *be* (as in *Jake fears being captured*) – instead, we get gerunds that are active in form but passive in sense – *Jake fears capturing* – by analogy of *Jake fears capture*.

The following sections are based on De Smet (2013).

5.3.4.2 Stage I: Emotion, avoidance, necessity and endurance verbs

The model for the earliest group of verbs to appear with the bare gerund is the bare abstract noun. Note that some of the Middle English and Early Modern English examples of such nouns in the list illustrate patterns that are no longer a straightforward option in PDE, and the same goes for passival gerunds:

- Emotion verbs, also called psychological ('psych') verbs:

(30) a. Jake enjoys/likes/loves/prefers [$_{NP}$meditation] as a form of self-healing (bare abstract noun)

      b. Jake enjoys/likes/loves/prefers [meditating] as a form of self-healing (bare gerund)

(31) a. Jake enjoys/likes/loves/prefers [$_{NP}$music in the background/tobacco smoke] (bare abstract noun)

      b. Jake enjoys/likes/loves/prefers [music playing in the background/the place reeking of tobacco smoke] (non-bare gerund)

- Avoidance verbs:

(32) a. Jake avoids/escapes/fears/risks [$_{NP}$capture/punishment/shipwreck] (bare abstract noun)

      b. [He] escaped drowning verye narrowely (*OED*, 1560; De Smet 2013: 174) (passival gerund)

      c. Jake avoids/escapes/fears/risks [being captured/being punished/being shipwrecked] (passive bare gerund)

- Necessity verbs, expressing that something is lacking; the subject of the necessity verb in this construction is usually inanimate. Again with passival gerunds:

(33) a. Her hair needs/requires/wants [$_{NP}$a wash] (indefinite noun)

      b. In somych (=inasmuch) . . . as an vlcere (=ulcer) is an vlcere, it requireth [$_{NP}$desiccacion]. . . (*MED*, ?a1425 **Chauliac(1)* (NY 12); De Smet 2013: 180) (bare abstract noun)

      c. Her hair needs/requires/wants [washing] (passival gerund)

(34) Those who wanted [a church consecrating], or a meeting to be held. (*OED*, 1868) (non-bare passival gerund)

- Endurance verbs, in a construction with *cannot* or *could not*:

(35) a. He cannot endure/bear [$_{NP}$criticism/banishment] (bare abstract noun)

      b. I would summ up the Particulars of this Second Head, if the Examiner's Performance could bear [recapitulating] (*OED*, 1699; De Smet 2013: 195) (passival gerund; note that the conditional implies a negative: . . . 'but it could not bear recapitulating')

      c. He cannot bear being criticised (passive bare gerund)

5.3.4.3 Stage II: Negative implication

At this stage, verbs start to form coherent semantic 'families', and the bare gerund is gradually extended to verbs that did not themselves collocate with a bare abstract noun, but had similar meanings to the established gerund 'families' – an example is the verbs of negative implication, which share a meaning component with the endurance verbs in the previous section. This means that the gerund is being extended beyond its original model.

• verbs of negative implication, with *cannot* or *could not* (cf. the endurance verbs). A typical PDE example is (36):

(36) I could not help laughing. (bare gerund)

Only one verb of this group provides a link with bare abstract noun complements: the now obsolete verb *forbear* 'refrain from':

(37) Quen þaim biheld at kinges here, was nan þat [NPlahuter] miht forbere
     when they beheld the king's army was none that laughter might forbear
     (*MED*, a1400; De Smet 2013: 173)
     'When they beheld the king's army, none of them could abstain from laughter'

Another member of this group, *defer*, did not collocate with bare abstract nouns but with definite nouns: *the search, the journey, the visit*, probably because its basic meaning of 'postpone'; what gets postponed is usually plans that were made earlier and are hence identifiable (De Smet 2013: 186). The remaining members of this group – *decline, help, omit* – do not collocate with abstract nouns, but appear with gerund complements in Early Modern English on the basis of their meaning only. *Help* is a relative newcomer to this group as it did not have the relevant meaning of negative implication when the group was first formed.

5.3.4.4 Stage III: Retrospective verbs, and proposal verbs

The following groups of verbs did not have a single member that collocated with bare abstract nouns, and did not appear with gerund complements on the strength of their meanings either. They represent a significant departure from the original model in that these new verbs collocate with definite NPs, and that the model is not the bare gerund but the non-bare gerund, especially the type with a possessive (as in *his being present* in (24b)). What must have facilitated this jump to entire new families of verbs is the fact that gerund complements had become extremely productive by this stage (seventeenth and eighteenth centuries).

The examples below show the model with a definite NP, the corresponding non-bare gerund, and the bare gerund, here a secondary development from the non-bare gerund rather than the original model (as it was for the verbs in Stages I and II).

- Retrospective verbs:

(38) a. I cannot but remember [_{NP}my Lord's equinimity in all these affairs] with admiration. (*OED*, 1663, Samuel Pepys Diary 8 March (1971) IV. 69) (definite NP)
   b. I remember/recollect/recall [his mother asking him that]. (non-bare gerund)
   c. I remember/recollect/recall [asking him that]. (bare gerund)

Proposal verbs collocate with both definite and indefinite NPs:

- Proposal verbs:

(39) a. Jake proposed/recommended/suggested [_{NP}a different course of action]. (indefinite NP)
   b. he was the man that did propose [_{NP}the removal of the Chancellor]. (CEMET; *The Diary of Samuel Pepys*, entry for 2 September 1667, <http://www.pepysdiary.com/diary/1667/09/02/>; De Smet 2013: 203) (definite NP)
   c. I to the office, whither Creed come by my desire, and he and I to my wife, to whom I now propose [the going to Chetham]. (*The Diary of Samuel Pepys*, entry for Saturday 29 June 1667, <http://www.pepysdiary.com/diary/1667/06/29/>, CEMET; De Smet 2013: 201) (non-bare gerund)
   d. Mr Warren proposed [my getting of *l*100] to get him a protection for a ship to go out, which I think I shall do. (*The Diary of Samuel Pepys*, entry for Monday 10 April 1665, <http://www.pepysdiary.com/diary/1665/04/10/>, CEMET; De Smet 2013: 201) (non-bare gerund)
   e. Another..wanted to act the ghost, which he proposed [doing in white shorts, and a night-cap]. (*OED*, 1826 B. Disraeli Vivian Grey I. i. iii. 21) (bare gerund)

Note that the gerunds at this stage have achieved functional equivalence with a finite clause expressing, for example, propositions:

(40) a. Jake proposed/recommended/suggested a different course of action
   b. Jake proposed/recommended/suggested taking a different course of action
   c. Jake proposed/recommended/suggested that we take_{subjunctive}/ should take a different course of action

5.3.4.5 Conclusion

This pattern of diffusion, then, can be summarised as follows: the gerund first appears as a bare gerund with verbs that collocate with abstract, 'voice-neutral' nouns that can have active as well as passive interpretations; its understood AGENT does not need to be identical in reference with the subject of the clause but can be generic, 'people in general'. The gerund starts its march in this tiny niche.

The verbs that take this bare gerund are recognised as sharing certain meaning components, and on the basis of this identification, the gerund is extended to verbs that never took the bare abstract noun.

These extensions, as well as the increasing use of gerunds in general (as the complement of prepositions, for instance), lead to new 'families' of verbs appearing with non-bare gerunds. Note that non-bare gerunds are even more clausal than bare gerunds, as they introduce an explicit subject (see also PDE 24a–c).

These extensions to new verbs make it difficult to identify a meaning for the gerund complement. But it is possible to identify components of such a meaning in oppositions as in (41a and b):

(41) a. Insert the screwdriver in the keyhole, then turn the screwdriver to the direction of where the lock opens. If this does not work, **try wriggling** it back and forth. (adapted from <http://monsterguide.net/how-to-pick-a-lock>)
      b. Try **to wriggle** it back and forth.

Although the alternative *try to wriggle* is perfectly grammatical, it introduces an element of uncertainty, not about the effectiveness of the wriggling action – which is present in both alternatives – but about whether wriggling is possible at all. This is the result of the semantic contribution of the *to*-infinitive, which in controlled complements (i.e. when the AGENT of the infinitive is inferred from the previous context rather than explicitly spelled out) refers to events and actions that are potential rather than actual, as we will discuss in more detail below. The contrast between (41a and b) shows that the *ing*-gerund has a holistic meaning, suggesting that the wriggling itself is expected to be achieved without a hitch; it is viewed as one of the options available to reach the required result ('picking the lock'). This holistic meaning of the gerund reflects its nominal origin.

5.3.5 *The present participle/gerund nexus*

5.3.5.1 *Adverbial clause re-analysed as argument*

The spread of the gerund as verb complement is complicated by the fact that there was another form in -*ing*, the present participle, which also came to be used as the complement of verbs.

An important source for present participle complements is the adverbial clause. An example of such a clause from the PDE text in (16) is (42):

(42) Results revealed many people now see becoming a home owner as so unrealistic that they've decided to splash money on temporary luxuries or intangible things, **further reducing their ability to buy property in the future**.

Example (43) is an adverbial clause from the seventeenth century (De Smet 2013: 115):

(43) Up, and to the office betimes, and there all the morning very busy, **causing papers to be entered and sorted**, to put the office in order against the Parliament (PPCEME; *The Diary of Samuel Pepys*, diary entry for 10 July 1666, <http://www.pepysdiary.com/diary/1667/07/10/>)

After some verbs and adjectives, this adverbial clause was reinterpreted as a complement, i.e. as a constituent that expressed an argument of the higher verb, or adjective, as in (44):

(44) He was busy sorting a sheaf of letters.

The difference between (43) and (44) is that *be busy* in (43) is complete; its single argument is catered for, and the clause after the comma can be deleted without affecting the sense of *busy*. In (44), without a comma, the *ing*-clause is a complement – an integral part of the clause which cannot be deleted without affecting the sense of *busy*.

Although being busy, happy or tired are complete in themselves as descriptions of certain states people may be in, there is an additional semantic role lurking in the background: the reason (or SOURCE) why they are busy, happy or tired. Although the present participle clause originally described the circumstances in which the state arose, which need not be the SOURCE, the implication must often have been that they were, and in time this led to the reinterpretation that the participle clause was a complement (De Smet 2013: 121):

(45) I am quite busy/happy/tired sorting this sheaf of letters for you.

Adjuncts that come to be reinterpreted as complements are a frequent source of complement clauses, both finite and non-finite. López-Couso (2007) charts the development of the conjunction *lest* (Old English *þy læs* (*þe*), Middle English *the lesse the, thi les the, lest*). This connective originally meant 'so that not', and introduced clauses of negative purpose. It was often used with verbs meaning 'fear, dread', and, as with *busy*, the inference that the clause following such verbs would explain what people were afraid of meant that *lest*-clauses started to be used interchangeably with *that*-clauses after such verbs (ibid.: 21):

(46) but bycause this texte of saynete Paule is in latyn, and hudhnnden commonely can but lyttell laten, I fere **leaste** they can-not vnderstande it. [CEHAND1A, Fitzherbert, *The Book of Husbandry*, 99 (a1534)] (López-Couso 2007: 14). (Cf.: I fear that they cannot understand it.)

This change in status, from adverbial clause to complement clause, can be put to the test, as there are syntactic operations that only work if a constituent is an argument of the verb, i.e. a complement, and not if it is an adjunct.

5.3.5.2 Diagnostic tests for complementhood

The diagnostic test for complementhood is that complements allow constituents to be moved out, while adjuncts do not. Consider the second clause of the paired examples in (47), which show an NP from inside an embedded clause being moved out of that clause by a syntactic operation – by *wh*-movement (constructing a question) in (47a), and by relativisation (constructing a relative clause) in (47b). The original position of the moved elements is illustrated by the italicised NP in the first clause of every pair, and by the gap (___) in the second clause:

(47) a. I think [$_{clause}$John will do *something*.] What do you think [$_{clause}$John will do ___]]?
      b. I bought [$_{NP}$pictures of *a house*.] The house that I bought [$_{NP}$a picture of ___] was my grandfather's birthplace.

In (48), a similar attempt to construct a question (a) and a relative clause (b) fails, as shown by the asterisks:

(48) a. Mary cried [$_{clause}$after John hit *Susan*. *Who did Mary cry [$_{clause}$after John hit ___]?
      b. I bought [$_{NP}$a book with *a slightly damaged cover*.] *The cover that I bought [$_{NP}$a book with ___] is slightly damaged.

The difference between (47) and (48) is that the moved NPs in (48) are extracted out of an adjunct – the *after*-clause in (48a) is not a complement of the higher verb *cry*, and the postmodification *with a slightly damaged cover* in (48b) is not a complement of *book* (as *book* does not contain a verb stem and hence has no semantic roles associated with it). In (47a), in contrast, the clause *John will do something* is a complement of *think*, and *the house* in (47b) is what is pictured, i.e. it is a participant of the verb stem within the nominalisation *picture*. If we perform the same test on the clause *sorting a sheaf of letters* in (46) by relativising the NP *a sheaf of letters*, the result is an acceptable sentence, showing that *sorting a sheaf of letters* is a complement of *be busy*:

(49) He looked up from a sheaf of letters which he was busy
      [$_{clause}$sorting ___]

In the absence of native speaker judgements, finding similar evidence of complement status in a historical corpus requires a bit of luck – the corpus of extant texts is limited, and not every construction that was possible is attested. A possible early example of a constituent moving out of the complement of *busy* is (50):

(50) On al maner that he myght, he was besy to haue Pees.
      (Michigan Corpus of Middle English Prose and Verse, English conquest of Ireland, from the 'Expugnatio hibernica' of Giraldus Cambrensis, MS. Rawl. B. 490, Bodl. Libr., p. 25, ch. 9)
      'In every possible way he could he was busy trying to make peace'

Although (50) has a *to*-infinitival clause rather than an *ing*-form, what it shows is that expressions of what someone was busy with were already complements rather than adjuncts of *busy* in Middle English: the manner adverbial *On al maner that he myght* has been **topicalised** – moved to clause-initial position – out of the clause *to haue Pees*. We cannot be 100 per cent certain, however, because it is still possible to interpret the manner adverbial as belonging to the clause *he was besy* rather than to the *to*-infinitival clause. But (50) gives an idea of the kind of data a more extensive investigation might want to look for.

5.3.5.3 The nexus

Adverbial adjuncts represent a nexus where gerund and participle meet and overlap. What complicates the notion that the *ing*-form after *busy* is originally a present participle complement is examples such as (51) and (52) that have PPs:

(51) Sain Jon was. . .bisi In ordaining of priestes, and clerkes, And in casting kirc werkes (*c*.1300 (MS a1400) English Metrical Homilies 112/2–4; Tajima 1985: 76)
'Saint John was. . .busy ordaining priests and clerics, and in planning church works'

(52) It was proved that the three Prisoners coming into the house of Temple, and calling for Wine, whilst Wilson and Pain were busie **in drinking**, Ellenor Davis makes use of the opportunity, taking the silver Salt-seller, marchs off unknown to her Companions, whereupon the said Temple missing his Salt seller, apprehends the said Wilson and Pain, as Accessary in the Theft (*OED* 1686, *Proceedings of the Old Bailey*; De Smet 2013: 113)

The most likely model for an *ing*-form inside a PP is the gerund, because of its nominal orgin. Note also the PP containing an *-ung* nominalisation in (20), here repeated as (53), a complement of the verb *bysi(g)an* 'busy':

(53) Hi   wurdon þa   ealle þurh   þa wundra onbryrde, and **on godes**
    they became then all   through the miracles excited   and in God-GEN
    herungum hi   sylfe   gebysgodon <ÆLS (Sebastian) 148>
    praises-DAT they themselves busied
    'They then all became excited because of the miracles and busied themselves in God's praises'

We noted in section 3.4.4 that such a PP with *in* was an alternative expression for a progressive; an example there was (23): *I was forced to keep Sir G. . . . in talk, while it was a doing*. The *ing*-complement after *busy* and *keep* (and after a number of other verbs with aspectual meanings like 'begin, continue, stop'), then, has its origins in *ing*-participles as well as in *ing*-gerunds, a reminder that any investigation into the development of complementation patterns should include any complements that were current at the time, also those that did not survive into PDE. Gerunds are aspectually neutral, and the durativity of *in talk* (and *in drinking* in (51)) is a component of the preposition *in* rather than the nominalisation or gerund that follows it – although the lexical aspect of the underlying verbs, *talk* and *drink*, must have duration to be compatible with *in*. But duration is also a crucial component of the progressive, as well as of the present participle complement, as we saw in the *smashing glasses* examples in (4) and (5) above.

5.3.5.4 Aspectualisers

The participle/gerund nexus is also relevant for the rise of the *ing*-form after the aspectualisers, verbs meaning 'begin'. Aspectualisers take events as complements, and they, too, express ongoingness and duration in that they can only refer to the beginning of an event if that event has duration. These verbs are found with bare and *to*-infinitives in Old English, and with *to*-infinitives and *ing*-forms in PDE. Both complements force a durative reading, or, if the non-finite verb expresses a punctual action, an iterative reading, as in this example, picked randomly from the internet:

(54) a. A fight ensued, during which one of the officers allegedly pulled out a handgun and began **hitting** the victim in the head.
     b. He began **to hit** the victim in the head.

The aspectualiser forces the reading that the victim was hit more than once, independent of which non-finite complement is used. Not every situation type lends itself to iterativity (see the discussion of lexical aspect in section 3.3); as with the *smashing glasses* examples in (4) and (5), singular subjects or objects prevent iterative readings of punctual events, witness these examples (based on Brinton 1988: 85):

(55) a. *A friend began to arrive/arriving at the party
     b. Friends began to arrive/arriving at the party

The difference between an *ing*-form and a *to*-infinitive has been claimed to be entailment (Freed 1979: 25ff.): the hitting-event in (54b) can be interrupted even before the first blow takes place, but this is not the case in (54a). This could be another indication that the gerund has preserved a holistic sense, as in the wriggling example of (41a) above.

5.4 The rise of the *to*-infinitive

5.4.1 Introduction

The *to*-infinitive developed much earlier than the gerund, which is why we cannot go into as much detail, and the semantic groups that came to take it as complement can only be sketched in broad outlines. What we know about its earliest history has so many similarities with that of the gerund, however, that the story of the *to*-infinitive is likely to have been a similar tale of gradual diffusion, from one group of verbs to another; and here, too, we can see the outlines of abrupt gear shifts where entirely new classes of verbs start to appear with this complement.

5.4.2 Origin of to-infinitives

To in the *to*-infinitive is a grammaticalised development from the preposition *to*, which of course still exists in PDE (*layering*, see section 2.7.1). We saw in the previous sections that the gerund must have originated in a bare abstract noun that expressed an action, situation or activity, and as such appeared in the complement of a small number of verbs. As an action noun, the noun contained a verb stem, and it is this feature that allowed it to become a verb, and hence a clause. The *to*-infinitive seems to have arisen in a very local niche, too: a PP with *to* in which the preposition *to* did not refer to distance in space but distance-in-time, the future.

The earliest function of this *to*-PP may have been that of an adjunct expressing purpose, as in (56). Neither the *to*-PP nor the *to*-infinitive (both in bold) are arguments of *undon* 'undo, open', as the argument structure of this verb only has room for the arguments *he* 'he' and *his muð* 'his mouth'.

(56) þæt he ... mihte ...undon his muð   **to wisdomes spræcum**, (*to*-PP)
     that he   might   undo his mouth to wisdom's   speeches
     and **to wurðianne God** (*to*-infinitive)
     and to praise   God
     <ÆHom 16, 184>
     '... so that he could ... open his mouth for words of wisdom, and to praise God'

There is no evidence of any other prepositions taking an infinitive as complement, or of an infinitive being used as an NP outside this *to*-PP, as subject or object, like some of the gerunds in (16). The etymology of the *to*-infinitive is often given as a bare infinitive in the complement of a preposition *to*, but this leaves the gemination ('doubling') of the -n- in the *to*-infinitive unexplained. The gemination points to the presence of an earlier -j-, probably part of a nominalising suffix. This parallells the origin of the gerund (see above, section 5.3.2), and indicates that the *to*-infinitive is not built on the bare infinitive, which was a much earlier formation, but on a verbal stem, like any other nominalisation:

(57) to (preposition) + ber- (verbal stem) + -anja (derivational suffix) + -i (dative sg) → Common Germanic *to beranjōi, Old English: *to berenne*, Middle English: *to beren/bere*, PDE: *to bear*.

(The *-anne* in *wurðianne* in (56) is a common variant of *-enne*). The fact that the *to*-PPs expressing purpose adjuncts in Old English invariably contain nominalisations of action nouns – *spræc* 'speech' in (56) is related to *sprecan* 'speak' – supports the hypothesis that the form that gave rise to the *to*-infinitive did so, too. See also (9) in section 5.1.

The preposition *to* governs the dative, and this is the case of the NP inside the *to*-PP *to wisdomes spræcum* in (56). The inflection on the *to*-infinitive has the same origin (dative case on the original nominalisation) but its behaviour in Old English, and the behaviour of the *du*-infinitive in Gothic, is that of a verb: its objects have accusative rather than genitive case; cf. the accusative *God* in (56).

5.4.3 Diagnostic tests for clausal status

One of the verbal behaviours that show that the *to*-infinitive is a very different animal from the *to*-PP it derives from is **preposition stranding**. The *to*-infinitive in (58a) has a stranded preposition *mid* 'with' (as also in the PDE translation *to nourish the body with*), while the *to*-PP in another version of the same passage, in (58b), does not:

(58) eall swa hwæt swa mihton beon gesewene lustfullice . . .
    all so what so might be   seen   desirable
    'whatever might appear desirable. . .'
    a. . . . þone   lichaman mid to gereordianne <GD (2) C 13.128.35>
        the-ACC body-ACC with to nourish
      '. . .to nourish the body with'
    b. . . . to þæs lichaman   gereordunge <GD 2 (H) 13.128.32>
        to the-GEN body-GEN   nourishment-DAT
      '. . . for the body's nourishment'

Stranding can only take place in clauses, not in phrases, so that the *to*-infinitival constituent must be a clause, and the *to*-infinitive itself a verb.

5.4.4 From adjunct to verb complement

The *du*-infinitive in Gothic is not found as complement, only as purpose adjunct (Köhler 1867). In Old English, as also in Gothic, purpose adjuncts take the following forms:

(59) *to*-PP:
    he sende hine   **to þrowunge**   for manna alysednysse
    he sent   him-ACC to torment-DAT for men's redemption
    <ÆCHom I, 16 232.2>
    'he sent him into torment for the redemption of mankind'

(60) *to*-infinitive:

[he] is ure hælend   crist. se ðe   com **to gehælenne   ure wunda**
he is our saviour   christ he who came to heal   our wounds
<ÆCHom I, 9 142.30>
'He is our Saviour, Christ, he who came to heal our wounds'

(61) subjunctive clause:

he com   to mannum   to ðy.   **þæt he wolde. beon gehyrsum**
he came to men   to that-INSTR that he wanted be   obedient
his fæder oð   dead <ÆCHom I, 14.1 214, 32>
his father until death
'he came to men to that end, that he wanted to be obedient to his
father until death'

Note that the *to*-PP invariably contains an action noun, i.e. a nominalisation of a verb-stem; *þrow-ung-e* in (59) is formed from the stem of the
verb *þrowian* 'to suffer'. We discussed movement as a test for complementhood in section 5.3.5.2. In (62), a constituent – in bold – has been
moved out of a *to*-infinitive, to make a *wh*-question:

(62) **On hwilcum godum** tihst þu us to gelyfenne _____? <ÆLS (George) 148>
In which   gods   urge you us to believe?
'In which gods do you urge us to believe?'

On hwilcum godum 'in which gods' cannot be an argument of the higher
verb *tihst* 'urge' in (62), as this verb is not attested with *on*-PPs; it does,
however, fit the complementation pattern of the infinitival verb *gelyfan*
'believe' ('believe in something'), which suggests that *on hwilcum godum*
has been fronted out of the *to*-infinitive *to gelyfenne*, its original position
is indicated by _____. This indicates that *to gelyfenne* is a complement, an
argument of verb *tihst* 'urge' and not a purpose adjunct.

  Tihst in (62) is from *tyhtan* 'urge', a member of a set of verbs in Old
English with meanings of 'persuade, urge'. They have the argument
structure and **subcategorisation frames** (i..e. the expression of the
complement) of (63):

(63) Semantic roles: AGENT, THEME, GOAL
    Subcategorisation frames:
    NPACC (THEME), *to*-PP (GOAL)
    NPACC (THEME), *to*-infinitive (GOAL)
    NPACC (THEME), subjunctive clause (GOAL)

The GOAL-argument in (63) has the same expressions as the purpose
adjunct in (59)–(61). Some 39 verbs of persuading and urging can
be found with these subcategorisation frames in Old English, and

they are the first clue as to the diffusion of the *to*-infinitive as verb complement.

The rise and spread of the *to*-infinitive happened long before the rise and spread of the gerund, and was in fact largely completed by the time of our earliest Old English texts. But it is possible to construct a scenario of its spread that is remarkably parallell to that of the gerund in section 5.3.4.

5.4.5 Stage I: Verbs of spatial manipulation

Many of the verbs of persuading and urging derive etymologically from verbs of spatial manipulation, and have basic meanings like PDE *force* in *They forced the ship to the shore* (*force* itself is an Old French loan; the vast majority of the 39 verbs of persuading and urging in Old English have not survived because of the extensive relexification of English after the Norman Conquest); this probably explains the accusative case of the THEME, as the deepest meaning is that of some inanimate object being pushed into a certain direction. This inanimate object was extended to human beings, as is also possible with PDE *force* (which has an *into*-PP in PDE rather than the *to*-PP of Old English):

(64) German Says Hypnotist Forced Him Into Crime (*New York Times* headline, 27 February 1947).

(65) A freak injury forced him into retirement.

The *into*-PPs in these PDE examples contain action nouns, with the implication that it is the human object that is forced to be the AGENT of these actions; these *into*-PPs can be rephrased as *to*-infinitives: *The hypnotist forced him to commit a crime, A freak injury forced him to retire*. Like the PDE *into*-PP frame, and the Old English *to*-PP adjunct in (59), the Old English *to*-PP frame in (63) invariably contains action nouns.

5.4.6 Stage II: Verbs of firing up

Apart from spatial manipulation verbs, the 39 Old English verbs of persuading and urging also contain a second coherent 'family' of verbs. Their etymology indicates core meanings like 'fire up, set fire to, inflame'; examples are *onælan* and *ontendan*. It is unlikely that they could take *to*-PPs in these meanings, and they probably acquired the frames in (63) only after they had extended their meanings metaphorically to 'fire someone up, inspire someone to do something'.

Both the *to*-PP and the *to*-infinitive may have appeared as complements with these verbs on the basis of these new metaphorically-extended directive meanings. This is entirely parallel to Stage II of the spread of the gerund in section 5.3.4.3.

5.4.7 Stage III: Verbs of commanding and permitting

The *to*-infinitive may then have spread to groups of verbs that are also not attested with a *to*-PP in Old English, but have a similar directive meaning – the verbs of commanding and permitting. These verbs derive from core meanings of 'give' – the RECIPIENT receives an order or a permission, cf PDE examples of (66a and b):

(66) a. Toy libraries and other sharing schemes allow [NPchildren] [NPaccess to a large variety of toys] (*OED*, 1990 *Lifestyle* Summer 28/2)

b. That reminded him to order[NPHeathcliff] [NPa flogging], and [NPCatherine] [NPa fast from dinner or supper] (Emily Brontë [1847] 1965, *Wuthering Heights*: 87).

These are ditransitive verbs with two NP arguments, and are found with the following subcategorisation frames in Old English:

(67) Semantic roles: AGENT, RECIPIENT, THEME
Subcategorisation frames:
NPDAT (RECIPIENT), NPACC (THEME)
NPDAT (RECIPIENT), *to*-infinitive (THEME)
NPDAT (RECIPIENT), subjunctive clause (THEME)

There are some 21 Old English verbs with meanings of 'command, permit' that appear with these frames, and of those only *forbeodan* 'forbid', *lætan* 'let, allow', *sellan* 'give, grant' and *tæcan* 'teach' have made it into PDE (although *sell* has narrowed its meaning to 'give in exchange for money' and hence no longer appears with clausal complements). A subgroup of this group also appear with AcIs. The example of *don* 'do, see to it' in (47) in section 4.6, probably also belongs to this group.

These verbs never occurred with *to*-PPs, so where did the *to*-infinitive come from?

5.4.8 Stage IV: Expressing 'dependent desires'

The original sense of direction of the preposition *to* allowed the action noun within a *to*-PP to refer to actions and events that are in the future, which was a good fit with the purpose adjunct, as such adjuncts referred to future GOALS. The GOALS of verbs of spatial manipulation when applied to people rather than to inanimate objects are more in the nature of directives: pressure is put to bear on people to perform an act. GOALS of directives can still be described as being in the future, but the focus is probably more on the fact that they are as yet unrealised. This is the meaning that takes both the *to*-PP and the *to*-infinitive to the *irrealis* domain of the subjunctive – any action that is feared, promised, ordered, hoped, expected, or insisted upon by someone (see section 4.8). The subjunctive encodes such actions in finite clauses that are the complement of verbs with meanings of fear, promise, order, hope, expect, or insist upon. All of these verbs share a meaning component of desire, the desire of some AGENT in the higher clause, and, as mere desires, their complements are potential rather than actual. We will follow Ogawa (1989) in referring to these complements as 'dependent desires'. Some PDE examples are given in (68) (dependent desire in bold):

(68) a. Exasperated police forces have taken to Twitter today to urge motorists **to clear their snow-covered windscreens**. (*Mirror News*, 20 Jan 2013)
   b. The police allowed motorists **to clear their snow-covered windscreens**.
   c. Motorists tried/promised **to clear their snow-covered windscreens**.

In (68b), a verb like *allow* has a complement that expresses someone's desire to do something which requires permission from an authority; in (68c), verbs like *try* and *promise* have a complement that expresses someone's desire (or at least commitment) to do something. In all of these cases, the preferred expression of the complement is a *to*-infinitive in PDE. In Old English, the *to*-infinitive as a complement to verbs with meanings as in (68a–c) is a marginal phenomenon, as the complement of choice for 'dependent desires' is a finite clause with a subjunctive verb. It is in Middle English that these roles come to be reversed: the *to*-infinitive becomes the preferred expression for a dependent desire, while the finite complement declines.

The diffusion of the *to*-infinitive from verbs of persuading and urging, where its model was the *to*-PP, to verbs of commanding and permitting where this model was not available allowed the *to*-infinitive to acquire a more abstract meaning, very similar to that of the subjunctive clause. The subjunctive clause may have provided a new model, so that the *to*-infinitive started to appear with verbs that not only had no *to*-PP but also had no directive meaning: verbs of intention with meanings like 'intend, hope, try, promise' – some 75 verbs, of which only a handful (e.g. *earnian* 'deserve, earn', *giernan* 'yearn', *leornian* 'learn', *secan* 'seek', *ðencan* 'think, intend', *a-*, *ondrædan* 'dread', *ceosan* 'choose', *forsacan* 'refuse', *deman* 'condemn', *onscunian* 'shun', *swerian* 'swear' and *understandan* 'understand, manage') have survived the relexification.

This situation ultimately led to a competition between the older finite (subjunctive) and the new non-finite (*to*-infinitival) clause, with the non-finite clause winning out. There are some early signs of this competition in Old English, where a late tenth-/early eleventh-century revision (manuscript 'H') of a ninth-century Old English translation of Gregory's *Dialogues* (manuscript 'C') systematically replaces subjunctive clauses expressing dependent desires, as in (69), with *to*-infinitival clauses, as in (70):

(69) . . . Dauid, þe   gewunade, þæt he hæfde   witedomes gast in him
         David who was-wont that he had-SUBJ of-prophecy spirit in him
         <GD 1 (C) 4.40.24>
      '. . . David, who was wont, that he had the spirit of prophecy in him'

(70) Dauid, þe   gewunode to hæbbenne witedomes   gast on him
      David who was-wont   to have   of-prophecy spirit in him
      <GD 1 (H) 4.40.22>
      '. . . David, who was wont to have the spirit of prophecy in him'

5.4.9 Stage V: Verbs of thinking and declaring

Towards the end of the Middle English period, the *to*-infinitive starts to appear with an entirely new set of verbs, the verbs of thinking and declaring. As an expression of a dependent desire, the *to*-infinitive does not have a subject of its own but depends on its AGENT being identified as identical in reference to (i.e **controlled** by) the subject or object of the higher verb:

(71) A freak injury forced him [subclause to retire] (object control)

(72) He wanted [subclause to retire] (subject control)

At the end of the Middle English period, we see the first *to*-infinitives that have explicit subjects of their own, like *their wives* in this PDE example:

(73) 49 per cent of women and a surprising 32 per cent of men
       reported that they were virgins at marriage. In spite of this,
       79 per cent of [the] . . . men believed [subclause **their wives** to have
       been virgins when they married]. (Microconcord Corpus)

What the men believe is that their wives were virgins when they married; *their wives* receives a semantic role from the predicate 'be virgins' rather than from *believe*. *Believe* only has room for two participant roles: someone who believes and the contents of the belief. The verbs that allow this construction constitute a distinct group, with meanings of 'thinking or declaring something to be the case'.

The construction in (73) is sometimes referred to as an AcI, or 'subject-to-object raising' (because the subject of the infinitive surfaces as the object of the higher verb) or 'Exceptional Case-Marking' (ECM) construction (because the NP *their wives* is assigned accusative case by a verb outside that clause). What is remarkable about this construction is that it occurs only rarely in the active form as in (73); a passive as in (74) is much more likely; indeed, many verbs, particularly verbs of declaring like *say* or *rumour*, can only take the construction when passivised:

(74) Investigations established that the security forces were directly responsible for the massacre, **which** was believed to be directed against supporters of the left- wing party, the Patriotic Union.

Note that verbs of thinking and declaring are all about expressing opinions, and the topic of those opinions would have been encoded by an adverbial in earlier English: people have opinions or hold beliefs *about* something. The passive ECM construction as in (74) allows speakers to express beliefs without having to position an adverbial in clause-initial position: *About this people believe/think/say that*... Instead, they can start with a subject: *This is believed/thought/said to be*... Adverbials in first position are far more likely to encode frame-setters in PDE, as in (23) in section 1.4.2, than discourse links, a topic that will be touched on briefly in Chapters 7 and 8.

Another interesting aspect of passive ECMs is that they renew a modal meaning of *sceolde* 'should' that had been lost. Old English *sceolde* could be used to indicate 'that the reporter does not believe the statement or does not vouch for its truth' (Mitchell and Robinson 1982: 115; see also under *sculan* (13) in Bosworth and Toller 1882):

(75) Ða   wæs ðær eac swiðe egeslic geatweard, ðæs   nama sceolde bion
      then was there also very   terrible doorkeeper whose name should be
      Caron <Bo 35.102.16>
      Caron
      'Then there was also a very terrible doorkeeper whose name is said to be
      Caron'

The most felicitous PDE translation has a passive ECM.

5.5 Summary of points

- This chapter charts the rise and spread of three non-finite complements: the gerund, the present participle and the *to*-infinitive.
- Although any account of the *to*-infinitive is necessarily more speculative than the other complements, the scenarios presented here show remarkable parallels between the *to*-infinitive and the gerund.
- Both the *to*-infinitive and the gerund appear to originate in action nouns, i.e. nominalisations that contain verb stems, and hence can encode events and actions.
- Both the *to*-infinitive and the gerund originate in a 'local' construction, a small niche in the system: the *to*-PP containing an NP with an action noun in the case of the *to*-infinitive, and an abstract bare noun in the case of the gerund.
- Both the *to*-infinitive and the gerund diffuse through the language by acquiring new models, the subjunctive clause in the case of the *to*-infinitive and the definite NP of retrospective verbs and proposal verbs in the case of the gerund.
- Both the *to*-infinitive and the gerund start out without an overt expression of the subject of the action they encode, but acquire these later – the *to*-infinitive in the ECM construction, and the gerund with posessives (*by his being present*, (24b)) and objects (*by him being present*, (24c)).
- There is some degree of overlap between the present participle and the gerund in the history of the *ing*-complement of predicates like *busy*.

Exercises

1. CHANGING COMPLEMENTS. Look up each of the following verbs in the *OED* and mark which clausal complements they have been found with in their recorded history. Write up a potted history for each, with the relevant *OED* examples, noting the dates each clausal complement was first attested, and speculate why.
expect, intend, mind, fancy, refrain, start, suggest.

2. HYBRIDS.

   a. The following gerunds seem to be hybrids. Which features are nominal features, and which are verbal?

   (i) This last action (as it appeareth) is verie easily performed by a skilfull Operator or cunning Chirurgian: neyther doth it require any great curiosity,[1] but a decent and artificiall[2] strong binding, meete[3] for the **plucking** of them out (as it is said) by the rootes [CESCIE2A]

(ii) Go on **wasting** of our blood and treasure (LC; Henry Robinson (1653), *Certaine Proposals in Order to a New Modelling of the Lawes*, London: Simmons; De Smet 149)

(iii) and then me thought I had reason to doe soo, for I did learne the Reasons of my **misliking** of you M. Hare, M. Southwell, and others in the Parliament House [CETRI1]

b. With respect to *mislike* in (iii), consider examples like (iv) and (v):

(iv) On the morrow being Wednesday, the people of that towne misliking of their proceedings, fought against them [CEHIST2A]

(v) Who..would most highly mislike of this divorce (*OED a*1575 N. Harpsfield *Treat. Divorce Henry VIII* (modernised text) 58) Reconsider the hybrid-status of (iii) in the light of (iv) and (v).

3. CAUSATIVES. Comment on the complements found in (i) and (ii).

(i) Pius Quintus ... was made beleeue that the Duke of Norfolke was a Catholike (*OED* 1602 W. Watson Decacordon Ten Quodlibeticall Questions 343)

(ii) I caused him bleed oftner then once (*OED* 1625 J. Hart Anat. Urines ii. iv. 73)

4. *ING*-FORMS IN EARLY MODERN ENGLISH. The text in (i) below constitutes a single sentence.

a. Read it carefully for meaning, taking into account that some words may have altered their meaning since this was written (look them up in the *OED* in case of doubt).

b. Identify the *to*-infinitives in (i), taking care to exclude instances of *to* that are prepositions and not the infinitival *to*. Note for every *to*-infinitive what its function is (purpose adjunct or verb complement), and, if it is a complement, which verb it is a complement of, and whether this verb has a meaning that conforms to the semantic groups set out in sections 5.4.5–5.4.9.

c. For every *ing*-form, say who is supposed to be its AGENT (i.e., what NP it is controlled by). Do the same for every *to*-infinitive.

---

[1] skill
[2] skillfully made
[3] suitable

d. Which *ing*-forms are present participles, and which are gerunds?
    Motivate your answer.

(i) This Bishopp Stokesley, being by the Cardinall not long before
     in the Starre Chamber openley put to rebuke and awarded to
     the Fleete [=the Fleet Prison], not brooking this contumelious
     vsage, and thincking that Forasmuch as the Cardinall, for lack of
     such forwardnes in setting forthe the kings divorse as his grace
     looked for, was out of his highnes favour, he had nowe a good
     occassion offred him to revenge his quarell against him, further
     to incense the kings displeasure towards him, busily travailed
     to invente some collorable[4] devise for the kings furtheraunce
     in that behalfe; which (as before is mencioned) he to his grace
     revealed, hoping thereby to bring the kinge to the better liking of
     himself, and the more mislikinge of the Cardinall (HC, Roper's
     Life of Sir Thomas More, 1556, 38–9)

5. THE *TO*-INFINITIVE AND THE GERUND IN COMPETITION? Consider (i)
    and (iia and b) below.

a. Identify the complements of the verbs *hinder* and *remember* in
    these examples.
b. Comment on Shakespeare's choice for the complement of *hinder*
    in (i); which complement would be more likely today? Use a
    PDE thesaurus, or the *Historical Thesaurus* in the *OED*, to draw
    up a list of verbs with similar meanings of hindering and pre-
    venting. Look up in the *OED* which complements these verbs
    have occurred with over the years, in these particular meanings.
c. How could you account for the choice of complement in the two
    PDE examples with *remember* in (iia and b)?

(i) Oh, who shall hinder me to wail and weep? (Shakespare, *Richard
     III*, Act 2, Scene 2)
(ii) a. He remembered to lock the door.
     b. He remembered locking the door.

6. EXPRESSING PARTICIPANT ROLES IN 'DEPENDENT DESIRES'. Consider
    the three examples (i–iii), all from the same Old English text.

(i) ðone   nydde Decius se kasere   deofolgeld   to begangenne.
     that-ACC urged Decius the Emperor devil-worship to practise-INF
     'the Emperor Decius urged him (lit. 'that one') to practise devil-worship'
     <Mart 5 1972)
(ii) se dema ... hine   þa   nydde to deofolgyld[a]   begonge.

---

[4] plausible

the ruler . . . him-ACC then urged   to devil-worships-GEN practice
'the ruler then urged him to the practice of devil-worship'
(Mart 5 756)

(iii)   þær   hy   mon nydde þæt hy   deofulgyld weorðedon.
there them-ACC one   urged that they idols   worshipped-SUBJ
'there people urged them that they should worship idols/there they were
urged to worship idols'
(Mart 5 2207)

a.   The verb in (i)–(iii) is *nydan* 'urge'. Which argument structure
and subcategorisation frames would you expect to find this verb
with in Old English? Do the examples in (i)–(iii) conform to
these frames?

b.   The final argument of these verbs describes the action that the
person who is the subject of *nydan* wants the person or persons
who are encoded as its object to carry out. Say for each example
what this action is, and which semantic roles it requires. How are
they expressed?

c.   There are observations in the literature that subjects of subjunctive clauses, unlike indicative clauses, are more likely to be
pronouns rather than full NPs (cf. Cole 2012 for Old English; de
Haas 2011: 181 for Middle English). Give an explanation for this
fact on the basis of (i)–(iii) and what was said about dependent
desires in this chapter.

7.   THE STRANGE CASE OF *ASK*. The *Paston Letters*, a Late Middle English
collection of correspondence, contains many examples of *to*-infinitives
that are no longer acceptable in PDE. One of them is (i), with *axe* 'ask':

(i)   Item, in eny wise, and[5] ye can, axe the probate of my fadyrs
wyll to be geuyn[6] yow (*Paston Letters*, Davis 1971: 338 ll. 41–2)

a.   How would you analyse the *to*-infinitive in (i): is it a complement of *axe* or is it a purpose adjunct, is it an object control
construction or an ECM? Look up *ask* in the *OED* for further
evidence to help you decide what you are dealing with here.

b.   Although *axe* 'ask' is a lexical survivor from Old English
ascian 'ask', it does not appear with a *to*-infinitival complement until Middle English. Why? Use the *OED* to support
your answer.

8.   GERUNDS AND PRESENT PARTICIPLES. It is not always possible to
make a clear distinction between gerund and present participle

[5]   if
[6]   given

complements, especially if complements spread beyond their original model. Consider the *-ing* complement in (i), from the text in (16):

(i)   A fifth of those saving deposits end up **abandoning** their attempts and **spending** the money.

Try to account for the appearance of the *-ing* complement after the phrasal verb *end up* on the basis of the information in this chapter and your own searches in the *OED* and the *Historical Thesaurus.*

Further reading

The rise of the gerund as verb complement, see De Smet (2013). For *-ing* complements in Middle English, see Moessner (1997). For *-ing* complements in PDE, see Rudanko (1996). The *-ing* form in PDE is a nexus of the present participle and the gerund; for its distribution in PDE, see Aarts (2006) and De Smet (2010). For the competition of the *to*-infinitive and the subjunctive clause as verb complement, see Los (2005), and as adjective complement, see Van linden (2010). For the history of aspectualisers like *gan* and the link with phrasal verbs, see Brinton (1988). For the infinitive in Gothic, see Köhler (1867). For cross-linguistic overviews of complementation, see Noonan (1985) and Dixon and Aikhenvald (2006). The etymology of the *to*-infinitive in (56) is due to van Loey ([1959] 1970) and the late Dirk Boutkan (p.c.) of the Department of Comparative Linguistics of Leiden University. The problem of the gemination in the *to*-infinitival inflection was pointed out by Jolly (1873: 150–54). There is a vast literature on the rise of ECM constructions in English, including Bock (1931), Fischer (1989, 1990, 1991, 1992a), Jespersen (1940), Lightfoot (1991), Warner (1982), Zeitlin (1908), van Gelderen (1993) and Fanego (1992). For the ECM construction in PDE, see Mair (1989). For a comparison of the C and H manuscripts of Gregory's *Dialogues*, see Yerkes (1982).

Note

1. AcI is an abbreviation of the Latin term *Accusativus cum Infinitivo.*

6 The structure of the clause

6.1 Introduction

We have so far discussed the first two of the three parameters of syntactic variation: (1) the expression of grammatical information in the morphology or the syntax (Chapters 2, 3 and 4); and (2) the expression of the arguments of the verb (Chapter 5). This chapter, and the next, will discuss word order change, parameter (3). Word orders are routines which provide speakers with a template for structuring their utterances, and hearers with expectations as to what the next constituent will be, which facilitates processing. An analytic language like PDE, which expresses much of its grammatical meaning by means of free words rather than by means of morphemes, has more items to line up – articles, auxiliaries, pronouns, conjunctions, infinitival markers like *to*, etc. – which makes developing routines even more pressing. The word order of PDE is quite strict; it is possible to construct sentences of twenty or more words that all need to be in a particular order; cf. (1), randomly taken from the internet:

(1)   But at that point, the picture began to change so rapidly that the symposium papers had to be revised for publication to remain abreast of international political developments. <http://www.nobelprize.org/nobel_prizes/themes/peace/sejersted/>

Word order variation is further restricted by the PDE speciality of *chunking* (see section 1.2). Adverbials offer some scope for variation in PDE, but this variation in position entails a change in meaning, at least for the place adverbials we discussed in section 1.4.2. Other word order operations can be said to be meaningful in that they serve discourse functions like helping hearers identify a new topic (see section 1.4.3), and some serve a purely syntactic function, like question formation (section 1.4.4).

English has undergone two major word order changes: a change in the basic ordering of the verb (V) and its objects (O) or complements;

and a change in the position of the finite verb. The change from O–V to V–O order will be discussed in this chapter, and the change in the position of the finite verb in the next.

This chapter will focus on the subclause rather than on the main clause. The reason is that the position of the finite verb in main clauses is often a derived position: finite verbs move to a position towards the beginning of the clause in main clauses. Subclauses are more likely to show the basic order of the various constituents; and even in the subclause, the basic Old English clause structure of O–V order is enhanced with a number of further derived slots where constituents from the O position move. Old English had special positions to the left of the V1' for pronouns and other constituents that represented 'old' information; these positions were lost in Middle English. There was also a position after the V for moving larger chunks, so that the hearer would encounter the V earlier, which would help processing.

Old English word order was quite flexible. Subjects, objects, complements and adverbials could be accommodated in various positions in the clause, at the beginning as well as at the end. The natural tendency in human language is that speakers start utterances with information that is known to the hearer, and leave information that is new until the end. Old English syntax, with its many positions, was very accommodating in this respect.

6.2 The text

We will use a famous passage from the Anglo-Saxon Chronicle: the story of *Cynewulf and Cyneheard*, which appears in the entry for the year 755 (although the copies in which the Chronicle has come down to the present day are dated much later). The central reportable event of this story exemplifies the heroic ideal of the relationship between a king and his retainers, a bond that is, or should be, stronger than that of blood. To avoid being distracted by unfamiliar lexical items, we will use a PDE transliteration of the text, with only minimal adjustment to help understanding. The numbered indexes should help you to keep track of who is doing what to whom. 'The king' refers to Cynewulf; 'the prince' refers to Cyneheard.

Cynewulf and Cyneheard in transliteration

Here (i.e. in this year, 755) Cynewulf₁ deprived Sigebryht₂ of his₂ kingdom, with the help of the West-Saxon councillors, for unjust deeds, except Hampshire; and he₂ had that until he₂ killed
5 the alderman₃ that with-him₂ longest remained; and him₂ then Cynewulf₁ into the-Weald drove,

and he$_2$ there stayed until that him$_2$ a swineherd$_4$ stabbed-to-death at Prefet's Flood; and he$_4$ avenged the alderman Cumbra$_3$; and that Cynewulf$_1$ often great battles fought against the Britons. And about 31 winters that that he$_1$ kingdom had, he$_1$ wanted drive-out a prince that was Cyneheard$_5$ called, and that Cyneheard$_5$ was that Sigebryht$_2$'s brother; and then discovered he$_5$

10 the king$_1$ with a small bodyguard$_6$ visiting his mistress$_7$ in Merton. And himself$_5$ there rode-out, and the bower outside surrounded [with his men$_8$] before him$_5$ the men discovered who with the king$_1$ were; and then perceived the king$_1$ that, and he$_1$ to the doorway went, and then admirably himself$_1$ defended, until he$_1$ on the prince$_5$ looked, and then lunged-out towards him$_5$, and him$_5$ much wounded. And they$_{5+8}$ all on the king$_1$ were hacking-away until that they$_{5+8}$ him$_1$ killed

15 had. And then because-of the woman$_7$'s screams discovered the king$_1$'s bodyguard$_6$ the disruption, and then thither ran whoever then ready was and quickest; and of-them$_6$ the prince$_5$ to-each money and life offered, and of-them$_6$ none it accept would. And they$_6$ still fighting were until they$_6$ all lay [dead] except one Welsh hostage, and that-one very wounded was. Then on morning heard that the king's retainers$_9$ who him$_1$ behind were [i.e. who had stayed behind,

20 who had not accompanied Cynewulf to his mistress's bower] that the king$_1$ killed was, then rode they$_9$ thither, including his alderman Osric, and Wiferth his retainer, and the men$_9$ that he behind him$_1$ left earlier, and the prince$_5$ in the place found where the king$_1$ killed lay, and [they$_{5+8}$] the gates to them$_9$ shut had and then there to went. And then offered he$_5$ them$_9$ their own choice of-money and land if they$_9$ him$_5$ the kingdom granted, and them$_9$ told that their$_9$

25 kinsmen$_8$ him$_5$ with were those$_8$ that him$_5$ from not-wanted [i.e. that did not want to part from him]; and then said they$_9$ that to-them$_9$ no kinsman dearer was than their lord$_1$, and they$_9$ never his killer$_5$ follow would, and then offered they$_9$ their kinsmen$_8$ that they$_8$ unharmed from [that place] departed; and they$_8$ said that the same to-their$_9$ companions$_6$ offered was, who earlier with the king$_1$ were; then said they$_8$ that they$_8$ that not considered any more than your$_9$

30 companions$_6$ who with the king$_1$ killed were.

They$_9$ then around the gates fighting were until they$_9$ there in broke, and the prince$_5$ killed, and the men$_8$ who him$_5$ with were all except one, that was the alderman's godson$_{10}$, and he$_{10}$ his$_{10}$ life saved and yet he$_{10}$ was much wounded.

(The *Anglo-Saxon Chronicle* A, 755, 1–38; edition Plummer)

The text has two protagonists, Cynewulf ('the king'), index 1, and Cyneheard ('the prince'), index 5; and a number of minor characters: Cynewulf's mistress, index 7, Cynewulf's bodyguard who went with him when he visited his mistress in Merton, index 6, Cynewulf's other retainers who had not gone with him to Merton, index 9, and Cyneheard's men, index 8.

6.3 The word order of the subclause

6.3.1 Introduction

We are starting with the order of the subclause rather than the order of the main clause because the basic order of the various constituents in the subclause is less likely to be obscured by movement of the finite verb, which we shall discuss in more detail in the next chapter.

6.3.2 Identifying subclauses

A subclause is a clause that is a constituent of another clause, i.e. it expresses a syntactic function (of subject, object or adverbial) of another clause. The boxes in Table 6.1 show a number of clauses from the *Cynewulf and Cyneheard* text, in transliteration, that contain a subclause. The verbs of these 'higher' or **matrix** clauses are shown in a separate box because of their important role in the identification of subclauses. In (a) and (f), the subclause encodes a role of the verb – what the retainers heard was that the king was killed, what they offered to their kinsmen was that they should depart unharmed from that place. These subclauses have been labelled with the syntactic function 'object', although this label is somewhat problematic; objects are prototypically NPs rather than clauses, and subclauses like the ones in (a) and (f) historically derive from adjuncts rather than arguments, much like the -*ing* complement of *busy* that we discussed in section 5.3.5.1. The other subclauses in Table 6.1 have the syntactic function of adverbial, as they do not encode roles of the verb but provide answers to questions of when the action in the higher clause took place (*how long did they hack away, how long did he defend himself admirably, how long were they fighting about the gates*) or under which conditions the action in the higher clause would hold (*they would offer them their own choice of land and money if they would grant him the kingdom*).

Apart from encoding a syntactic function of the higher clause, subclauses can also post-modify a noun. This type of subclause is called a relative clause. An example is (g): the clause *who earlier with the king were* postmodifies the noun *companions*; the entire NP *their companions who earlier with the king were* is an indirect object in the higher clause.

Table 6.2 shows these subclauses further analysed into constituents of their own, with subjects (S), objects, complements and adverbials (XP) and verbs (V).

A conjunction *that, until* (*that*), or *if,* starts these clauses off, as a sign that what follows is a (finite) subclause. The constituents that follow

Table 6.1 Subclauses and their matrix clauses

	Beginning of matrix clause	Verb(s)	Subclause
a.	Then on morning the king's retainers	heard	OBJECT: that the king killed was
b.	And they all on the king	were hacking-away	ADVERBIAL: until that they him killed had
c.	and then admirably himself	defended	ADVERBIAL: until he on the prince looked
d.	They then around the gates	fighting were	ADVERBIAL: until they therein broke
e.	then offered he them their own choice of money and land	offered	ADVERBIAL: if they him the kingdom granted
f.	then they their kinsmen	offered	OBJECT: that they unharmed from that place departed
g.	that the same their companions	offered was	RELATIVE CLAUSE: who earlier with the king were

Table 6.2 The basic order of the clause

	Conjunction	S	XP	V
a.	that	the king		killed was
b.	until that	they	him	killed had
c.	until	he	on the prince	looked
d.	until	they	therein	broke
e.	if	they	him – the kingdom	granted
f.	that	they	(unharmed) from that place	departed
g.		who	(earlier) with the king	were

have the order Subject–Object(s)–Verb(s), i.e. the basic O–V order that will change to V–O in due course. Note that the XP position covers not just direct objects (*they killed HIM, they granted him THE KINGDOM*) but also indirect objects (*they granted HIM the kingdom*), prepositional objects (*he looked ON THE PRINCE, they departed FROM THAT PLACE*) and subject complements of copula verbs (*who were WITH THE KING*). *Unharmed* in (f) and *earlier* in (g) are adverbials (*they departed from that place IN AN UNHARMED CONDITION, they were with the king AT AN EARLIER TIME*) and show the basic position of adverbials in the SOV structure, i.e. before the object(s). The tables that follow will present this SAOV order as the basic skeleton of the clause.

6.3.3 Special positions for old information

Not all objects are found in the designated slot for objects in the SAOV order. Object pronouns are found in positions more to the left than full NP objects. Table 6.3 shows two derived positions to accommodate them – here shown as shaded: the high pronoun position before the subject, and the 'scrambled' object position to the left of the adverbial. The term 'scrambling' is a traditional one, a label for objects that precede adverbials in Dutch and German, and reflects the assumption that the objects that end up here started out in the underlying object position – the O in the SAOV order – but have 'scrambled' over the adverbial position. Unlike Dutch and German, Old English pronouns can 'scramble' out of their PPs, as in (c) in Table 6.3. This movement is shown by ___$_i$ in the original position of the moved pronoun, with the pronoun itself being marked by an index ($_i$) linked with this original position. *With him* starts out in the O slot because it is a subject complement (*they were with him*), and complements are also found in that slot.

The scrambling position is not exclusive to pronouns but may also host definite NPs. The generalisation appears to be, as in Dutch and German, that the scrambling position is for old information – NPs denoting entities that are known to the hearer, usually because they occur earlier in the text.

The addition of these two 'derived' positions introduces an element of uncertainty in which elements are in which slots in individual Old English clauses. It is not always clear where the various constituents go – there may be more than one option, especially in the absence

Table 6.3 Derived positions for pronouns and scrambled objects

Conjunction	High pronoun	S	Scrambled object	A	O	V
a. until that	him	a swineheard				stabbed-to-death
b. before	him	the men				discovered
c. that		their kinsmen	him$_i$		with ___$_i$	were
d. that	to-them	no kinsman			dearer	was
e. until		they	there$_i$	in ___$_i$		broke

of 'diagnostic' elements that have fixed positions, like adverbials for scrambling. We have no way of knowing whether *him* in (2), also from the transliterated text, is in the scrambled position or in the O position:

(2)   until that they him killed had

Similarly, having identified a high pronoun position in Old English, we cannot be sure that this position is only for object pronouns; it might be for pronouns in general, in which case the subject pronoun *they* of (e) could have moved there as well, from the S slot. Such **analytic ambiguity** is not just a problem for us as linguists, but also for new generations of Old English speakers in the acquisition process. The frequency with which diagnostic elements appear in their input may change, which means that new generations may arrive at somewhat different grammars, which may eventually result in quite major changes – in the case of English, a VO instead of an OV grammar, for instance.

6.3.4 Extraposition

There is another 'derived' position in Old English (and in Dutch and German), for which the diagnostic element is the verb, more specifically the non-finite verb in a verbal periphrasis with BE, HAVE or modal verb. This derived position is the right-most box in the examples of subclauses in (a–f) in Table 6.4, again from the transliterated text.

The shading shows that the constituents in that box do not originate there but have been moved there from other positions by what is traditionally called **extraposition**.

Note the form of the extraposed constituents: an NP containing a relative clause in (a); a PP in (b); a relative clause in (c): a PP in (d) and (e); and a relative clause again in (f). Extraposition survives in PDE for clauses, and for lengthy NPs (in which case the label 'heavy NP shift' is sometimes used). In the PDE example of (3), the extraposed clause is a part of a large NP, the NP *evidence that he is drunk*. In (4), we have heavy NP shift. The clause in (3) and the NP in (4), both in bold, have been shifted from their original positions (indicated by ___) to the end of the clause:

(3)   Evidence _____ will be presented **that he is drunk** (Ross 1968: 67).

(4)   He threw _____ in the dustbin **all the documents that contained incriminating evidence**.

What motivates such movement in PDE? In (5), the large NP *evidence that he is drunk* is a subject, and hence could be expected to appear at the beginning of the clause:

Table 6.4 Introducing extraposition

	High pronoun	S	Scrambled object	A	O	V	Extraposed constituents
a. until		he			—i	killed	the alderman that with-him longest remained_i
b. until that	him	a swineheard		—i		stabbed-to-death	at Prefer's Flood_i
c. before	him	the men _i				discovered	who with the king were_i
d. until		they all		—i		lay (dead)	except one Welsh hostage_i
e. that	to-them	no kinsman			dearer _i	was	than their lord_i
f. that		the same			to-their kinsmen _i	offered was	who earlier with the king were_i

(5)   Evidence that he is drunk will be presented.

Note that the most informative part of this clause – *that he is drunk* – is not in the most felicitous position for such new information, as it does not conform to the natural flow of information which is from old to new. Example (6) offers this more natural flow:

(6)   I will present evidence that he is drunk.

Pronouns are old information by definition, with an antecedent in the previous discourse; first and second person pronouns (*I, we* or *you*) do not require an antecedent at all, as speakers (*I* or *we*) and hearers (*you*) are always 'given' in the context of any utterance. *Evidence that he is drunk* is new information. The order in the PDE sentence in (6) is SVO, and the functions of subject and object match quite naturally to old and new information, respectively. The 'problem' in (5) is that the speaker apparently wants to keep the AGENT of the presenting action out of the discourse, for whatever reason; the identity of the AGENT may be irrelevant, or the speaker does not want to commit him or herself to any knowledge of the AGENT's identity. The mechanism used is the passive, which suppresses the AGENT that would have been the subject of the verb, and turns the object into a subject – but we noted that the result of this operation, in (5), is not felicitous from the viewpoint of information flow. Extraposition of the clause, as in (3) offers a way out of this dilemma. The reason for extraposition in (3), then, is information structure.

The heavy NP shift in (4) is probably motivated by the problem of processing such a long NP rather than its information status (although length and information status are difficult to separate – long NPs are also likely to be informative). The verb *throw* requires a PATIENT and a GOAL. The normal order would be PATIENT first, then GOAL – but the length of the NP that encodes the PATIENT means that it takes some time before the hearer encounters the GOAL, which is encoded as a short PP. Having this short PP first makes it easier for the hearer to tick that participant off, so to speak, and the NP that follows is almost immediately identified as the other obligatory item, without having to wait until the end – *the documents* is enough of a clue that this is an NP. There is an alternative for heavy NP shift, and that is to leave the head – *the documents* – in its original position, and only extrapose the postmodification of the noun *documents*, i.e. the relative clause *that contain incriminating evidence*. The result, in (7), is a split NP, as in (3). A dash ___ indicates the original position of this clause.

(7)   He threw all the documents ____ in the dustbin that contained incriminating evidence.

This choice – of moving the entire NP (let us call this option 1) or moving only the post-modification and leaving the head in place (let us call this option 2) – is only available to a limited number of constructions in PDE, but it is more widely available in Old English, where any postmodification may extrapose: for the relative clauses in (a), (c) and (f) in Table 6.4, as well as for the PP that postmodifies the adjective *dearer* in (e). In (a), repeated as (8a), the writer has selected option 1, but option 2, as in (8b), would also have been possible:

(8)   a.   he had that until he _____ killed [$_{NP}$the alderman that with-him longest remained]

      b.   he had that until he [$_{NP}$the alderman _____] killed [that with-him longest remained]

Below are the options for (c) (in 9a and b), and for (f) in (10a and b):

(9)   a.   before him _____ discovered [$_{NP}$the men who with the king were]

      b.   before him [$_{NP}$the men _____] discovered [who with the king were]

(10)   a.   the same _____ offered was (to) [$_{NP}$ their kinsmen who earlier with the king were]

      b.   the same (to) [$_{NP}$ their kinsmen _____] offered was [who earlier with the king were]

Examples (9 and 10) both involve NPs containing a relative clause as postmodification of the noun head. In (e) of Table 6.4, the postmodification *than their lord* is a truncated clause postmodifying an adjective, *dearer*. Options 1 and 2 are given in (11a and b) (AP stands for Adjective Phrase):

(11)   a.   and then said they that to-them no kinsman _____ was [$_{AP}$dearer than their lord]

      b.   and then said they that to-them no kinsman [$_{AP}$dearer _____] was [than their lord]

Note that option 2 is only available to postmodifications. Clauses and PPs that are not post-modifying another head can only be extraposed in their entirety, as in (b) in Table 6.4, here repeated as (12a); option 2 in (12b) is not possible (which is why it is marked with an *):

(12)   a.   until that him a swineherd _____ stabbed-to-death [at Prefet's Flood]

      b.   *until that him a swineherd [at _____] stabbed-to-death [Prefet's Flood]

Is extraposition in Old English also motivated by information structure and by processing, just like the PDE cases of extraposition in (3) and heavy NP shift in (4)? The processing burden of long NPs is even more relevant for Old English than it is for PDE because of the position of the object. Languages with OV-orders have a potential conflict between ease of processing for the receiver of the message, and the rules of syntax. The rules of syntax require the object to precede the verb; but as processing a string of words pivots on the verb, which comes with roles like AGENTS and PATIENTS that need to be identified and ticked off, processing halts until that verb is reached. Lengthy constituents before the verb delay processing, and have a cost in terms of what needs to be kept in memory before the hearer encounters the verb, and who is doing what to whom can be resolved. The concept associated with this processing motivation for extraposition in PDE is 'weight' – it is the 'heaviness', the sheer length of the constituent rather than its information status that makes it show up in the post-field. Options 1 (extrapose the entire constituent) and 2 (only extrapose the postmodification) resolve this conflict between syntax and processing.

Dutch and German favour option 2, and in those languages Option 1, extrapose the entire constituent, has become a marked order for NPs and APs containing postmodifiers. Option 1 has come to signal an elevated style in Dutch, to be used only in particular registers. Earlier stages of these languages, however, show that option 1 was less marked and more widely available, as in Old English.

6.3.5 And-*clauses*

Clauses starting with *and* 'and' or *ac* 'and, but' in Old English may have their verb in clause-final position, as if they are subclauses, even if they are conjoined to a main clause and hence a main clause themselves. Table 6.5 presents some examples from the *Cynewulf and Cyneheard* text. As in the earlier tables, derived positions are shaded.

Main clauses could be expected to show movement of the finite verb (see Chapter 7), but here the verb stays in V. There are a number of possible explanations. One is that *and* and *ac* have a different status in Old English – that they are not exclusively coordinating conjunctions, like *and* and *but* in PDE, but could also be subordinating conjunctions. Another one is that finite verb movement does not (only) mark the main or subordinate status of a clause but has a range of other functions. We will come back to these clauses in Chapter 8.

Table 6.5 *And*-clauses in *Cynewulf and Cynebeard* in transliteration

AND	High pronoun	S	Scrambled object.	A	O	V	Extraposed constituents
and	he			there ___i		stayed	until . . . i
and		that Cynewulf		often ___i	great battles	fought	against . . . i
and		Ø	the bower_i	outside ___i	___i	surrounded	before . . . i
and		he		to the doorway		went	
and		Ø		then admirably ___i	himself	defended	until . . . i
and	of-them	the nobleman			to-each money and life	offered	
and	of-them	none			it	accept would	
and		Ø	the nobleman	in the place ___i		found	where . . . i

6.4 Modelling

6.4.1 Right-headed VP and IP

A basic template of the SOV order as in Tables 6.1–6.5 in an X'-structure might look like this:

(13)

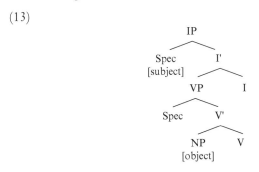

The adverbial position (before the object in Tables 6.3–6.5) is shown in (14a); the VP in (14a) has grown an extra V'-level to accommodate an adverbial. X'-projections can grow extra intermediate 'bar' (X')-levels for optional material, optional in the sense 'not structurally required'. Verbs require subjects, and, if transitive, objects; prepositions require NP complements; but adjectives modifying nouns, or adverbials modifying verbs, are optional in this sense, even though they often encode important information and a sentence would lose much of its meaning if they were left out. Nouns can be premodified by more than one adjective, and verbs by more than one adverbial; and N'- or V'-levels can be expanded to accommodate them.

The structures in (14a and b) represent the situation in Dutch and German and the situation in PDE, respectively, and it is likely that they also represent the initial and the final stage of the word order change in English. The IP and VP projections are the mirror image of IP and VP in the PDE structures in section 4.3, and the switch in 'headedness' (heads to the right of the complement become heads to the left of the complement) in the VP is reflected in a change in basic word order, from OV to VO.

The I-head, too, must have started out in final position. The final position of the I-head is historically linked to the final position of the V-head; the clause-final V in Tables 6.3–6.5 would have been a single verb in earlier times, and hence the carrier of finiteness, the information in the I-head, but with the rise of the verbal periphrases discussed in Chapter 3 and 4, the finiteness information increasingly came to be

(14)

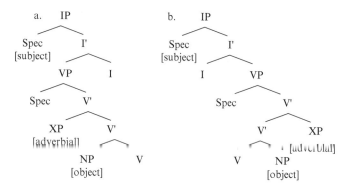

expressed not on the lexical verb, but on an auxiliary. How far along Old English was in these changes in headedness will be discussed below (for the VP) and in Chapter 7 (for the IP).

6.4.2 Verb raising

With the rise of verbal periphrases, the question arises of how the auxiliary verb and its complement are to be ordered: Vv (non-finite complement-finite verb) or vV (finite verb-non-finite complement). As a complement of the auxiliary verb, the non-finite verb can have been expected to appear in the complement position XP, giving Vv. This order is found in Old English, but vV orders are also found, as in (15):

(15) & hie   alle on þone Cyning **wærun feohtende** [vV] oþ   þæt hie hine
       and they all on the   king   were   fighting   until that they him
       ofslægenne hæfdon [Vv] <The Anglo-Saxon Chronicle A, 755, 16; edition Plummer>
       killed   had
       'And they continued to hack away at the king until they had killed him'

We know that the vV order in *wærun feohtende* 'were fighting' is not due to the finite verb moving to a position outside the IP; the position of *on þone Cyning* 'on/at the king' shows the clause has subclause order. This is not unexpected as it is an *and*-clause (see section 6.3.5). The IPs of both clauses contain a (finite) auxiliary (v) and a (non-finite) lexical verb (V) (given in bold), in vV and Vv order, respectively. These orders are well attested in the Modern West Germanic languages, and co-exist, particularly with the perfect periphrasis as in (15). The variation here is assumed to be the result of a word order operation known as 'verb raising'.

Vv must have been the earlier order historically because the participle must have been in the complement position of the auxiliary verb's
V, and evidence from Gothic suggests Vv order for that early Germanic
language (Eythórsson 1995). However, by the time of Old English, vV
is also found, as the result of verb raising in which the V of the complement – VP$_2$ in (16a and b) – moves to the auxiliary verb, the V of VP$_1$:

(16)

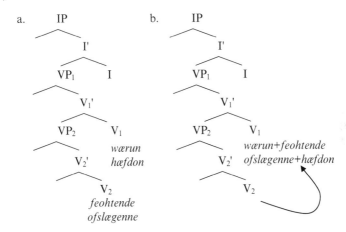

This is a case of 'head-to-head' movement, like I-to-C movement in
section 4.3, and cross-linguistically common.

The Vv order of *ofslægenne hæfdon* 'killed had' in (15) could be the
result of the absence of verb raising, as in (16a); but, to complicate
matters, not all cases of Vv order are necessarily the result of a failure of
verb raising. There are various pieces of evidence that the verb raising
from its original complement position in (16a) may attach either to the
right or to the left of the higher verb, as shown with *ofslægenne hæfdon* in
(16b). Verb raising leads to **clause union** of VP$_1$ and VP$_2$, as if VP$_2$ is no
longer a clause after it has lost its V to verb raising. Elements inside VP$_2$,
arguments of V$_2$ that would not be able to move out of a fully clausal
VP$_2$, may be found moved out of that VP once it has been diminished
by verb raising. Although this process appears to resemble the simplified
structure in section 4.8 that was due to the grammaticalisation of the
auxiliary verb, verb raising is also robustly attested with verbs that
show no sign of becoming auxiliaries, like perception verbs. Here is an
example with the perception verb *hieran* 'hear' taking an AcI complement (see section 5.1); the vV combination that is the result of verb
raising is given in bold:

(17) in þære stowe wæs gewuna,   þæt man hwilum   ymb fisc
      in that place was customary that one sometimes about fish
      gehyrde sprecan, &   þær   næs   næfre nan   gesewen. <GD 1(C) 1.11.16>
      heard   speak-INF and there not-was never none   seen
      'In that place it was customary that one sometimes heard [someone] mention fish, but
      none was ever seen.'

Ymb fisc 'about fish' is an argument of *sprecan* 'speak, tell' but separated
from it by *gehyrde* 'heard'; *sprecan* has been raised to adjoin *gehyrde*.

6.5 The change from OV to VO

6.5.1 Postverbal objects

If a long object NP is extraposed in its entirety, i.e. the option labelled
'option 1' in section 6.3.4, the result is V–O order; we saw an example
of this in (8a) above, here repeated as (18), this time from the original
Cynewulf and Cyneheard text rather than from the transliteration:

(18) he hæfde þa oþ   he ofslog [$_{NP}$þone aldormon þe   him lengest wunode]
                   S   V   O
      he had   that until he killed   the alderman   that him longest remained
      <ChronA 755.1>
      'He held that [=Hampshire] until he killed the alderman who had remained
      with him longest'

If the order in (18) is the result of extraposition, the underlying order is
still OV. As we know that the underlying order changed to VO at some
point, the question is when instances like (18) started to be analysed as
underlying VO. It seems likely, then, that extraposed objects as in (18)
kick-started this change. The rates found for objects in postverbal position in Old English are very high. Pintzuk (2002: 287) reports an overall
rate of 36.6 per cent postverbal full NP-objects in finite subclauses in
Old English, and Los (2005) reports the same figure for postverbal full
NP-objects in non-finite subclauses (*to*-infinitives). These are high rates.
How do we know whether such postverbal objects are cases of underlying OV with extraposition, or cases of underlying VO, the new order
that became dominant in Early Middle English? We could look at the
length of the NP, and speculate that only long NPs, for instance NPs
with postmodifiers, can be postverbal as a result of extraposition, while
the short ones must be postverbal because the underlying order is VO.
The problem is that the motivation for extraposition may be different
from extraposition in the modern West Germanic languages, with not

only processing a factor ('weight') but also information status ('new') or perhaps some other stylistic reason (contrast?) for positioning the NP towards the end of the clause. The rates of postverbal objects go up with the passage of time, with Late Old English having higher rates than Early Old English, but the motivations for extraposition may have changed as well.

In the face of such imponderables, it might be better to see what happens to elements that cannot extrapose. If they do not extrapose at an early stage but do later on, this might show the change to underlying VO more clearly.

6.5.2 Postverbal pronouns and particles

Postverbal NPs that are extremely unlikely to be the result of extraposition are pronouns, where considerations of 'weight' and information status do not apply: pronouns are light elements, and by definition 'old' information (Pintzuk 1999; Koopman 2005).

Not just any postverbal pronoun is evidence for underlying VO order: pronouns may appear to the right of a verb if the verb has moved. As verb movement is particularly likely with finite verbs (see Chapter 7), pronouns to the right of non-finite verbs are the best evidence. Postverbal pronouns after non-finite verbs are unsafe as evidence if they are found in Middle English copies of Old English manuscripts, where the copyist could have changed an OV order in the original text to a VO order in his or her copy, following his or her own Middle English VO grammar. Pronouns may also appear in unlikely positions in a clause if they are contrastively stressed; cf. PDE (20) below. In PDE, non-pronominal objects can either follow a phrasal verb, as in (19a), or intervene between the verb and its particle, as in (19b); but pronominal objects can only intervene, as in (19c), not follow, as in (19d):

(19) a. 'Smart' gadgets could *give away* more information about your lifestyle than you are comfortable with.
   b. 'Smart' gadgets could *give* more information about your lifestyle *away* than you are comfortable with.
   c. 'Smart' gadgets could *give* it/you *away*.
   d. *'Smart' gadgets could *give away* it/you.

But examples like (20) show that pronouns may occasionally be found in the prohibited position, provided that there is strong contrastive emphasis:

Table 6.6 Pronouns following non-finite verbs in Early and later Old English, based on Table 3 in Koopman (2005: 58)

	Postverbal pronouns	%
Early OE	20/1222	1.6
Late OE	107/2124	5.0

(20) If you force your confidence upon me, Mr. Headstone, I'll give up every word of it. Mind! Take notice. I'll give it up, and I'll give up **yóu**. I will! (Dickens [1865] 1919, *Our Mutual Friend*: 673; *give up* could mean 'reveal, divulge' in Dickens' day.)

If instances from Middle English copies, or instances that are clearly contrastive, are excluded, as was done in Koopman (2005), the figures that result are those given in Table 6.6.

What is interesting about the 107 instances from the later texts is that there is a particular environment that favours postverbal pronouns: the second of two coordinated VPs as in (21) (pronoun in bold):

(21) Þa heton þa consulas Hasterbale þæt heafod of aceorfan, & aweorpan
    then ordered the consuls Hasdrubal the head off cut   and throw
    hit beforan Hannibales wicstowe
    it before Hannibal's camp
    'Then the consuls ordered Hasdrubal's head to be cut off and to be thrown before Hannibal's camp' <Or 4.10.105.34> (Koopman 2005: 55)

The second characteristic of postverbal pronouns is that they are rarely found on their own in these coordinated clauses, but are accompanied by other material. This suggests that many of these postverbal pronouns are there for a stylistic reason, the result of a conscious choice. Koopman gives (22) as an example of clear parallelism between the first and the second conjunct, from one of Ælfric's letters (Koopman 2005: 56). The first infinitive, *forgifan* 'forgive', is followed by an extraposed object, *eallum þam mannum* 'all the men', which may have prompted the same order of 'infinitive – pronominal object' in the second clause:

(22) And he sceal forgifan eallum þam mannum, þe him ær   abulgon, and
    And he must forgive all   the men   who him earlier offended and
    biddan **hym** forgifnysse
    ask   them forgiveness
    'and he must forgive all the men who had offended him and ask them for forgiveness' <ÆLet 3, 17> (Koopman 2005: 56)

Ælfric has been described as a 'conscious stylist' (Hurst 1972), and we will see another example of his style below.

The trend visible in Table 6.6 continues in Middle English. The fragment in (23) from the Middle English *Orrmulum* has four pronominal objects (*itt* 'it', in bold), all referring to the same entity (Orrms own text); but only the first and third *itt*s are clear evidence of VO – they appear to the right of non-finite verbs:

(23) Forr þatt I wollde bliþelig þatt all Ennglisshe lede
     for   that I would gladly   that all English   people

      wiþþ ære shollde lisstenn **itt**, wiþþ herte shollde **itt**
      with ear should listen   it,   with heart should   it

      trowwenn, wiþþ tunge shollde spellenn **itt**, wiþþ
      trust,   with tongue should spell   it with

      dede shollde **itt** follghenn.
      deed should it follow.
      [CMORM 113.33] (Trips 2002: 112)

      'That is why I want all English people to listen with their ears, to trust it with their hearts, to spell it with their tongues and to follow it with their deeds.'

The other two cases have *itt* to the left of the non-finite verb and could be analysed as base OV order, with movement of the finite verb *shollde* 'should'.

The *Orrmulum* is verse, not prose, and constituents may appear in unusual positions for metrical reasons; but its high rates of pronominal objects following non-finite verbs suggests that VO order is the base order by this time.

The second diagnostic is provided by the position of particles in verb+particle combinations. The expected position of the particle is as in (24):

(24) And seo helle þone deofel **ut** a- draf,
     and the hell the   devil out PREF-drove
     'and Hell drove out the devil' [CONICODC 282.274] (Los et al. 2012a: 140)

The diagnostic is based on the assumption that the particle does not move out of its original position, which is preverbal, either because the particle is part of the V, in a set combination like PDE phrasal verbs (*ut-a-drifan* 'drive out'), or because *þone deofel* 'the devil' and *ut* 'out' in (24) form a kind of resultative small clause, with a copular relationship: *the devil is out* (see section 5.1). As the small clause is the complement of the

V, in the preverbal O (complement)-slot of Tables 6.3–6.5, the particle can be expected to appear preverbally in OV syntax.

As with the pronouns, the V needs to be non-finite, for the same reason: finite verbs may have moved to the left, leading to a postverbal particle either in the original V position (if particle and verb form a phrasal-verb-like combination), or in the position preceding that V-position (if particle and object form a resultative small clause). An example is (25), where the finite verb *draf* 'drove' has moved, leaving the particle behind. *Ut* 'out' is in the same position in both (24) and (25).

(25) Eadwine eorl com mid land fyrde and draf hine **ut**. <ChronLaud 1066>
      Eadwine earl came with land army and drove him out
      'Earl Eadwine came with a land army and drove him out'

The theory is that any particle following a non-finite verb cannot be in a derived position, as particles do not move; if non-finite verbs do not move either, such a particle must point to an underlying VO structure. An example of such a particle is (26), from the *Cynewulf and Cyneheard* episode in another manuscript of the Anglo-Saxon Chronicle than the one from which the text in 6.2 was taken.

(26) he wolde adræfan **ut** anne æþeling. . .
      he would drive out a prince
      'he wanted to drive out a prince'
      <ChronB (T) 82.18–19 (755)> (Pintzuk 1999: 116)

The position of the object *anne æþeling* 'a prince' is not at issue here – it has been extraposed (together with its following relative clause, not shown here). What is interesting is the position of the particle, which now follows the non-finite verb. If we assume that particles cannot move, the postverbal particle in (26) indicates underlying VO. This analysis is supported by the fact that instances like (26) become more frequent in Late Old English, and the norm in Middle English (as it is in PDE), as Koopman (2005) shows (see Table 6.7).

Koopman (2005) notes that the great majority of particles are found in the work of Ælfric (38 out of 41), and represent 35 per cent of Ælfric's total use of particles in the texts investigated. As in the case of pronouns, Koopman notes that the postverbal particles are favoured in a particular environment, in this case the AcI, where the particle appears after the bare infinitive that is one of the components of the construction. One such instance is (27), with an AcI after *hatan* 'order, command', a verb of commanding and permitting (see section 5.4.7) that encodes peremptory commands that come close to outright causation (Royster 1918: 83–84; Los 2005: 133).

Table 6.7 Postverbal particles in Early and later Old English, based on Table 3 in Koopman (2005: 58)

	Postverbal particles	%
Early OE	11/229	4.8
Late OE	41/156	26.2

(27) ac   ða apostoli heton   lædan **forð** þone diacon and þæt cild forð
      but the apostles commanded lead   forth the deacon and the child forth
      beran þe   ðær   acenned wæs
      carry which there born   was
      'but the apostles ordered the deacon to be led forth and the child which
      had been born there to be carried forth' <ÆCHom II, 38.284.158>
      (Koopman 2005: 57)

A closer look at this example reveals that the first *forð* 'forth' in (27) appears postverbally as part of a particular rhetorical device, *chiasmus*: the deacon is an adult and can be *led* forth, while the baby has to be *carried* forth; chiasmus, a rhetorical device that juxtaposes structures with mirror-image syntax, expresses the contrast between these different modes of locomotion: V–forth–object and object–forth–V. Ælfric is known to favour chiasmus (Ohkado 2004; Sato 2012).

The parallelism between Tables 6.6 and 6.7 is very suggestive: there is certainly a change. Whether this change can be identified as the first beginnings of a switch to underlying VO depends on how we weigh and interpret the following points: (1) the postverbal pronoun shows some skewing with respect to the environments it occurs in, which suggests it is a stylistic feature; the development of conventions for written styles are very interesting in their own right, but whether they tell us something about the underlying structure depends on whether we accept or reject the notion that writers can 'bend' the syntax of their language to produce word orders that are not normally possible; (2) the same goes for the postverbal particles; (3) our assumptions that particles do not extrapose are based on evidence from Dutch and German, languages in which the rules of extraposition have become more restricted in the course of time; unlike pronouns, particles are heavily stressed and not automatically old information. The fact that particles stay put in present-day Dutch and German does not necessarily entail that they stayed put in Old English; and (4) if underlying VO was increasingly possible, we would expect to find not only pronouns and particles, but also stranded prepositions in postverbal position. We do find some examples of such prepositions, but far fewer than postverbal pronouns or particles.

6.5.3 Postverbal stranded prepositions

Prepositions stranded by relativisation, the formation of a relative clause, are always found in their original preverbal position in OV languages like Dutch and German. The same is true for Old English. In PDE, stranded prepositions follow the verb.

Relativisation moves a constituent and leaves a gap in the structure. When the moved constituent is an NP in the complement of a preposition, such movement strands the preposition. A PDE example is (28b and c), with (28a) showing a similar clause without the relativisation:

(28) a. Their incredibly luxurious hotel was equipped with its own gold bar vending machine.
      b. [$_{NP}$The gold bar vending machine [$_{CP}$(that) the hotel was equipped **with** ___]] was out of order. (Preposition stranding: NP-shaped gap)
      c. [$_{NP}$The gold bar vending machine [$_{CP}$**with** which the hotel was equipped ___]] was out of order. (No preposition stranding: PP-shaped gap)
      d. [$_{NP}$The gold bar vending machine [$_{CP}$(that) the hotel **with** equipped was ___]] was out of order. (Preposition stranding in OV base order)

Examples (28b) and (28c) show the gap in the relative clause; in (28b), the NP inside the with-PP is relativised, and the preposition *with* is left stranded; in (28c), the entire PP has been relativised, and *with* has been taken along to the Spec,CP of the relative clause. We saw an example of preposition stranding by question formation in (30a) in Chapter 1.

The structures in (29a and b) show how the headedness of the VP, as introduced in (14a and b) above, accounts for the difference in stranding. In (29a), PP–V order parallels the NP–V order of (14a), the OV order. If the NP moves out of the PP because of relativisation, and the preposition is stranded, the result will be P–V, preverbal stranding, and this is the stranding we see in Old English. In (29b), V–PP order parallels the V–NP order of (14b), the VO order. If the NP moves out of the PP because of relativisation, and the preposition is stranded, the result will be V–P, postverbal stranding, and this is the stranding we see in PDE.

(29)

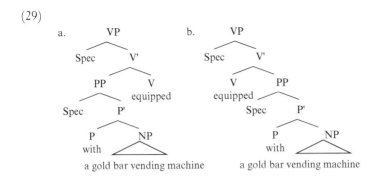

As PDE is a VO language without finite verb movement, a PP such as *with a gold bar vending machine* will always follow rather than precede the verb (here *equip*), which is why the preposition *with* will always follow rather than precede *equip* when stranded (*was equipped with*). As an OV language, Old English stranded prepositions precede rather than follow the verb, as in *with equipped was* in (28d). An Old English example, from Ælfric's rhythmic prose which I have marked by full stops (see section 1.5.3), is (30) (stranded preposition in bold):

(30) Þær wæron gehælede . Þurh ða halgan femnan . fela adlige menn,
     there were healed through the holy maiden many ailing people
     swa swa we gefyrn gehyrdon . and eac ða þe hrepodon .
     as we before heard and also those who touched
     þæs reafes ænigne dæl. þe heo **mid** bewunden wæs .
     the-GEN shroud-GEN any-ACC part-ACC that she with winded was
     wurdon sona hale
     became at-once whole
     <ÆLS (Æthelthryth) 113>

   'Many ailing people were healed by the holy maiden, as we heard earlier, and those who touched any part of the shroud that she had been wrapped in also regained their health immediately'

The relative clause fits Ælfric's pattern of rhythmic half lines. A search of the parsed Old English Corpus yielded just two cases of a preposition stranding in postverbal position, as opposed to hundreds of preverbal strandings. One of these is (31), from the same text as (30), and almost identical in phrasing; like (30), this relative clause also measures out a half-line. The stranded preposition again is in bold:

(31) Þa wæs seo wund gehæled. Þe se læce worhte ær . ac swilce
     then was the wound healed which the doctor made earlier; also like

þa gewæda . þe heo bewunden wæs **mid** . wæron swa ansunde .
the shrouds that she winded   was with were   so   sound

swylce hi   eall niwe wæron. <ÆLS (Æthelthryth) 93>
as-if   they all new were

'Then the wound which the doctor had made turned out to be healed,
just like the shrouds that she was wrapped up in were as free from
damage as if they had all been newly made'

It is interesting that we find this rare construction in Ælfric, the conscious stylist, although we cannot recover his reasons for using it, the
relative with the preverbal preposition in (30) apparently fits the metre
just as well, so why did he not use it in (31)?

Like postverbal particles and postverbal pronouns, postverbal
stranded prepositions become much more numerous in Middle English,
with some texts exhibiting a 50:50 variation in pre- and postverbal
stranding (Kroch and Taylor 2000a).

6.5.4 *Information structure as a diagnostic for change*

Although it is tempting to see the conflict between the rules of syntax
and ease of processing as motivating the change to base VO order
that takes place around 1200, it cannot be a sufficient cause, precisely
because there is the escape-hatch of extraposition. Dutch and German
show the same conflict but have remained OV. As option 1 – extrapose
a constituent in its entirety – also existed in the earlier West Germanic
languages, which did not switch to base VO, ease of processing cannot
be the main ingredient in any scenario of the switch in Early Middle
English. Quite small independent developments may have had an
impact; the wholesale loss of the anticipatory pronouns in the correlative constructions that will be discussed in Chapter 8 might be one of
them, as these pronouns provided clear evidence in acquisition that the
language was underlyingly OV, even though the *that*-clause that it was
linked with would always be extraposed.

Recent investigations look at the information status of pre- and postverbal objects, and whether the rates of new versus old postverbal NPs
change through time. If one of the motivations for extraposing objects
is information structure, with new objects more likely to extrapose than
old objects, changing rates in the information status of postverbal objects
could indicate not only a change in syntax but also a motivation for
change. Suppose that there are two mechanisms that can lead to postverbal objects: (1) extraposition from underlying OV; (2) underlying VO.

We take a sample of 100 postverbal objects from Early Old English texts and analyse their information status. We find that 50 out of 100 postverbal objects are 'new'. When we do the same for a sample of 100 postverbal objects from Late Old English texts, we find that only 25 out of 100 are 'new'. If information structure accounted for 50 per cent of postverbal objects at the early stage, and the motivations for extraposition remain stable, it follows that 50 (25+25) out of 100 objects at the later stage are due to extraposition, and 50 are due to underlying VO, showing that the rate of underlying VO has increased. Initial results suggest that rates of new versus old postverbal objects change: they are higher at the earlier end of Old English than at the later end (Taylor and Pintzuk 2012).

6.6 Summary of points

- Orders in the Old English subclause follow a basic pattern of Subject–Adverbial–Object(/Complement)–Verb (SAOV).
- Clauses that start with *and* 'and' often exhibit this order as well, regardless of their clausal status (main clause or subclause).
- There are at least three derived positions in this basic pattern: a high position for pronouns, a position for scrambling (old/'given' information only), and a clause-final position after the V for extraposed constituents.
- The options for extraposing constituents are extensive in Old English and not restricted to lengthy constituents only, as in PDE.
- Like the other early West Germanic languages, Old English can either extrapose a constituent in its entirety, or only extrapose a postmodification inside a constituent.
- Extraposing objects in their entirety results in V–O orders. As the switch from underlying OV to underlying VO orders was complete in Middle English, the question is how far advanced the variation between these orders is in Old English. Possible diagnostics discussed in this chapter are pronouns and particles following non-finite verbs, preposition stranding, and whether informationally-new objects are more likely to follow the V than old or 'given' objects.

Exercises

1. ANALYZING SUBCLAUSES. Consider the following Old English clauses, all taken from the *Cynewulf and Cyneheard* text transliterated in section 6.2. Analyse the six clauses in italics in the template of Table 6.5. Note any analytical ambiguity (i.e., instances of there being more than one slot for a particular constituent).

(i)   & þa þider   urnon *swa hwelc swa þonne gearo wearþ & radost,*
       and then thither ran   whoever   then ready was   and quickest

(ii)   & *hiera   se æpeling gehwelcum   feoh   &   feorh gebead,*
       and of-them the prince to-each   money and   life offered

(iii) & *hiera   nænig   hit geþicgean nolde.*
       and of-them none   it accept   not-would

(iv)   *oþ hie   alle lægon   butan anum Bryttiscum gisle*
       until they all lay [dead] except one   Welsh   hostage

(v)   *þæs cyninges þegnas þe   him beæftan wærun*
       the king's   retainers who him behind were

(vi)   *þur ve cynning ofslægen was*
       that the king killed was

2. ANALYZING MORE COMPLEX SUBCLAUSES.

   a. Do the same for the following subclauses (in italics) from *Ælfric's Catholic Homilies*, including any subclauses within these subclauses. Note any problems.
   b. Construct an X'-tree structure for the underlying order of the subclause in (ii), along the line of tree (14a).
   c. Provide a PDE translation of this paragraph.

   (i)   Us sæde soðlice beda *þæt se eadiga Cuðberhtus ða ða he wæs eahta wintre*
          us tells truly   Bede that the blessed Cuthbert, when he was eight winter's
          cild   arn swa swa him his nytenlice yld tihte, plegende mid his efenealdum.
          child ran, like him his ignorant age urged, playing with his companions.

   (ii)   God ... asende him to[1] an ðrywintre   cild *þæt hit[2] his dyslican plegan*
          God   sent him to a three-winter's child that it   his foolish games
          mid stæððigum wordum wislice ðreade
          with grave words wisely rebuked

   (iii) geðeod þe   to gode *ðe ðe to biscope his   folce geceas*
          turn yourself to God who you as bishop of-his people chose

   (iv)   Hwæt ða cuþberhtus þa   gyt mid his plegan forð arn *oð   þæt his lareow[3]*
          Well then Cuthbert   then yet with his games on ran until that his teacher
          mid biterum tearum dreoriglice wepende ealra ðæra cildra   plegan
          with bitter tears sadly   weeping all the children's games
          færlice   gestilde
          suddenly stopped

   (v)   hi ealle ne mihton mid heora frofre   his dreorignysse adwæscan
          they all not could with their comforting his sadness   quench

----
[1] *asende him to* 'sent to him'
[2] *hit* refers to the child, as *cild* is a neuter noun
[3] *his lareow* refers to the three-year-old child

ær   ðan þe   cuðberhtus hit⁴ mid   arfæstum cossum gegladode.
until that that Cuthbertit   with kind   kisses cheered-up
Text from <ÆCHom II, 10, 81.7–22>

Further reading

For the OV/VO change, see Taylor (2005), Pintzuk and Taylor (2006), Taylor and Pintzuk (2012), Trips (2002), Foster and W. van der Wurff (1997), and van der Wurff (1997). Verb Raising in Germanic has been discussed in Den Besten and Edmondson (1983), Rutten (1991), and Fanselow, G. (1989). For clause union, see Wurmbrand (2001). An account of why verb movement might fail in Old English *and*-clauses is presented in Bech (2012).

---

⁴ *hit* again refers to the child, see note 2

7 Verb-Second

7.1 Introduction

Old English, like Dutch and German today, shows an **asymmetry** in main and subclause orders, illustrated here with a series of 'transliterations' from Dutch in (1a and b):

(1) a. Celebrities **dig** their family secrets up in this new TV series.
     b. ... that celebrities in this new TV series their family secrets up-**dig**.
     c. Their family secrets **dig** celebrities in this new TV series up.
     d. In this new TV series **dig** celebrities their family secrets up.

The main clause in (1a) looks like the SVO order of a PDE main clause, but the subclause has the verb in an entirely different place. There is a general consensus that this asymmetry is best explained by assuming that the SOV order of the subclause in (1b) shows the underlying order, and the main clause deviates from this order in a systematic way. The similarity of the main clause in (1a) to a PDE clause, then, is deceptive: PDE main clauses start out as SVO, whereas the clause in (1a) actually starts out as (1b), and arrives at (1a) by means of two movement rules: (1) the finite verb moves into second position (which in the case of a phrasal verb like *dig up* means that the particle *up* is left behind), and (2) a constituent from the clause is **topicalised** into first position. This constituent may be moved from any position in the clause, and may have any syntactic function; in (1a) it is the subject that has been topicalised, in (1c) it is the object, and in (1d) it is the adverbial. These two movement rules have been labelled collectively as 'Verb-Second'.

Note that (1a–d) has a phrasal verb at its core, a combination of a particle and a verb. Such verb+particle combinations have been used as evidence for finite verb-movement for Dutch (Koster 1975): they start out together in clause final position, as in (1b), but the finite verb moves away in main clauses, leaving the particle behind (as in (1a), (1c) and (1d)).

What is the function of finite verb-movement? In Dutch and German, finite verb-movement appears to be a syntactic device, obligatory in all main clauses, so that it can no longer signal anything more specific than the bare fact that we are dealing with a main clause and not with a sub-clause. The choice as to which constituent to put first – the subject, the object, or the adverbial – is up to the speaker. This choice depends on a force field of conflicting demands. The first position of a main clause has been called a 'cognitively privileged position' (Lambrecht 1994: 31–2) – how we start a sentence is important. We can use the first position to link to the previous sentence, which will produce an utterance in which the flow of information goes from what is already known to the hearer to what is new. But we can also start with information that is unexpected and new.

We said in Chapter 1 that syntax evokes expectations about what the next words in an utterance will be. Having basic word order patterns in a language is handy on the production side, as it presents speakers with set routines that they can follow; it eases things on the processing side, too, as the choice of what the next word will be becomes smaller as the sentence progresses, and this helps hearers to anticipate and decode what is said. Both speakers and hearers have a stake in predictability, which makes it easy to see how word orders can syntacticise, i.e. become automatic. Creative speakers will exploit hearer expectations by not playing by the book, by making hearers sit up and take notice precisely because their expectations are not met. If there is a general tendency for utterances to go from given to new, speakers may create a shock effect by starting with information that is completely new. Such innovations which are meant to create a special communicative effect may acquire a momentum of their own when taken up and systematised by subsequent generations of speakers.

This is how different types of information may come to compete for the first position: given information, to provide a suitable 'point of departure' that complies with the natural tendency to have the informa-tion in a sentence flow from given to new, and new information that a speaker may position there for extra prominence. The information, given or new, may be contrastively focused in that position or not, in accordance with the speaker's communicative needs. Languages tend to develop main and subclause asymmetries precisely for that reason: it is particularly the main clause that has to satisfy these various, often conflicting, communicative requirements. This is why main clauses may develop special constructions not found in the subclause, and why subclauses tend to preserve older orders (Bybee 2001). This fits in with a scenario in which finite verb-movement is a relative innovation in Germanic, a departure from the basic template of Subject–Adverbial–Object–Verb (SAOV) that suffices for many Old English subclauses, as we saw in the previous chapter. The innovation introduced two syntactic operations onto this basic SAOV template: movement of the finite verb, and movement of a constituent to the first position. In modern West Germanic, finite verb-movement is a sign of main clauses and a lack of finite verb-movement is a sign of subclauses. But this is not true of Old English, where verb-movement apparently signalled something more specific than marking the clause as a main clause.

This chapter will present the Old English facts in a framework that, although speculative, tries to account for these facts in a meaningful way, where the two landing sites for verb-movement – the second place and the third place – are interpreted as showing the outcome of two different motivations for movement, in line with the competition for the first position signalled by Lambrecht. Although the verb shows up in the third position under certain well-defined circumstances, this, too, is the result of finite verb-movement. We will continue to refer to the entire phenomenon of finite verb-movement, including Verb-Third, as Verb-Second, for reasons that will become clear in section 7.4.

7.2 Verb-movement to the second position

The fact that Verb-Second in Old English does not operate in the same way as in the other West Germanic languages is clear from main clauses like (2), where the finite verbs (in bold) are clause-final:

(2)   Ðas ðry tungel-witegan hi   to Criste **gebædon,**   and him getacnigendlice
      those three astrologerss   them to Christ prostrated   and him symbolic
      lac **offrodon** <ÆCHom I, 116.7>
      gift offered

      'Those three wise men prostrated themselves to Christ and offered him symbolic gifts'

We saw in the previous chapter that verbs can remain in clause-final position in *and*-clauses, which accounts for the position of *offrodon* 'offered'. The position of *gebædon* 'worshipped' in (2) shows that verb-movement may also fail in other main clauses. It is not clear why. A conscious stylist like Ælfric may well have exploited the flexibility of Old Englush word order to create two perfectly parallel clauses.

The finite verb almost invariably moves to the second position in questions as in (3) and in declarative clauses introduced by a negative element (as in (4)). Finite verbs appear in bold:

(3) Hu **mæg** he ðonne ðæt lof   & ðone gilp   fleon
     how may he then   the praise and the vainglory   avoid
     'How can he then avoid praise and vainglory. . .?'
     <CP 9.57.18> (van Kemenade and Westergaard 2012: 88)

(4) ne **mihton** hi nænigne   fultum æt him begitan
     not could they not-any   help from him get
     <Bede 48.9–10> (Kroch and Taylor 1997: 303)
     'They could not get any help from him'

PDE still marks questions (see (5)) and declaratives starting with a negative element (see (6)) in this special way:

(5) Why **did** the management refuse to provide more food at the
     buffet?

(6) Never at any point **did** the customer indicate that she wanted to
     stay within a fixed budget.

Where PDE differs from Old English is that only auxiliaries can
undergo this movement, not lexical verbs (see Chapter 4), which is why
do-support is required if there is no auxiliary (*did* in (5) and (6)); this
movement is called subject-auxiliary or I-to-C movement in PDE. It
extends to sentences starting with certain adverbs, like *only*, or *rarely*,
that have scope over the entire clause:

(7) Only after I had been in the room for a few minutes **did** I realise
     that everyone was staring at me.

(8). Rarely **did** I hear such overtones of gratitude as went into the
     utterance of this compound noun. (Green 1980: ex. (32e), cited in
     Birner and Ward 1998: 157)

Elements like *only* and *rarely* pattern like *never* in (6) because their
meaning contains a negative component. It is not just that they can be
rephrased with a negative (*only after* equals *not immediately*, *rarely* equals
not often) but, like *never*, they also 'license' **negative polarity items** that
need to be in the scope of negation:

(9) a. *I received any letters.
     b. Never have I received any letters.
     c. Rarely have I rarely received any letters.
     d. Only then did I receive any letters.

The semantic link between negation and questions is that both involve
variables. Questions create a variable x that requires a value, the
'answer', which in (5) could be the fact that the management thought

the customer wanted to stay within a fixed budget. An undefined variable x evokes a set of possible values for x. Negation, too, involves a variable, as it activates its positive alternative: by saying 'not x' the speaker automatically evokes x. What negation and questions have in common, then, is that they evoke alternatives, and this is exactly what focus is about. As *never, only* and *rarely* are also focus-sensitive elements, the relevant generalisation could be that the verb originally moved to the second position to mark off a focus domain, i.e. to make the first position of the clause available as a position for a focused constituent.

Although questions and negative first elements still require finite verb-movement, focus-sensitive elements like *only* and *precisely* have an alternative expression, the stressed-focus *it*-cleft:

(10) **It was** only after I had been in the room for a few minutes **that** I realised that everyone was staring at me.

This structure has two clauses, not one, which means that it is syntactically more complex. Instead of *did* we have the conjunction *that* in what has become a separate clause, while a new main clause allows the focused constituent *only after I had been in the room for a few minutes* to be positioned at the end of the clause, which is a default position for new information in PDE. The stressed-focused *it*-cleft is an Early Modern English innovation (see Ball 1991; Komen 2013).

Contrastively-focused adverbials in first position, as in the PDE example in (11), are no longer accompanied by auxiliary movement from Early Modern English onwards; being in presubject position in PDE is apparently enough:

(11) In Germany the prospects are good, but in America they are losing money. (Krifka 2007: 45)

We briefly discussed such adverbials in section 1.4.2. This use of adverbials has been called frame-setting (Chafe 1976); these adverbials are forward-looking rather than backward-looking: they denote the domain in which the following proposition, in this case *the prospects are good*, holds. They do not establish a relation with the previous discourse. This is an important difference with the first-position adverbials that we will consider in the section 7.4.

7.3 Modelling movement to the second position

Approaches that model word order in tree structures have identified the second position of the finite verb in the modern West Germanic

languages as the C-head, with Spec,CP as the position of the first constituent; this idea was introduced and briefly discussed in section 4.4.1.
Positioning verbs in a complementiser slot is not intuitive, and needs
some argumentation. Let us recapitulate the tenets of this type of modelling. In section 2.7 we introduced the X'-format:

(12)

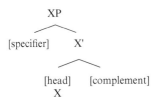

Heads – X in this structure – can be functional as well as lexical; lexical
heads are verbs, nouns, adjectives and prepositions, building VPs, NPs,
APs and PPs; functional heads are K for case (see section 2.7) or I for
inflection (see section 4.3), building KPs and IPs. The specifier position
of functional heads is typically a landing site for moved constituents, with
the trigger for movement often seen to reside in that functional head X.
The agreement of the subject with the finite verb, for instance, which
survives even in PDE *he/she/it walk-s* versus *I/you/we/they walk-ø*, can be
modelled in the IP, with the subject ending up in the specifier-position
(Spec, IP) and agreement features – person and number – in the head of
that IP, the I-head. The subject is located in Spec, IP in order to make
a connection with the agreement features in I. The verb in V contains
only lexical information and depends for its realisation on the agreement
information in I.

Complementisers are located in a functional head C and build a functional projection CP in the highest position of the clause; we met this
projection in section 4.3.4 where we translated subject-auxiliary inversion as head movement from I to C. CPs are, in effect, clauses. Example
(13) shows the general structure of CP and IP with suggestions of possible fillers. The subject is mentioned twice because it starts out inside
the VP, where semantic roles like AGENT and PATIENT are assigned to
the subject and object. The subject then moves to Spec,IP to allow it to
pass on its agreement-features to the I-head. The I-head is able to share
information with the next head down, V, which is how subject-verb
agreement, as in *he walks*, is achieved in PDE:

(13)

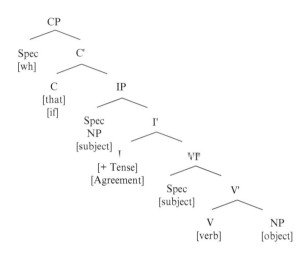

The structure in (13) shows that we need another projection on top of a main clause IP in PDE, as this is where we can position questioned constituents (see again section 4.3.4). We also require it for the PDE sentences in (6)–(8); (7) is here repeated as (14):

(14)   Only after I had been in the room for a few minutes **did** I realise that everyone was staring at me.

As *do*-support in PDE translates as I-to-C movement, *did* is in C, and this movement has 'opened up' the Spec,CP position as a host for the focused constituent *Only after I had been in the room for a few minutes*. Where PDE differs from Old English is the fact that the chain of head-movement from V has been broken: I-to-C is still possible, but V-to-I is no longer possible for lexical verbs (section 4.6).

   The question remains why we identify this topmost projection as CP, also for a main clause, if the C in main clauses is not filled by a complementiser but by a verb. A possible answer is the way in which functional information can be expressed. Consider the conditional clauses in (15). They can be formed by merging *if* in C, as in (15a and b), but it is also possible to signal a conditional by subject-auxiliary inversion. In PDE this is only possible with the auxiliaries *should* (15d) or *had* (16b):

(15)   a. If your boss enters the room while you are playing a game, hit the boss-key immediately.
       b. If your boss should enter the room while you are playing a game, hit the boss-key immediately.

c. *Enters your boss the room while you are playing a game, hit the boss-key immediately.

d. Should your boss enter the room while you are playing a game, hit the boss-key immediately.

(16) a. If he had managed to hit the boss-key in time, he would not have been fired.

b. Had he managed to hit the boss-key in time, he would not have been fired.

C in PDE can apparently be filled by a complementiser (*if*) or by an auxiliary, but not by a lexical verb. This is I-to-C movement (as in (17)) but without the possibility of *do*-support:

(17)

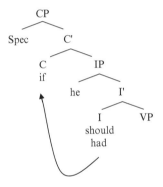

The restriction to auxiliaries is what we would expect, given that there is no V-to-I movement in PDE – but there was earlier, before the rise of *do*-support (section 4.6). This leads us to expect that conditional clauses could also have been marked by lexical verbs moving to C (V-to-I-to-C movement) before that watershed in the sixteenth century. This is borne out by Old English instances like (18) (the fronted finite verb of the conditional clause, the **protasis**, appears in bold):

(18) **Gewite** seo sawul ut. ne mæig se muð clypian. þeah ðe he ginige
      go-SUBJ the soul out not may the mouth call though that he gape

      'Should the soul go out, the mouth cannot call though it be wide open'
      <ÆCHom i.262.126> (from Mitchell 1985: §3679, quoted in Molencki 1999: 109)

The verb *gewite* 'depart' is in C in the protasis; it is in the subjunctive (see section 4.8), as is usual for conditional clauses. The verb *mæig* 'may' in the **apodosis** is also in C, as is usual for main clauses; the protasis is the first constituent of that main clause, in Spec,CP. A late instance of a fronted lexical verb as a signal of a conditional clause is (19):

(19) I could not love thee (Deare) so much, **Lov'd** I not Honour more
      (*OED*, 1649 R. Lovelace Lucasta 3; *OED*, *if*)
      Cf. if I did not love Honour more.

We noted in section 4.8 that functional information can be expressed in three ways: (1) a bound morpheme merged in the relevant functional head, which requires another head to move to that functional head (*merge* and *move*); (2) a free form moving to the relevant functional head (*move*); and (3) a 'bespoke' free form merged in the relevant functional head (*merge*) (Roberts and Roussou 2003). For the C of conditionals this is exemplified by complementisers being expressed by a 'bespoke' element *if* (*merge*) and by movement of another head, in this case the auxiliary verbs *had* or *should* (*move*), or by the subjunctive in (18) (*merge* and *move*). The connection between C and a moved head (V in Verb-Second) fits in this general schema of expressing a functional head.

The functional information in the C-head, then, says something about the clause-type: it marks a clause as interrogative, declarative, conditional (with *if* or I-to-C movement), or as a complement (with *that*). This is not necessarily what V-to-I-to-C set out to do when it first arose; the original motivation for I-to-C in the interrogative and negative element-initial clauses may well have been for no other purpose than to create a focus position. This movement may have been reanalysed as clause-typing at a later stage.

To sum up, V-to-I-to-C movement is not so very different in Old English from what it is in PDE. It is still triggered by questioned constituents and other focus-sensitive elements. What is lost is the V-to-I part of the chain: in PDE, there is still I-to-C movement, but lexical verbs can no longer move to I, as marked by the introduction of *do*-support. There is a further change in that focus markers like *only* and *rarely* in first position with I-to-C movement are experiencing some competition from stressed-focus it-clefts, as in (10); *only* and *rarely* in first position with I-to-C movement have become somewhat marked, and a conscious stylistic choice rather than default syntax.

What has changed since Old English is another type of verb-movement, the type of movement that marks the Old English version of Verb-Second as more complicated than the Verb-Second rule in Dutch or German. This is the topic of the next section.

7.4 Verb-movement to the third position

There is a second type of movement in Old English in which the verb is probably not in C but in a head lower down. This type of verb-movement does not mark off a focus domain, and the first constituent is not a *wh*-phrase or a negative element. At first sight, the verb appears to be in second place, too, much like the main clause finite verb in the other West Germanic languages as shown in the transliterations in (1a–d) above. The finite verb is given in bold.

(20) egeslice **spæc** Gregorius be ðam <WHom 10c, 48> (Warner 2007: 88)
      and sternly spoke Gregorius about that
      'and Gregorius spoke sternly about that'

(21) On   twam þingum **hæfde** God þæs mannes saule gegodod
      in   two   things had   God the man's soul endowed
      'With two things God had endowed man's soul.' <ÆCHom I, 1.20.1>

(22) Be   þam **awrat** Moyses se   mæra heretoga, In principio fecit Deus
      About those wrote Moses the great general, In principio fecit Deus

      celum et terram (<ÆHom I, 70, 46>; van Kemenade 2009: 99–100)
      celum et terram

      'About those words Moses the great general wrote: In principio fecit
      Deus celum et terram. . .'

(23) On ægðer þæra   boca.   **sind** feowertig cwyda buton ðære forespræce
      on either those-GEN books-GEN are   forty   sermons except the   preface
      'in each of those books are forty sermons, not counting the preface'
      <ÆCHom II Pref 2.37>

The difference with the focus movement of the previous section becomes clear when we look at cases that have pronominal rather than nominal subjects, and compare them with (3) and (4) above; (3) has been repeated as (25) for comparison:

(24) Æfter þysum wordum he **gewende** to þam ærendracan <ÆLS (Edmund) 83>
      After these words   he turned   to the messenger
      'After these words he turned to the messenger'

(25) Hu **mæg** he ðonne ðæt lof &   ðone gilp   fleon
      how may   he then   the praise and the   vainglory avoid
      'How can he then avoid praise and vainglory. . .?'
      <CP 9.57.18> (van Kemenade and Westergaard 2012: 88)

Note the difference between (24) and (25) in the position of the pronominal subject. When the first constituent is not one of the focus-categories, and the subject is a pronoun, the verb ends up in third rather than second position as in (24). The word order in (24) may look deceptively like its PDE translation, but unlike PDE, (24) involves verb-movement, which becomes clear when there is a non-finite verb, like *geswutelod* 'manifested' as in (26); finite and non-finite in bold:

(26) Eft   embe geara ymbrenum   he **wearð** on his fulluhte on þisum dæge
      again about years course   he was   on his baptism on this   day
      middanearde **geswutelod** < ÆCHom I 104.21 >
      world   shown
      'Again, in the course of a number of years, he was, at his baptism,
      manifested on this day to the world'

The non-finite verb stays in the clause-final V-slot (cf. Tables 6.3–6.5 in Chapter 6), but the finite verb has been fronted.

The consensus at the moment is that the verb is in the same low position in (20)–(24) and (26), the shaded column in Table 7.1.

If movement to the higher position, C, may originally have been motivated by the need for focus-marking, what could have motivated movement to the lower position?

A possible motivation may have been to demarcate old, 'given' information from new information. This would explain the different positions of pronominal and nominal subjects: pronouns are by definition old information, while nominals and names need not be, and the two categories end up to the left and the right of the moved finite verb. The adverbial in first position in this configuration is often a PP containing an NP that is not new as in the frame-setters in (11) but **anaphoric**, i.e. it refers back to previously mentioned items, or to a previously established time or place: *Be þam* 'About those' in (22), *On ægðer þæra boca* 'in either of those books' in (23), *Æfter þysum wordum* 'after these words' in (24). When these adverbials are not PPs but single adverbs, they are often from the *þ/s*-set that derives from a demonstrative stem *þa-* (see *OED the, then, there, thus*) or *sa-* (see *OED so*). This makes them ideal forms for the adverbial first position in the 'given' information domain that is demarcated by the verb in the configuration of Table 7.1.

Note that Spec,CP is a derived position; constituents do not start out there, but in the position of the SAOV-basic order that is appropriate to their syntactic function (see Chapter 6). This holds for cases of V-to-C movement as well as for V-to-F movement.

It is not clear whether such a motivation is still in place as a productive process in Old English. The pattern may well have become

Table 7.1 Positions for pronominal and nominal subjects, with examples in transliterations

Example	1 Spec, CP	2 C	3	4	5 Spec, IP	6 I	7 VP
20	sternly			spoke	Gregorius		
21	with two things			had	God		the man's soul endowed
22	about those			spoke	Moses		[Latin text]
23	in each of those books			are	forty sermons		
24	after these words		he	returned			to the messenger
26	in the course of a number of years		he	was			at his baptism on this day to the world manifes-ted

entrenched and syntacticised. The adverbials *egeslice* 'sternly' in (20) and *On twam þingum* 'with two things' in (21) are not anaphoric, and the name *Moyses* 'Moses' in (22) is not new information in the context. When the first constituent is not a questioned constituent or a negative element, the verb may even not move at all, as we saw in (2) – even though *Ðas ðry tungel-witegan* 'those three wise men' is clearly anaphoric.

7.5 The adverbs *þa, þonne, þær* and *nu*

The adverbs *þa* and *þonne*, both meaning 'then', are anaphoric, and refer back to a particular period (the initial *þ-* marks them as deriving from the same deictic roots as the demonstratives). As such, they could be expected to behave like the other anaphoric adverbials, with pronominal subjects intervening between them and the fronted finite verb, but they do not – they are only occasionally found in the configuration of the template in Table 7.1. Their usual pattern is actually the one for focus, with the finite verb in C, also when the subject is a pronoun. An example is (27):

(27) þa   **worhte** he sylf   Cristes rodetacen   mid his fingrum.
      Then made he himself Christ's sign-of-the-cross with his fingers
      ongen   þam gledum.
      amongst the flames <GD1 (C) 11.87.14>
      'Then he himself made Christ's sign of the cross with his fingers amongst the
      flames.'

Table 7.2 lines up all the *þa*-clauses in the *Cynewulf and Cyneheard*
episode we discussed in the Chapter 6. Pronominal and nominal subjects are both found after the finite verb; the labels prefield, middlefield
and postfield are traditional labels for sections of the main clause in
Dutch and German.

If we accept the given/new demarcation as a possible motivation
for the rise of this type of verb-movement, how can we account for the
anomalous behaviour of *þa* and *þonne*? Etymologically, they seem to go
back to the same root as the *þ*-forms of the demonstrative paradigm of
Table 2.4 in section 2.6, and their meaning 'then' appears to be just as
anaphoric as the demonstratives, and as the adverb *þær* 'there'. If *þær*
makes a link with a place mentioned in the previous discourse, and *þa*
and *þonne* make a link with a time that has been established previously,
they would both be good candidates for filling the Spec, CP slot in
Table 7.1 and behave like the adverbials in (21)–(24) and (26) in triggering V-to-F rather than V-to-C. *þær* conforms to the pattern in Table 7.1,
but *þa* and *þonne* overwhelmingly do not. The finite verb is always in
second place, whether the subject is nominal or pronominal.

One way of looking at this is to think of *þa* and *þonne* as narrative
operators, signalling a special type of clause that expresses the actions
on the main line of the narrative. As negative constituents and interrogative elements also signal special clause types, the content of CP and
its head C would then express the function of clause-typing. We will
return to *þa* and *þonne*, and *þær*, in Chapter 8.

7.6 Modelling movement to the third position

If the finite verb in clauses like (20)–(24) does not move as high as C, where
does it move to? What are the positions 3 and 4 in Table 7.1? We would
expect 4 to be a functional head, as the typical landing site of V ('head-to-
head movement') and 3 to be that head's specifier – a position for pronominal subjects to move to that is higher than the Spec,IP position which is the
standard position for subjects – which means that we need one additional
projection. The tree below adds this projection as FP (for Functional
Projection) without being specific about what the label should be.

Table 7.2 þa-clauses in *Cynewulf and Cyneheard* in transliteration

Prefield		Subject	Middlefield			V	Postfield
þ_A	Finite verb		Scrambled 'given' objects	Adverbials	Object(s)		Extraposed constituents
þa	discovered_i	he [Cyneheard]	the king_j	with-small bodyguard on woman-tryst in Merton		—_j	—_i
þa	perceived_i	the king			that	—_i	
þa	lunged-out_i	Ø		toward him		—_i	
þa	discovered_i	the king's bodyguard			the disruption	—_i	
þa	heard_i	—_j			that>	—_i	the king's retainers who him behind were_j <that the king killed was
þa	rode_i	they		hither		—_i	
þa	offered_i	he	them		their own choice of money and land		
þa	said_i	they				—_i	that to-them no kinsman dearer was than their lord
þa	offered_i	they	to-their kinsmen			—_i	that they unharmed from there departed
þa	said_i	they				—_i	that the same to-their kinsmen offered had-been, who earlier with the king had-been

(28)

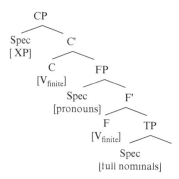

One suggestion in the literature (Haeberli 2002) is that this mystery projection is AgrSP, following a proposal by Pollock (1989). IP is associated with finiteness, but that concept has two components: agreement (of the subject and the verb) and tense. Pollock proposed to separate these two out into an Agr(eement)S(ubject)-phrase (AgrSP) and a T(ense)-Phrase (TP).

7.7 Early verbs in subclauses

7.1.1 Introduction

Having two positions for the finite verb instead of one is not the only difference between Verb-Second in Old English and in the modern West Germanic languages. The asymmetry between main and sub-clause, with Verb-Second being strictly a main clause phenomenon in West Germanic, and subclauses keeping their finite verbs in clause-final position, is only found as a strong tendency in Old English. Not only do we find main clauses without verb-movement, we also find finite verbs showing up early in the clause in subclauses. As it is not clear whether finite verbs in early positions in the subclause are due to movement of that verb, we will refer to them by the neutral label of 'early verb'. This section will suggest a number of analyses for such early verbs.

7.7.2 Main-clause-like subclauses

7.7.2.1 Se-relatives
One of the factors influencing early verbs in Old English is clause-type. One clear subclause type with high rates of 'early' verbs are relative clauses of the *se*-type. An example of this type from the *Cynewulf and Cyneheard* fragment is (29):

(29)   he wolde   adræfan   anne æþeling se   was Cyneheard haten
       he wanted drive-out a nobleman   who was Cyneheard called

Although this is best translated in PDE as a relative clause (*he wanted to drive out a nobleman who was called Cyneheard*), it is quite likely that this is not a relative clauses in the PDE sense but a main-clause-like **paratactic correlative**: *He wanted to drive out a particular nobleman. That one was called Cyneheard.* Although this sounds strange in PDE, it would not sound strange in Modern Dutch or German, where demonstratives can refer to human referents. The 'early' verb in (29), in that case, may well be just another case of movement of the finite verb to F. Another example of a *se*-relative, this time with a non-human referent, is (30):

(30)   ðære sawle mihta syndon þas feower fyrmestan and sælestan; *prudentia*,
       of-the soul powers are those four first and best *prudentia*

       þæt is snoternysse, **þurh þa** heo sceal hyre scippend understandan
       that is intelligence through that she shall her creator understand

       and hine lufian, and tosceaden god fram yfele. <ÆLS (Christmas) 157>
       and him love, and distinguish good from evil

       'the powers of the soul are those four, first and best: *prudentia*, that
       is intelligence. Through that/through which she [i.e. the soul] shall
       understand her creator, and love him, and distinguish good from evil.'

Modern readers will tend to translate the PP in bold in (30) as a relative, 'through which', and this is followed by coding practices in parsed corpora, so that cases like (30) boost counts of early verbs in subclauses. The problem is that adverbial links containing demonstratives, like the examples in Table 7.1 above, have become rare in PDE, so that the translation 'Through that', as the beginning of a separate main clause, has become infelicitous. Example (30) conforms perfectly to the template of Table 7.1, however, and the main clause interpretation receives further support from Dutch and German, which have retained the possibility of such adverbial links, and have even evolved a dedicated set of 'pronominal adverbs' to express them, parallel to the expression *thereby* in PDE.

Se-relatives as in (29) and (30) contrast with relatives that contain the particle *þe*, as in (31), also from *Cynewulf and Cyneheard*:

(31)   he hæfde þa   oþ   he ofslog þone aldormon   þe   him lengest wunode
       he had   that until he killed the   alderman   ÞE   him longest remained
       'he held that [i.e. Hampshire] until he killed the alderman who had stayed
       with him longest'

As the particle *þe* is a general sign of embedding in Old English, not only for relative clauses but also for other types of subclauses, the higher rates of finite verbs in final position for this type of relative is in line with the tendency for finite verbs in subclauses to stay put.

7.7.2.2 Assertions

The second type of main-clause-like subclauses consists of complement clauses and clauses that provide explanations ('reason clauses'). These clauses are much more likely to have early verbs than other adverbial clauses or embedded (or indirect) questions. The reason might be that complement clauses and reason clauses are more likely to represent assertions that something is the case, and assertions are associated with main-clause-like behaviour. This could mean that finite verb-movement to F as in section 7.4 is not aligned with the syntactic status of the clause (main versus subclause) but with assertion versus non-assertion. We will return to this in Chapter 8.

7.7.3 Extraposition

There are a number of constructions that might result in an 'early' verb that does not involve verb-movement to the second or third position. One is extraposition, which we encountered in the previous chapter; recall from section 6.3.4 that lengthy, 'heavy' constituents in object or complement position delay the encounter with the verb in an SOV language, which makes it more difficult to process the sentence. Old English has two options of dealing with such constituents: move the entire constituent to the end of the clause, beyond the verb, so that the verb is encountered first (we called this option 1), or move only the postmodification of that constituent and leave the head in its original position (option 2). Option 1 will result in an early verb (*wolde* in the example in (32) below); the extraposed constituent appears in bold:

(32) Se frumsceapena man and eall his ofspring wearð adræfed of   neorxena-wanges
      the first-created man and all his offspring were driven   from paradise-GEN

      myrhðe, þurh   ungehyrsumnysse, [. . .], and ðurh   modignysse,
      joy   through disobedience   and through   pride

      ðaða he **wolde** beon **betera ðonne hine se Ælmihtiga Scyppend gesceop**.
      when he wanted be   better than him the Almighty Creator created
      <ÆCHom I, 118.23>

'The first-created man and all his offspring were driven from the joy of paradise through disobedience and through pride, when he wanted to be better than the Almighty Creator created him.'

Note that option 2 would have resulted in (33):

(33) ðaða he betera wolde beon ðonne hine se Ælmihtiga Scyppend gesceop.
       when he better wanted be   than him the Almighty Creator created

It is not only 'heavy' material that can be extraposed but also very informative material; although *þe*-relatives tend to have clause-final verbs, as we saw in the previous section, this is often not the case if they introduce names (relative clause in bold):

(34) On þæs caseres   dagum **þe wæs gehaten Licinius** wearð astyred
       in that emperor's days   that was called   Licinius was   stirred-up
       mycel ehtnys ofer þa Cristenan
       much persecustion over those Christians
       <ÆLS (Forty Soldiers) 4> (Traugott 1992: 27)
       'In the days of the emperor who was called Licinius there was much persecution of the Christians'

Note that Licinius follows the non-finite verb, which shows that this is extraposition rather than movement of the finite verb, which would have resulted in *þe wæs Licinius gehaten*. Although the name *Licinius* is not a heavy constituent, and the OV order *þe Licinius wæs gehaten* would not present a processing problem for which extraposition could offer a better alternative, the writer, Ælfric, has still extraposed it, possibly to give it more prominence.

7.7.4 Verb projection raising

Another construction that results in early verbs is verb projection raising (VPR), a raising of more than just V. VPR has been suggested as an analysis for certain early verbs in subclauses in West Flemish, another West Germanic language (Haegeman and van Riemsdijk 1986). VPR is a variant of verb raising, an operation on sequences of verbs in clause-final position that we discussed in section 6.4.2. Consider (35) (relevant verb in bold):

(35) Hu God þa mæstan ofermetto and þæt mæste angina   on swa heanlice
       how God the greatest pride   and the greatest undertaking in such worthless

       ofermetto geniðerade, þæt se,   se þe him ær   geþuhte þæt him nan sæ
       pride   humbled   that that-one that that him earlier seemed that him no sea

wiþhabban ne   mehte þæt he hiene mid scipun and mid his fultume afyllan
keep   not might that he it   with ships and with his army   fill

ne mehte, þæt he eft   wæs biddende anes lytles troges æt   anum earman
not might that he afterwards was asking   a   little boat   from a   poor

men, þæt   he **mehte** his feorh generian. <Or 5.48.13> (van Kemenade 1987: 59)
man so-that he might   his life   save.

'So did God humble the greatest pride and the greatest undertaking in such
worthless pride that he [i.e. Xerxes], who earlier thought that no sea could
keep him from covering it with ships and with his army, found himself begging
for a little boat from a poor man so that he might save his life.'

The finite verb *mehte* 'might' could show up in this early position in the
clause because the entire VP *his feorh generian* 'save his life' has been raised:

(36)

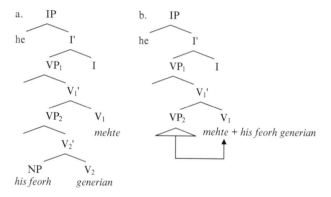

Evidence from Modern West Germanic languages that exhibit VPR
suggests that it is not possible to raise VPs if the object is a pronoun,
which would mean that the early verb *wolde* 'would' in the Old English
subclause (37) cannot be the result of VPR:

(37)   and seo modor behet him þæt heo **wolde** hine læran
       and the mother promised him that she would him teach
       'and the mother promised him that she would teach him'
       <ÆLS 25.173> (cf. Pintzuk 1999: 73)

If we assume that VPR in Old English was subject to the same restrictions
as in the modern West Germanic languages, instances of early verbs in
subclauses like (37) cannot be explained by VPR or extraposition.

7.7.5 Left-headed IP

A third possibility is that IP can be both right-headed (as in (38a)) and left-headed (as in (38b)) in Old English:

(38)

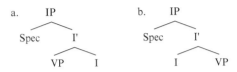

As we assume that IP is left-headed in PDE – witness the trees in section 4.3 for I-to-C movement in PDE questions – there must have been two switches in headedness in the history of English: a switch in the headedness of the IP, and in the headedness of the VP (resulting in the OV/VO change as discussed in section 6.5). PDE does not have any right-headed projections.

7.7.6 Conclusion

This section has outlined various aspects of the structure of the Old English clause that may lead to finite verbs ending up early in sub-clauses. Some of these explanations rely on phenomena that match cross-linguistic findings, such as the main clause nature of complement clauses and reason clauses, some rely on phenomena found in the modern West Germanic languages, like verb projection raising and paratactic relative clauses, and others on general characteristics of the Old English clause, such as the existence of a postfield for extraposed constituents. There was a lot of scope for Old English writers and translators to position sentence constituents, and to develop their own preferred style.

7.8 Charting the decline of Verb-Second

7.8.1 Introduction

Verb-Second starts to decline in the fifteenth century, for reasons that are as yet not fully understood. Fischer et al. (2000: 133) cite a number of studies that try to chart the decline. These report wildly varying rates of Verb-Second, within individual periods, individual text types, and even within the output of individual writers. The reasons why the decline is so hard to chart is that we should not be looking at just any finite verb in second place. The word order pattern that is lost is the one described in sections 7.4 and 7.5 in terms of V-to-F movement. This means that we should exclude patterns of finite verbs in 'early' positions in main clauses that are not due to this particular movement but due to I-to-C movement or to another construction. Once finite verb-movement becomes a receding option rather than canonical syntax, speakers may use it as a special construction with a discourse function, or even as a 'metatextual' sign to signal an 'elevated' style. This section discusses instances that might distort the picture of the decline and would probably be best excluded from the investigation.

7.8.2 Interrogative and negative clauses

Finite verbs in second place triggered by interrogatives and negatives in earlier English, which still trigger I-to-C movement in PDE (see section 7.2), should be kept apart.

It is interesting to note that such negative elements waver for a while in the Early Modern English period in whether they trigger subject-auxiliary movement or not, before the situation is resolved and such movement once more becomes obligatory (Nevalainen 1997). An example of where subject-auxiliary movement fails is (39):

(39)   but bycause we be not gouerned by that Law, **neither** I haue my Trial by it, it shal be superfluous to trouble you therewith [CETRI1, THROCKM I, 68 (a1554)] (Nevalainen 2006: 114)

7.8.3 Then, now, there, thus, so

We saw in section 7.5 that the adverbs *þa* and *þonne*, both meaning 'then', triggered verb-movement to the higher position: they are followed by the verb in Old English even if the subject is a pronoun. This behaviour persists well into Early Modern English with the adverbs *then, now, there, thus* and *so*:

(40)   Attourney: My Lords and Maisters, you shall haue Vaughan to justifie this heere before you all, and confirm it with a Booke Oth. Throckmorton: He that hath said and lyed, will not, being in this case, sticke to swear and lye.
Then **was** Cutbert Vaughan brought into the open Court.
Sendall: How say you, Cutbert Vaughan, is this your own Confession, and wil you abide by all that is here written?
[CETRI1, THROCKM I, 67 (a1554)]

(41) C. is the appointed pricke, from whiche vnto the line A.B. I must
      draw a perpendicular. Therefore I open the compas so wide, that
      it may haue one foote in C, and thother to reach ouer the line,
      and with that foote I draw an arch line as you see, betwene A. and
      B, which arch line I deuide in the middell in the point D. Then
      drawe I a line from C. to D, and it is perpendicular to the line
      A.B, accordyng as my desire was. [CESCIE1B P E4R, The xxxiij
      theoreme (a1551)]

This pattern is restricted to just these lexical items.

7.8.4 Stance adverbs

So-called 'stance' adverbs in first position – like *soþlice* 'truly' or *witodlice*
'certainly' – are not as integrated into the clause as adverbials of place,
time or manner, and do not 'count' as the first constituent in terms of
Verb-Second. The same goes for adverbs that function as text structuring elements, like *furthermore.*

7.8.5 Verbs of saying

Verbs of saying regularly show verb-subject order, from Early Modern
English into PDE:

(42) 'You have made me very wretched,' **whispered** Fred Lamb,
      pressing my hand with much passionate agitation. He looked
      remarkably well. (Harriette Wilson (1825), *The Game of Hearts:*
      Harriette Wilson and Her Memoirs: 208).

They also represent a category that should be excluded from the data.

7.8.6 Nominal and pronominal subjects

Nominal and pronominal subjects need to be kept distinct, as we saw
in section 7.4 that the verb may show up in third place if the subject is
a pronoun. The examples to look for are cases of V-to-F with nominal
subjects, as this is where the decline should manifest itself most clearly.
Note that we increasingly see the verb in second place with pronominal
subjects (verb in bold):

(43) and to þese lordes **gaue** he mech of þe liflod of þe duke of
      Gloucetir, erl of Warwik, and erl of Arundel. [CMCAPCHR
      209.3751 (15th C)]

'And to these lords he gave much of the livelihood of the Duke of
Gloucester, the Earl of Warwick and the Earl of Arundel.'

7.8.7 Discourse functions

Another problem for charting the decline of Verb-Second is the fact that
a resurrected or 'exapted' version of Verb-Second continues to be used
after its decline as a canonical word order pattern. The very fact that
there is word order variation within a speech community precipitates
new functions for orders that are no longer seen as canonical; some of
the wildly different rates of Verb-Second in the oeuvre of the fifteenth-
century writer John Capgrave (for some figures, see for example Eitler
2006) can be explained by the fact that he uses Verb-Second in his
chronicle as a text-structuring device, to mark the beginning of a new
section:

(44) So was he taken and sent to Couentre, þere drawen and hanged.
      Men sey þat he was sent be on William Marys, þat was outelawed
      and dwelled in a ylde betwix Cornwayle and Wales – þei þat
      dwelle þere clepe it Lundy. In xxii ȝere of Herry **was** Edward
      þe First born in þe feste of Seynt Bothulp, and he was baptized
      of Otho, legat, and confermed be Seint Edmund, þan bischop of
      Cauntirbury. [CMCAPCHR 120.13–17]
      'In that way he was captured and sent to Coventry, and there
      drawn and quartered. Men say that he was sent by one William
      Marys, who was outlawed and dwelled in an island between
      Cornwall and Wales; they that live there call it Lundy. In the 12th
      year of Henry, Edward I was born on the feast of St Bodulph, and
      he was baptized by Otho, legate, and confirmed by St Edmud, the
      bishop of Canterbury.'

Another new discourse function has been suggested for the position of
the verbs in bold in (45):

(45) And because he was desirous for godly purposes somtyme to be
      solitarye and sequester hymselfe from wordly company, a good
      distance from his mansion house **builded** he a place called the
      Newe Buildinge [. . .] in which as his use was upon other dayes to
      occupye himselfe in prayer and studye togeather, soe on Frydaye
      there usually **continued** he from morninge to eveninge spending
      his tyme only in devoute prayers and spiritual exercises. [. . .]
      Thus **delighted** he evermore not only in virtuous exercises to be
      occupied himselfe, but alsoe to exhorte his wife and children and

houshoulde to embrace and followe the same. (Roper's *Life of Sir Thomas More*, written *c.*1555, first printed in 1626; quotation from edition of 1910: 219–20; Fludernik 1996: 593)

Fludernik (ibid.) points out that the fronting of the lexical verb in (45) appears to mark a conclusion, a summing-up after a string of argumentative points. Note the position of the pronominal subject in (45), and also in the examples below; movement to the lower position (F) that is a feature with first constituent objects and adverbials in Old English, as we saw in section 7.4, is not part of this resurrected version.

7.8.8 The elevated style

In later Modern English, I-to-C starts to mark an elevated style, as in (46) and (47), where we find I-to-C movement with first constituents containing focused adverbials:

(46) Or, to give the full meaning of the words, at the sacrifice of the beauty of the translation- In a mere shadowy being **doth** man walk to and fro; For a mere breath **do** they so tumultuate. . . [pusey-186x, 278.8–9]

(47) Pastor Fricke, a man of ability, well trained and highly gifted, was an ardent missionary. He was never too tired to look up some member or wavering soul that needed the church, and many a mile **did** he walk in heat or cold to bring one more to church and Christ. <http://knoxcotn.org/old_site/churches/firstlutheran1919/biographies/fricke.htm>

The elevated style is also found in nineteenth-century Bible translations:

(48) A light **shalt** thou make to the ark, and to a cubit **shalt** thou finish it upward; and the door of the ark shalt thou set in the side thereof; [erv-old-1885,6,1G.223-225]

The fact that (V-to-)I-to-C movement still occurs in these restricted styles is one of the major difficulties of charting the decline of Verb-Second in the history of English.

7.8.9 The 'late subject' construction

The PDE construction often referred to as 'subject-verb inversion' should also be kept distinct, as the order Verb-Subject is probably not due to verb-movement but to extraposition of the subject. The subject is not separated by the finite verb alone but by the entire verbal string (given in bold); cf. (49):

(49) In the iron trade, enormous quantities of material are used for the manufacture of boilers and pipes; while the manufacturers of paint, putty, and other materials also do a brisk trade with market growers. To these **must be added** the various gas companies and colliery merchants, who provide thousands of tons of coke or anthracite coal to feed the furnaces attached to the glasshouses. [weathers-1913,1,7.154-156]

This construction has been present in English from Old English onwards; an example can be found in (34), here repeated as (50); verbal string in bold:

(50) On þæs caseres   dagum þe wæs gehaten Licinius **wearð astyred**
      in that emperor's days   that was called Licinius was   stirred-up
      mycel ehtnys   ofer þa Cristenan
      much persecustion   over those Christians
      <ÆLS (Forty Soldiers)> (Traugott 1992: 27)
      'In the days of the emperor who was called Licinius there was much persecution of the Christians'

A fourteenth-century example is (51):

(51) by this cercle equinoxial **ben considered** the 24 howres of the clokke
      'by this equinoxial circle are denoted the 24 hours of the clock'
      (Chaucer, *Astrolabe*, Robinson 1957: 548, II. 32–3; Eitler 2006: 189)

In PDE, 'late subjects' are the only option, as finite verb-movement is no longer possible with lexical verbs, and the construction is used for presenting subjects in the clause-final end-focus position if they contain new information:

(52) To the left of the altar one of the big wall panels with rounded tops opens, it is a secret door like in a horror movie, and out of it **steps** Archie Campbell in a black Cassock and white surplice and stole. (Updike 1990: 840, from Birner and Ward 1998: 158).

But cases of late subjects are almost impossible to distinguish from Verb-Second in Old and Middle English when there is only a single verb (verb in bold):

(53) Of þese seuene heuedes **comen** alle manere of synnes (*Book of Vices and Virtues*, Francis 1942: 11.8; Warner 2007: 94).

from these seven heads come all manner of sins
'From these seven heads spring all manner of sins'

Of þese seuene heuedes is a clear link to the previous discourse ('given' information) and the subject is non-pronominal, so the conditions are met for V-to-F movement. But (53) is also positioning new information that will be the topic of the next sentence in clause-final position. This second function is where V-to-F movement as in Table 7.1 – demarcating given from new information – overlaps with the late subject construction. With V-to-F movement gone, the late subject construction appears to fill the same niche, witness (49) above, where we also have a link to the previous discourse (*To these*). This clause-initial adverbial is not a contrastive frame-setter, as in (11).

7.9 Causes of the decline

7.9.1 *Language-internal causes*

The presence of inflections on a verb are important cues in language acquisition that the language in question has verb-movement: the inflection sits in a head in the functional shell on top of the VP (whether we want to call that head I, T, AgrS, etc.), and the verb in V moves to that head to pick it up. Inflections are subject to phonetic reduction and erosion, and the story of English is the story of the loss of inflection – verbal inflection, case inflection. Without inflection, the verb may continue to move, and the meaning of that functional head may continue to be expressed by that movement, rather than by the inflection, as we saw in the story of the subjunctive and the modals (Chapter 4). The rise of *do*-support in the sixteenth century showed that I-to-C movement endured, but V-to-I movement did not, and the high frequency of periphrastic expressions for tense, mood and aspect in the fifteenth century may well have obscured the evidence for such finite inflections as then remained.

We mentioned the loss of the pronoun *thou* in the sixteenth century, and its distinctive-(*e*)*st* verbal inflection, which marked both present and past tense; we also mentioned the position of adverbs, like *always* and *never* which mark the left edge of the VP, and provided evidence for the speaker that any finite lexical verbs preceding them were in I rather than in V (example (33) in section 4.4.5). In PDE, such adverbs always follow the lexical verb. These causes are language-internal, the result of changes in one system (the morphology) having consequences for another (the syntax).

7.9.2 Language-external causes

A good case can be made that the earliest loss of V-to-F was in the North; although Old Norse had a rule of finite verb-movement it did not exhibit the nominal/pronominal subject distinction as described in section 7.4, and it may well have been the contact situation of Old English speakers and Old Norse speakers in the Danelaw area that led to the loss of this distinction in the northern dialect (see Kroch et al. 2000). The rise of the wool trade led to massive immigration into London from the North and the Midlands in the late fourteenth century and beyond, which provided a second occasion in which speakers with the northern rule of finite verb-movement came into contact with speakers who had preserved the nominal/pronominal subject distinction in V-to-F. Language or dialect contact is a language-external cause.

7.10 Summary of points

- Word order in the main clause often differs from that of the subclause in Old English. One way of explaining this asymmetry is to view the subclause as preserving an older order, and the main clause as having innovated; main clause innovations can be explained by the heavier functional load of main clauses, particularly if the innovations affect the beginning of the clause, as in Old English.
- The main clause/subclause asymmetry is due to movement of the finite verb in the main clause. There are two types of finite verb-movement in Old English, one of the verb to C, and one of the verb to a lower position, here called F. The difference between the two types comes to the fore if the subject is a pronoun.
- In this chapter, the label Verb-Second refers to these two types, even though the verb may surface in third position with V-to-F.
- The first type has survived into PDE as 'subject-auxiliary inversion' (I-to-C movement), in roughly the same environments: questions, negation, and focus-markers like *only*.
- A small set of adverbs also trigger movement to C in Old English, most notably *þa* 'then'.
- The second type was not as consistent as the first type, and has not survived; this is the type of Verb-Second that declines in the fifteenth century.
- Some of the functionality of this second type, i.e. positioning new subjects late in the clause, was shared by another construction that was also available in Old English, the 'late subject' construction.

This construction survives up to the present day as 'subject-verb inversion'.

- The decline of Verb-Second is difficult to chart because of the difficulty of teasing out 'late subject' constructions from V-to-F movement, and because of the fact that V-to-F appears to have acquired a number of stylistic functions after it was no longer an option in 'regular' syntax.

Exercises

1. PUZZLING OVER DATA. Consider the following data. What are the options for the analysis of the position of the verbs in each example, and why? Some points to bear in mind:

   - The difference between V-to-C and V-to-F in Old English.
   - The date: Verb-Second (as V-to-F) declines rapidly as canonical syntax in the fifteenth century but survives (or is resurrected) as a marked stylistic construction.
   - The behaviour of pronominal subjects.
   - The behaviour of adverbs with meanings like 'then, thus, so, now'.
   - The loss of V-to-I in the sixteenth century (as manifested by the rise of *do*-support).
   - The overlap between V-to-F and 'late subject' constructions and the ability of both to facilitate new, lengthy or informative subjects in a late position in the clause.
   - The fact that V-to-F targets the finite verb only and not the entire verbal string.
   - The nature of first constituent adverbials: links to the previous discourse or frame-setters?

The relevant finite verbs are given in bold.

   (a) By þus suche tormentes þou **schalt** somtyme se me wyth sayntes in blis. (*OED*, c.1430 Life St. Kath. 45)
   (b) In ech of hem he **fint** somwhat That pleseth him, in this or that. (*OED* 1390 J. Gower Confessio Amantis II. 210)
   (c) Bot yhon tre **cum** þou nawight to, Þat standes in midward.
       But yon tree come you not   to that stands in middle
       (of) paradis
       Paradise
       (*OED*, a1300 Cursor Mundi 654)
   (d) However, in your case, Robert, a confession would not do. The money, if you will allow me to say so, is ... awkward. Besides,

if you did make a clean breast of the whole affair, you would never be able to talk morality again. And in England a man who can't talk morality twice a week to a large, popular, immoral audience **is** quite over as a serious politician. There would be nothing left for him as a profession except Botany or the Church. (Oscar Wilde, *An Ideal Husband*, 1895, 46.187–191)

(e) It is Goddis will, it sall be myne,
Agaynste his saande[1] **sall** I neuer schone,[2]
To Goddis cummaundement I **sall** enclyne,
That in me fawte non be foune.
(York Mystery Plays x. 245, *c*.1410; Smith 1885)

(f) He fawte[3] ageyn Anlaf, kyng of Erlond, and ageyn Constantyn, kyng of Scottis, at Banborow, where, þorow[4] þe prayeres of Seynt Ode, a swerd fel fro heuene into his schaberk. He maried on[5] of his douteris onto þe Emperour Octo, and þat same emperour sent him þe swerd whech Constantine fawt with – in þe handelyng[6] þerof **was** closed on of þoo[7] iiii nayles þat were in Cristis handis and feet. He sent him eke þe spere of Constantyn- þe hed þerof was in Cristis side – and mech more oþir þing. [*c*.1460; CMCAPCHR 92.1824–7]

(g) and þese men preise God nyte & day in holy songis & ympnis[8] whech þei continuely be vsed too. And þis Iudas eke[9] may be referred on-to þoo heremites þat Seynt Augustin mad ny iij ȝere be-for þat he was bischop at Ypone, and mad þere cha-nones. This mater is proued with grete euydens in þe book whech I mad to a gentil woman in Englisch, and in þe book whech I mad to þe abbot of Seynt Iames at Norhampton in Latin, whech boke I named Concordia, be-cause it is mad to reforme charite be-twix Seynt Augustines heremites and his chanones. In þese same bokes **may** men se þe names of þe first faderes of þis order of heremites, whech heremites Simplician sent witȝ Augustin on-to Affrik. [CMCAPSER 145.20–146.24 (*c*.1452)]

---

[1] order
[2] shrink with dread
[3] fought
[4] through
[5] one
[6] hilt
[7] those
[8] hymns
[9] also

(h)   And at that Parlyment the Erle Marchalle was made Duke of
       Northefolke; and in that Parlyment **was** moche altercacyon
       by-twyne þe lordys and the comyns for tonage and poundage.
       And at that Parlyment **was** grauntyd that alle maner of alyen-
       tys shulde be put to hoste as Englysche men benne in othyr
       londys, and ovyr that condyscyon **was** the tonage grauntyd;
       the whyche condyscyon was brokyn in the same yere by the
       Byschoppe of Wynchester, as the moste pepylle sayde, he
       beyng Chaunseler the same tyme, and there-fore there was
       moche hevynesse and trowbylle in thys londe. [CMGREGOR
       157.691–695]

(i)   . . . and three pavylyons **stood** thereon, of sylke and sendell of
       dyverse hew. And withoute the pavylyons **hynge** three whyght
       shyldys on trouncheouns of sperys, and grete longe sperys
       stood upryght by the pavylyons, and at every pavylyon dore
       stoode three freysh knyghtes. [CMMALORY 198.3091–3095]

(j)   Lilium speciosum, which also forms an important part of
       the trade in Lily bulbs with Japan, was introduced from that
       country in 1833; but since that year the Japanese growers
       of Lilies have sent us varieties of this species which are so
       superior in the size, form, and colouring of their flowers as to
       surpass those of the typical white and coloured forms and to
       render them of quite secondary importance.
       Of much interest **is** Iris Kaempferi, which was introduced to
       this country from Japan in 1857, and attracted much attention
       when the large handsome and richly coloured flowers were
       first presented to public notice at the exhibitions, and began to
       make their appearance here and there in private gardens. For a
       time they failed to make the headway that was anticipated . . .
       [1913: weathers-1,15.328–332]

(k)   The investigation is appended to this paper. The composite
       forms, Figs. 4 and 5, represent the actual bell Fig. 3 as nearly
       as may be. At the top is a circular disk, and to this **is** attached
       a cylindrical segment. The expanding part of the bell is repre-
       sented by one Fig. 4, or with better approximation by two Fig.
       5, segments of cones. [1890, strutt, 3,329.231–235]

(l)   Up, and several people to speak with me. Then **comes** Mr.
       Caesar, and then Goodgroome, and what with one and the
       other. Nothing but Musique with me this morning, to my great
       content. (*The Diary of Samuel Pepys*, entry for 17 December
       1666, <http://www.pepysdiary.com/diary/1666/12/17>)

(m)   These wordes he **sayde** vnto them and abode still in Galile.

But as sone as his brethren were goone vp, then **went** he also vp vnto the feast: not openly but as it were prevely. Then **sought** him the Iewes at the feast, and sayde: Where is he? And moche murmurynge **was** ther of him amonge the people. [CENTEST1 (Tyndale's *New Testament*) John 7:10–12 1526–1536)]

Further reading

The seminal work on Verb-Second in Old English is van Kemenade (1987). Pintzuk (1999) demonstrates that Verb Second is not as clearly asymmetrical in Old English as it is in the modern West Germanic languages: subclauses have 'early verbs' too. The debate in this period focuses on the question of whether Old English sides with Yiddish and the Scandinavian languages in having symmetrical Verb-Second, i.e. verb-movement in both main and subclause. In theoretical terms, this debate translated as IP-V2 systems (Yiddish and Scandinavian) versus CP-V2 systems (Dutch and German). In the latter, V moves to C in all main clauses, while IP-V2 systems lack CP and V moves to I. The corollary of this analysis is that Spec,IP in IP-V2 systems must be argued to be multifunctional in order to host material other than just subjects. IP-V2 systems would be expected to have similar constituents in first position in both main and subclause, which is not the case in Old English (van Kemenade 1997). Although there are 'early verbs' in subclauses, and verb-movement in main clauses often fails (Haeberli 2002), Old English main and subclauses still show an asymmetry, with the majority of subclauses having finite verbs in a late position in the clause, while the majority of Old English main clauses have finite verbs in C or F. A consensus appears to have been reached that Old English does not fit the mould of either Yiddish and Scandinavian or Dutch and German, and that it has two landing sites for verb-movement rather than one. A hypothesis of what may have been the original motivation for these landing sites is set out in Los (2012). Another account is Kiparsky (1995), who links it to the emerging subordination system (hypotaxis), a subject to which we turn in Chapter 8. For information structure, see Birner and Ward (1998), Lambrecht (1994) and Krifka (2007). The difficult task of teasing apart the decline of Verb-Second in Middle English is undertaken by Warner (2007) and van Kemenade and Westergaard (2012). A detailed account of the earlier literature on the decline is set out in Eitler (2006). My use of the neutral terms 'early verbs' and 'late subjects' are due to Schlachter (2012) and Warner (2007) respectively.

8 Syntax and discourse

8.1 Introduction

We have seen examples in the previous chapters that speakers can assign functions to certain constructions that give out signals to the hearer. In section 1.4.2, clause-initial place adverbials were seen to have a contrastive effect in PDE, as if the frame-setter *In York* in *In York Paulinus was welcomed with open arms* evoked alternatives – in this case, places where Paulinus was not welcomed with open arms. These pragmatic effects are utilised in conversation by speakers as a sign to the hearer that they want to 'hold the floor'. Consider (1), from Krifka (2007):

(1) A: What do your siblings do?
     B: [My [SISter]$_{Focus}$]$_{Topic}$ [studies MEDicine]$_{Focus}$,
        and [my [BROther]$_{Focus}$]$_{Topic}$ is [working on a FREIGHT ship]$_{Focus}$
        (Krifka 2007: 44)

In the first clause of B's response in (1), *sister* is inferred by the earlier mention of *siblings* and hence 'given' rather than new information; *studies medicine* is the new information of the sentence, in the expected 'end-focus' position. But *sister* also has a type of focus, an intonational focus which indicates an alternative to the topic 'my sister', namely 'my brother', and this prosodic marking is used by the speaker as a signal to the hearer that the answer is not finished with the first topic (the sister) but will also include information on another topic (the brother) (ibid.). Note that we have gone beyond the level of the clause here – this is discourse rather than syntax or information structure.

   To give some examples of the kind of functions that need to be marked in discourse, let us review the functions that have cropped up sporadically in this book so far. We saw in section 1.4.3 that Left-Dislocation can be used in spoken discourse to introduce a new topic. We saw in section 7.8 that the declining rates of V-to-F movement had led to a reinterpretation of Verb-Second as an optional, rather than a

215

canonical order, and this paved the way to assign it various functions: a fifteenth-century text appeared to use it to mark the beginning of a new section; a sisteenth-century text appeared to use it to mark a wrapping up, a conclusion; and a nineteenth-century text appeared to use it to mark the elevated style that was deemed appropriate for Bible translations.

This chapter will look at the sort of discourse functions speakers may want to mark, particularly in narratives, and how the expression of these functions may have an impact on syntax. A key function needed in narratives is **grounding**, i.e. signalling which events are foregrounded, part of the main storyline, and which are backgrounded, events that explain why or when the foregrounded events happen.

8.2   Grounding, assertion and subordination

We saw in Chapter 1, in revision (4) of the simple text in (3) about Christian the lion, that a system of hierarchically-ordered main and subclauses can make even a very short story much easier to take in. The problem is that events on the main storyline are rarely self-contained and self-explanatory; a bald statement as in (2) raises questions in the mind of the audience about the circumstances of the event:

(2)   Anthony and John bought a lion cub in Harrods.

Such circumstances usually involve another event; as events require verbs, the result will be another clause. The result is two clauses that are intimately connected, with one the main event, and the other the embedded event.

(3)   When Anthony and John lived in London in the swinging sixties, they bought a lion cub in Harrods and named him Christian.

This brings us to the topic of syntactic signalling of grounding by subordination.

Languages have various ways to signal to the hearer which is the main event and which is the embedded event. Semantically, embedding refers to the fact that it is possible to identify a main event and an embedded event; the complex sentence in (3) is about the buying event, not about the living event. Semantic embedding can be signalled linguistically, and, in time, such linguistic signals can become part of a system of syntactic subordination, in which the embedded event is not only semantically but also syntactically embedded in a subclause. In such a system, a clause marked as subclause will be less autonomous, less independent, and not able to occur on its own; it will be more integrated into the main clause, expressing a semantic role that belongs to the higher verb. Its syntactically dependent status can also be signalled by incompleteness: there will be a gap in the structure, as in the case of relative clauses or indirect questions, and subclauses generally show less marking of participant roles. The *to*-infinitival clause in (4) below does not have its own expression of the AGENT of the verb *release*; instead, we infer that this AGENT can be identified as a participant of the higher verb *travel*. The same goes for the 'dependent desires', clauses that are the complement of verbs with meanings of fear, promise, order, hope, expect, or insist upon that we discussed in section 5.4.8; they are generally expressed by *to*-infinitive clauses in PDE, and similarly depend on the higher clause for the identification of the AGENT. These dependent desires are generally expressed by a finite clause, with a subjunctive verb, in Old English; as finite clauses require subjects, the AGENT will be expressed in such clauses, but it will always be a pronoun that refers back to the subject or object of the higher clause, so it is just as much dependent on the higher clause as the unexpressed AGENTS of *to*-infinitives.

In PDE, subclauses are signalled by an introductory element, like *When* in (3), by non-finiteness, as in the purpose clause *to release Christian into the wild* in (4), or by finite verb movement, as in the conditional clause *should you want to see it* in (5):

(4)   Anthony and John travelled to Kenya to release Christian into the wild.

(5)   The footage of their reunion is available on the internet, should you want to see it.

These three ways – 'bespoke' element, marking on the verb, and word order – are frequent strategies to signal syntactic subordination in languages. These three means correspond to the three expressions of functional heads we saw in sections 2.7, 4.8 and 7.3. The relevant functional head for information about clausal status is C, but the next head down, I, can also be roped in to signal subordination as it is associated with finiteness. We have seen that Spec,CP is an important position in main clauses, marking interrogatives (sections 1.4.4 and 4.3.4), and this position, too, is relevant to the development of subordination in English.

It needs to be stressed that the cognitive concepts of main and embedded events can also be expressed by means that do not require syntactic subordination. In Old English, there is a system of linking clauses that do not show syntactic signs of embedding – it is **paratactic** rather than **hypotactic** – but make connections to the main event by a correlative element – a demonstrative or an adverb that occurs in both the main event clause and the embedded event clause. This paratactic correlative system disappeared in Early Middle English. We will discuss it at length, as it provides a number of clues how the subordination markers in PDE came about.

If the conceptual asymmetry between the main event and the embedded event is not marked in the syntax of a language, they can still be identified in many cases by their semantics. In narratives, main events belongs to the main storyline, and we can use the concepts of **foregrounding** and **backgrounding**. We will see that there is overlap, but not a perfect match between syntactic main clauses and foregrounded events. One of the reasons why the alignment is not a perfect fit is the fact that there is a semantic category that out-ranks foregrounding, and that is assertion. Consider (6):

(6)   The spirit of the times was such that no one batted an eyelid when two young men bought a lion cub in Harrods in the swinging sixties.

Example (6) embeds an event on the main storyline into a comment. What is asserted in (6) is that buying or selling a lion cub from a department store was not a strange thing to do in the 1960s. We can test this by adding a tag-question:

(7)   The spirit of the times was such that no one batted an eyelid when two young men bought a lion cub in Harrods in the swinging sixties, wasn't it?

The tag-question questions the assertion rather than the purchasing-event itself. Note that the assertion in (7) provides circumstantial information and can be taken as an explanation of some sort. As such, it is backgrounded information in terms of the story – but the information is coded by a main clause. The use of such assertions in narratives often lead to events on the main storyline being expressed by subordinate clauses; an example is main clauses like *It befell that* 'it happened that' in Middle English, which are used to mark a new episode (Brinton 1996).

If we take the concept of assertion as a semantic criterion for main events, some degree of misalignment between semantic and syntactic subordination can also be demonstrated for PDE. A PDE reason-clause can be questioned by a tag-question, as in (8), from Chafe (1994: 439), quoted in Cristofaro (2003: 35):

(8)   a. I decided to buy it, because it has such a big memory.
      b. I decided to buy it, because it has such a big memory, hasn't it?

Reason-clauses are syntactically subordinate, but their strong sense of assertion makes them good candidates for encoding main events, occasionally leading to main-clause behaviour.

A similar competition of foregrounding and assertion leading to a misalignment is seen in PDE clefts. Examples (9a–c) show a lexical item that usually plays a key role in structuring narrative texts, *then*, in a range of syntactic constructions.

(9)   a.   We got together about 18 months ago, before the Earth Summit in Rio. **Then** we realised we were terrifically compatible/We **then** realised we were terrifically compatible.

      b.   We got together about 18 months ago, before the Earth Summit in Rio. **That was when** we realised we were terrifically compatible.

      c.   We got together about 18 months ago, before the Earth Summit in Rio. **It was then** that we realised we were terrifically compatible. (BNC, K32:1051)

The first thing to note is that these sentences have the same **truth conditions**. This means that the same state of affairs in the sociophysical world has to be the case for these clauses to be true. This state of affairs is that the couple realised that they were compatible at that particular moment. This means that the constructions in (9b) and (9c) add something to the meaning of these clauses that goes beyond the lexical meaning of the individual words. What they add at the level of the clause is the special information structure of clefts: indications to the hearer/reader about which parts of the sentence are assumed to be known to them and which parts carry the new point.

What makes (9a) awkward is that *then* in first position apparently makes what follows into a separate event (cf. Prince 1978: 902); it fails to make a specific connection with the time of the earlier clause in PDE (unlike its Old English counterpart *þa*, as we will see below). The **reversed pseudo-cleft** in (9b) is better able to create a link with a specific time established in the previous discourse by pulled apart the linking component (*that*) and the time-component (*when*) of *then*.

A **stressed-focus *it*-cleft** as in (9c) also does the job, but it also has a foregrounding effect of the content of the following *that*-clause, triggering the expectation that the events described in this clause are key events, possibly the 'central reportable event' that is the *raison d'être* of every narrative, the reason the story is worth telling in the first place (Labov 1972). Its function in (9c) appears to be an announcement of where this story is going, and what the climax is going to be. The speaker is stepping back from the narrative to provide a **meta-comment**, conveying the message 'What I am telling you now you should consider the "point" of the story, and the reason why I am telling it at all' (Stein 1990: 36).[1] We have a combination here of assertion in the main clause and foregrounding in the subclause.

A final example of assertion taking precedence over foregrounding is relative clauses. Relative clauses, too, can express foregrounded events, in spite of being syntactically subordinate (relative clause in bold):

(10) . . . and the Sky was ting'd with a very unusual yellowish Colour, which perhaps might be reflected from a great Quantity of Snow, **that soon after fell for near a quarter of an Hour** . . . (1721 Lang_s3b; Denison and Hundt 2013: 141)

This chapter will zoom out from the clause to the discourse and look at what individual clauses are trying to achieve in discourse, and how these functions mesh with the available means to mark them syntactically as main or subordinate. We will then consider how clauses are connected, and how such connections may change over time.

8.3 Foregrounding and peak marking

As foregrounding is such a major vector in distinguishing main from embedded events, we will devote the next sections to a detailed discussion of how main events are marked in the *Cynewulf and Cyneheard* episode introduced in Chapter 6.

The text contains, as expected in a narrative, a number of different clause-types. Apart from complement clauses introduced by *þæt* 'that', adverbial clauses introduced by *oþ þæt* 'until' or *gif* 'if', and relative clauses introduced by a demonstrative or by the particle *þe* (see the various tables in Chapter 6), the text contains clauses that do not start with such complementisers but with *and* 'and' or *ac* 'and, but', clauses that are not marked by complementisers and hence candidates for main clause status. A third main clause candidate is clauses starting with *þa* 'then'. There are also two other clauses starting with time adverbials: *her* 'here, i.e. in this year' and *ymb xxxi wintra* 'around 31 winters'. The distribution of these clause types over the narrative is uneven; *þa*-clauses in particular cluster in the middle of the text and are absent from the beginning and the end. Such clustering phenomena usually point to a discourse function. The *and*-clauses are almost all verb-final, while the *þa*-clauses are almost all verb-second. The two clause-types are distributed over the various narrative units as follows (Table 8.1).

Note that there are no *þa*-V clauses in unit (i), the scene-setting, and unit (xi), the aftermath. This fits with the notion that *þa*-V clauses are a

Table 8.1 Narrative units and clause-types in *Cynewulf and Cyneheard*

Unit	Function	Content	Clause types
i	Scene setting	Explanation why Cynewulf and Cyneheard are enemies	*her*-clause; *ymb*-clause; verb-final-*and*; V2-*and*
ii	Cyneheard arrives in Merton	Cynewulf is in Merton with only a small bodyguard; Cyneheard seizes this opportunity, rides over and surrounds the bower	*and þa*-V-; verb-final-*and*
iii	First fight	Cynewulf starts to defend himself from the strategic position of the doorway of the bower, but when he identifies Cyneheard among his attackers, he loses his head and rushes out towards him, which causes him to be killed	*and þa*-V-; verb-final-*and*; verb-final *and þa*-; *and þa*-V-; verb-final-*and*
iv	Cyneheard's first offer	Cynewulf's small bodyguard is alerted to what is going on by Cynewulf's mistress and they run to the scene; Cyneheard tries to persuade them not to intervene by bribes and promises	*and þa*-V-; verb-final *and*
v	Second fight	They refuse and fight, but are outnumbered and killed, apart from a single man, a British hostage	verb-final-*and*, verb-final-*ac*
vi	Cynewulf's other retainers arive in Merton	Cynewulf's other retainers hear about the catastrophe the following morning; they arrive on the scene to find their king dead	*and þa*-V-; *þa*-V-; verb-final-*and*
vii	Cyneheard's second offer	Cyneheard tries to persuade them to accept him as their new king, saying that some of their kinsmen have already accepted him as their lord and are part of his entourage	*and þa*-V-; verb-final-*and*
viii	Cynewulf's retainers' refusal: CENTRAL REPORTABLE EVENT	Cynewulf's retainers refuse to accept him, saying that their lord was dearer to them than any kin, and they will never follow their lord's killer	*and þa*-V-; verb-final-*and*

Table 8.1 (continued)

Unit	Function	Content	Clause types
ix	Cynewulf's retainers' offer CENTRAL REPORTABLE EVENT	Cynewulf's retainers, in turn, offer their kinsmen who are in Cyneheard's entourage free passage	*and þa-*V-; *and*
x	Cyneheard's retainers' refusal CENTRAL REPORTABLE EVENT	these kinsmen also refuse to leave their lord, Cyneheard	*þa-*V-; midway switch to direct speech
xi	Aftermath	They fight, Cyneheard is killed, and so are the two groups of retainers, apart from a single young lad	S-*þa-*verb-final; verb-final-*and*; V2-*and*-

device for foregrounding events. The *þa*-V clauses are not distributed randomly in the discourse, but cluster together in the narrative units that discuss key events rather than background or scene-setting. The verb-final *and*-clauses all express events on the same chronological line as those expressed by the *þa*-V clauses, i.e. they are also foregrounded, and like *þa*-V clauses, they are primarily found in the body of the narrative; in contrast, the *and*-clauses with the verb in second position are found in the scene-settting part and in the conclusion.

We now come to a common methodological problem in investigating discourse functions in historical texts. The units in Table 8.1 are headed by *þa*-V clauses. If I wanted to strengthen the case for *þa*-V as specifically marking the start of a narrative unit, I could have adjusted my division into units accordingly, dividing up units (iii) and (vi) in more segments, which would have given me a perfect fit. The risk of such circular reasoning looms large in historical investigations. What we need to make a convincing case is some meaningful clustering of other features that give a more objective measure of the presence of a particular discourse function at that particular period.

To give an idea of what these features could be, here are some examples from the literature. Lenker (2000) supports her hypothesis that Old English items like *witodlice* and *soþlice*, 'truly, really, certainly, verily', mark **episode boundaries** by pointing to the fact that they significantly often head paragraphs and co-occur with visual cues in the manuscripts like illuminated initials. To avoid the circularity of identifying peaks in Old English saints' lives by the occurrence of the linguistic devices whose status as peak markers is precisely the issue that needs to be established, Wårvik (2013: 173) determines before she starts her investigation that she will define 'peaks' as the typical turning-points in such texts, like 'the miracles, conversions, victories or defeats, martyrdoms and other such crucial deaths of main characters' – these are the typical 'central reportable events' of saints' lives. Brinton (1996) backs up her hypothesis of the discourse function of Middle English *gan* 'begin, go' as a device for marking salient turns of event in the narrative by pointing out that a list of the actions expressed with *gan* in Chaucer's *Troilus and Criseyde* reads like a plot synopsis.

The ten *þa*-V clauses in *Cynewulf and Cyneheard* were tabulated in Table 7.2 in section 7.5 of the previous chapter, and if it is possible to read them as a plot synopsis, that would constitute more solid evidence that *and þa*-V clauses and V-final *and*-clauses have distinct functions, even though they both express foregrounded events. I leave the reader to judge whether Table 7.2 reads as a synopsis of the *Cynewulf and Cyneheard* episode. The difference between the *and*-events and the *þa*-V events appears to be not so much foregrounding versus backgrounding as key-events versus sub-events – if the *þa*-V clauses read as a plot synopsis, *þa*-V events and *and*-events need to be taken together to show the full plot. In modern terms, we might expect *þa*-V to signal the start of a paragraph, and *and*-events to signal cohesion within that paragraph.

The *and þa*-V clauses cluster particularly thickly in units (xiii)–(x), the part of the story that contains the 'central reportable event', i.e. that the bond between a lord and his retainers is, or should be, even stronger than the bonds of kin. This is the **peak** of the narrative (Longacre 1983: 24), the climax, and the reason the story is worth telling in the first place. We find more *and þa*-V clauses here because we have a number of key events in quick succession. They represent foregrounded rounds of bargaining, mostly expressed in MAIN CLAUSE – COMPLEMENT SUBCLAUSE pairs:

(11) a. And then offered he₅ them₉ their own choice of-money and land . . .
 b. and them₉ told that their₉ kinsmen₈ with him₅ were
 c. and then said they₉ that to-them₉ no kinsman dearer was than their lord₁
 d. and they₉ never his killer₅ follow would,
 e. and then offered they₉ their kinsmen₈ that they₈ unharmed from that place departed;
 f. and they₈ said that the same to-their₉ companions₆ offered was,

g. then said they$_8$ that they$_8$ that not considered any more than your$_9$ companions$_6$

The remaining subclauses are background information: a conditional clause (12a) and a set of *þe*-relative clauses (12b–d) that serve to pinpoint the identity of the various bands (i.e. they are **restrictive** relative clauses) rather than take the narrative further:

(12) a. if they$_9$ him$_5$ the kingdom granted,
       b. those that did not want to part from him;
       c. who earlier with the king$_1$ were;
       d. who with the king$_1$ killed were.

That (12b–d) are *þe*-relatives rather than *se*-relatives is unlikely to be a random choice. *Þe* is a 'universal embedder' that even in Old English appears to be a clear sign of a following subordinate clause (see section 7.7.2.1, and, below, section 8.5). The four subclauses in (12), then, are subordinate both from a syntactic and a discourse point of view. We will return to hypotaxis and parataxis below. But first we will consider another way in which clause status aligns with discourse functions, in the run-up to the peak.

8.4 Creating suspense

8.4.1 The durative main clause+ oþ-clause pair

Another clause-type that is suspiciously thick on the ground in *Cynewulf and Cyneheard* is clauses starting with *oþ* ' until' or *oþ þæt, oþþe* 'until that'. Table 8.2 shows these clauses in transliteration.

The clauses in Table 8.2 all have the structure MAIN CLAUSE – *Oþ*-CLAUSE, with the main clause presenting an open-ended durative event (having possession of something, living somewhere, defending oneself, hacking away, fighting, fighting), and the *oþ*-clause presenting either a punctual event (killing, stabbing to death, catching sight of someone, killing, breaking through defences) or, at the very least, an event that is telic (*Until they all lay dead* has an end point which will be reached when the last person is killed). The durative nature of the main clause is further emphasised by a verbal periphrasis of BE+present participle to describe the fighting: *wærun feohtende/feohtende wæran/feohtende wæron*. This is the construction that developed into a full-blown progressive in Late Middle English (see Chapter 3). These durative clauses help to build narrative tension that culminates into an event on the main storyline; this narrative device persists into Late Old English (see

Table 8.2 *oþ/oþ þæt*-clauses in *Cynewulf and Cyneheard* in transliteration

Unit	Function	*oþ*-clauses in transliteration
i	Scene setting	and he$_2$ had that **until** he$_2$ killed the alderman$_3$ that with-him$_2$ longest remained;
		and he$_2$ there stayed **until** that him$_2$ a swineherd$_4$ stabbed-to-death at Prefet's Flood
ii	Cyneheard arrives in Merton	
iii	First fight	and then admirably himself$_1$ defended, **until** he$_1$ on the prince$_5$ looked
		And they$_{5+8}$ all on the king$_1$ were hacking-away **until** that they$_{5+8}$ him$_1$ killed had
iv	Cyneheard's first offer	
v	Second fight	And they$_6$ still fighting were **until** they$_6$ all lay [dead] except one Welsh hostage
vi	Cynewulf's other retainers arive in Merton	
vii	Cyneheard's second offer	
viii	Cynewulf's retainers' refusal: CENTRAL REPORTABLE EVENT	
ix	Cynewulf's retainers' offer CENTRAL REPORTABLE EVENT	
x	Cyneheard's retainers' refusal CENTRAL REPORTABLE EVENT	
xi	Aftermath	They$_9$ then around the gates fighting were **until** they$_9$ there in broke, and the prince$_5$ killed

e.g. Wårvik 2013). This means that the *oþ*-clauses are likely to encode foregrounded events, in spite of being syntactically subordinate. This is another example of misalignment between semantically and syntactically subordinate clauses.

The distribution of *oþ*-clauses over the narrative units is just as skewed as that of the *þa*-V clauses we discussed in the previous section, almost to such an extent that they represent a negative image of the *þa*-V clauses. The *oþ*-clauses are completely absent from the peak in units (viii)–(x), a reminder that the narrative peaks are sometimes marked more by what is absent than what is present (ibid.: 170). The clauses in Table 8.2 create the suspense leading up to the peak, but once we've reached the peak the pace quickens, leaving no space for open-ended durative situations as represented by the main clause preceding the *oþ*-clause. These durative situations slow the pace down, which is the opposite of what is required at the peak.

We saw in Chapter 3 that there were a number of ways in which imperfective aspect and ongoing-ness could be expressed before the rise of a grammaticalised progressive, and all of these potentially can be drafted in to increase suspense. In the following two sections we will concentrate on linguistic expressions for duration and imperfective aspect already briefly touched on in Chapters 3 and 5: the use of a construction with a verb of motion, commonly *cuman* 'come'+infinitive, and the AcI with perception verbs, in combination with a Verb-First construction, to create suspense in *Beowulf*; and the use of the verbs *onginnan* and *beginnan*, both meaning 'begin', also in combination with a Verb-First construction, in the work of Ælfric.

8.4.2 Durative motion verbs, AcIs and Verb-First in Beowulf

In *Beowulf*, too, we find imperfective constructions that slow the narrative down as a build-up to key events. Consider this passage describing the monster Grendel's first approach to the hall. The finite verb is in first position, a dramatic device that often marks the start of a narrative unit in *Beowulf*, much like the function of *þa*-V in *Cynewulf and Cyneheard*. Suspense is created by the use of the motion verb *gewitan* 'depart'+infinitive and an AcI (see section 5.1) with *findan* 'find'. Relevant verbs are given in bold:

(13) **Gewat**   ða   **neosian**, syþðan niht   becom,
     departed then visit   after   night came

     hean huses,   hu   hit   Hringdene
     high houses   how it   Ring-Danes

     æfter beorþege   gebun   hæfdon.
     after beertaking settled had

     Fand þa   ðær   inne æþelinga gedriht
     found then there in   of--nobles band

     swefan   æfter symble;   sorge   ne   cuðon,
     sleep-INF after feast   sorrow not knew3PL

     wonsceaft wera. <Beo 115–17>
     misery   of-men

'Then after night came, [Grendel] went inspecting the tall house – how the Ring-Danes had settled in after the beer-drinking. Then he found therein a band of nobles sleeping after the feast; they had no thought of sorrow, of the misery in store for men.'

Richardson (1994: 317), discussing this passage, comments: 'We do not suppose that Grendel saw the men sleep in the hall, but rather that he perceived them in what our military leaders might call an ongoing dormative situation.' The durative situation of their sleeping is interrupted by the drama of Grendel's attack. The attack itself is described with past tense verbs (in bold) in verb-final *and*-clauses, again marking foregrounded actions, as in the *Cynewulf and Cyneheard* episode:

(14)   Wiht   unhælo,
                creature   evil

grim ond grædig, gearo sona   **wæs**,
grim and fierce   ready at-once was

reoc ond reþe, ond on ræste **genam**
savage and cruel and in rest   took

þritig þegna.   <Beo 117–19>
thirty thanes

'The creature of evil, grim and fierce, was quickly ready, savage and cruel, and seized thirty thanes from their rest.'

Foregrounded events usually have completed, perfective aspect, which explains these simple past tenses. Grendel then leaves the scene, and the pace of the narrative slows down again (as we also saw in the aftermath of *Cynewulf and Cyneheard*), again by using *gewat*+infinitive, but this time without Verb-First:

(15)   Þanon eft   **gewat**
          thence again departed

huðe hremig to ham **faran**,
booty proud to home go-INF

mid þære   wælfylle   wica   **neosan**. <Beo 119–21>
with the   slaughter-fill dwelling visit-INF

'From there he went travelling back to his home, proud of his plunder, seeking his dwelling with that fill of slaughter.'

Combinations of Verb-First and ongoingness-expressions to create suspense can be found throughout the poem.

As with finite verb movement in conditional clauses (*If he had managed* versus *Had he managed*, see section 7.3), Verb-First in Germanic is analysed as V-to-C, i.e. another head is moved to the C-head to express that head, in order to mark a certain clause-type. This clause-type is clearly defined in PDE as a conditional subclause, but it has been more difficult to pinpoint the function of Verb-First when it occurs in a main clause. Verb-First in the Germanic languages has been described as indicating 'lively narrative' (see for example Kiparsky 1995: 163; Thráinsson 1985: 177), foregrounding and 'vividness of action' (Stockwell 1977. 291). Mitchell notes that it can denote a turning-point in the narrative, a transition, or a change of pace, 'just as a new paragraph does in MnE prose' (Mitchell 1985: §3933). The many faces of Verb-First can be explained by the fact that linguistic devices that build up tension in a narrative may 'devaluate' through overuse, at which point the speaker will draft in other expressions to do the same job. This is why discourse marking tends to be ephemeral and short lived, and explains why Verb-First in *Beowulf* appears to have a similar function to *þa*-V in the *Cynewulf and Cyneheard* episode.

8.4.3 Durative onginnan/beginnan 'begin' and Verb-First in Ælfric

Ælfric, writing towards the end of the Old English period, also uses Verb-First to create suspense before a peak. We will discuss one of the devices he uses to create duration: the verbs *onginnan* and *beginnan* 'begin'. Consider (16), describing an event in the life of St Martin. Martin has been captured by a band of brigands, one of whom is assigned to rob and guard him. As soon as he is left alone with this man, the force of Martin's personality and his faith in God make such an impression on his guard that he becomes a convert to the faith of Christ, and frees his captive. This sudden turn in the plot, in which Martin, outnumbered by his enemies, wounded and bound, manages to completely reverse his hopeless position, is a peak, and we would expect the run-up to the peak to be marked by devices that create suspense. In this particular passage, the device is a combination of the verb *beginnan* 'begin' and a Verb-First construction; there is a further clause-final *ongann* 'began' in the next clause, with a bare infinitive as complement. The peak itself is marked by *hwæt* 'lo' and *sona* 'at once':

(16) **Begann** ða **to secgenne** þam sceaðan geleafan. and mid
     began   then   to say   the ruffian faith   and with

Table 8.3 *onginnan* and *beginnan* in Verb-First and *þa*-V constructions in Ælfric (Los 2000)

Verbs	*þa V* with bare infinitive	*V1* with bare infinitive	*þa V* with *to*-infinitive	*V1* with *to*-infinitive
Onginnan	17	1	3	4
Beginnan	6	1	9	5
Totals	23	2	12	9

boclicere lare   hine læran ongann; **Hwæt** ða   se sceaða
scriptural doctrine him teach began   lo   then the ruffian

sona   gelyfde. on ðone lifigendan god. and tolysde   ða   benda
at-once believed in the living   god and released the bonds
<ÆCHom II, 39.1 290.70–1>

'[he] began then to explain the faith to the ruffian and began to
guide him with scriptural doctrine; Lo, then the ruffian at once
believed in the living god and untied the bonds . . .'

The figures for bare infinitives and *to*-infinitives with *onginnan* and *beginnan* in combination with Verb-First and *þa*-V in Ælfric's writings are skewed (see Table 8.3).

What explains the preference for *to*-infinitives in Verb-First constructions? Aspectualisers with meanings like 'begin' are often roped in as suspense devices because they focus the audience's attention on the beginning of an action, the implication being that that action is going to be interrupted – presumably by a key event, or even a peak. This resembles the time-frame use of the progressive in later periods (see for instance example (44) in section 3.6: *So while this knight was making himself ready to depart, there came into the court the Lady of the Lake*). Ælfric uses *onginnan* or *beginnan*+bare infinitive particularly in *þa*-V clauses, as foregrounded events, as in (17). As foregrounded events usually have completed, perfective aspect, it could well be that the bare infinitive with these aspectualisers has come to imply that the action is completed rather than just begun (note that *ongann* in (17) cannot easily be translated by *begin* in PDE; the same is true for the many instances of the Middle English foregrounder *gan* [Brinton 1996]). With Verb-First a device to create suspense just before a peak, this perfective aspect makes *onginnan* or *beginnan*+bare infinitive unsuitable, as the stage-setting event marked by Verb-First is going to be interrupted by the peak event before it reaches completion:

(17) þa   ongann se apostol hi   ealle læran   ofer twelf monað.
      then began   the apostle them all teach   for twelve months

      ða deopan lare be   drihtnes tocyme. to ðyssere woruld
      the deep   lore about lordGEN coming to this   world
      <ÆCHom II, 18 170.27>

      'Then the apostle taught (*began to teach) them all for twelve
      months the profound doctrine of the Lord's coming to this world'

Ælfric's narratives no longer use *þa*-V for peak marking, only for foregrounding, the simple sequencing of events without any of these events
being singled out for special emphasis.

8.5 Correlative linking

8.5.1 Introduction

The previous sections have shown that clause-types may be used for
various discourse purposes. Clause-type marking involves the left edge
of the clause, and this marking can give rise not only to systematic syntactic marking of subordination, but also to a greater degree of embedding (hypotaxis). This section will discuss a type of clause-linkage in
Old English that is still paratactic rather than hypotactic, and may give
us clues as to how syntactic subordination arises.

  Hypotactic subclauses may fill syntactic functions in a higher clause,
like object (complement clauses and indirect questions) or adverbial
(conditional clauses, or clauses expressing concessions or reasons; or
clauses expressing time, place, manner or purpose of the action of the
main clause). The third type of subclause, relative clauses, postmodify
nouns, or entire sentences (sentential relatives).

  In what follows, we will use the terms 'main event' and 'embedded event' as semantic notions, without committing ourselves to any
pronouncements as to the syntactic status (main or embedded) of the
clause that encodes the embedded event, as this status is precisely what
is at issue here. The correlative element in the main-event-clause will
be marked by a subscript 1, and in the embedded-event-clause by a
subscript 2. In each case, it is the element marked by 2 that marks what
will later become a subordinate clause, i.e. it is the precursor of a complementiser, a conjunction or a relative pronoun.

8.5.2 *Complement clauses*

Unlike PDE, complement clauses in Old English may have an anticipatory pronoun in the clause that expresses the main event, usually a
demonstrative like *þæt* 'that'. This anticipatory element, marked by a
subscript 1 in (18), links to a *þæt* in the clause that expresses the embedded event. In (18), there are two such clauses. The *þæt* that introduces
them has been marked by a subscript 2:

(18) & þa   sona   sændon hi   ærendracan to þam Godes þeowe Equitie & him
     and then at once send   they messengers to the God's man Equitius and him

     þæt₁ bodedon, þæt₂ seo nunne wære   inhæted   mid unmætum feferadlum
     that told   that the nun   was-SUBJ heated-up by   excessive fevers,

     &   þæt₂ heo geornlice bæde   Basilies neosunge þæs muneces.
     and that she eagerly   asked-SUBJ Basileus'coming of-the monk
     <GD 1 (C) 4.29.7>

     'and then they at once sent messengers to God's servant Equitius and told
     him that the nun was burning with excessive fevers, and that she was asking
     eagerly for the coming of the monk Basileus'

Þæt is a neuter accusative form of the demonstrative pronoun *se* (see
Table 2.4 in Chapter 2); the neuter form should probably be considered
a kind of default choice in the absence of a (gendered) noun as antecedent. *Þæt₁* is not a fossilised invariant form in Old English, as the case it
appears with depends on the case assigned by the verb. Many verbs take
accusative objects, but some take genitive objects, in which case *þæt₁*
duly appears in the genitive case, as in (19):

(19) & heo þa sona   þæs₁ gefægnode,   þæt₂ heo hæfde ealles þæs gæres
     and she then at once that-GEN rejoiced   that she had   all-GEN the year-GEN
     bigleofan.
     supply <GD 1 (C) 9.69.12>
     'and she then at once rejoiced over the fact that she had a whole year's
     supplies'

The anticipatory element, then, is clearly a pronoun. These constructions with anticipatory demonstratives are correlatives: two (or more)
clauses are connected by means of a similar element. Such elements
are typically demonstratives, but personal pronouns as in (20) are also
found.

(20) ne sæde ic **hit** ær,   **þæt** he wære   deofol nalles   munuc?

not said I it earlier that he were-SUBJ devil, not-al-all monk
<GD 1 (C) 4.29.16>
'Didn't I say it earlier, that he was a devil, and not at all a monk?'

8.5.3 Adverbial clauses

Adverbial clauses, too, can be introduced by an anticipatory element,
either adverbs that make a referential connection, like *swa* 'so, as', *þa*
'then', *þær* 'there', or the *se*-demonstrative in the instrumental case *þy*, or
adverbial prepositional phrases that contain demonstrative pronouns, as
in the purpose clause of (21):

(21) þa wæs he gelæded to þam Godes were, **to þan₁ þæt₂** he gewilnode & abæde
      then was he led   to the God-GEN man to that that he desired   and asked
      him þa helpe þæs   halgan mannes   þingunga. <GD 1 (C) 10.77.20>
      him the help the-GEN holy-GEN man-GEN intervention-GEN
      'Then he was led to the man of God in order to desire and ask the aid of the
      holy man's intervention for himself'

Such anticipatory PPs often develop into phrasal conjunctions in PDE
(cf. *in order that/in order to*) or even single-word conjunctions (e.g. Old
English *þa hwile þe* which becomes *while* in PDE, or Old English *þy læs*
(*þe*) which has given us *lest*), but in Old English they are found separated
from the *þæt₂*-clause as in (22) and (23). Like the anticipatory elements in
the previous section that can appear in any of the designated positions
for (pronominal) objects, the PPs appear in the various positions that the
syntax makes available for adverbials: Spec,CP as in (22), the preverbal
object position as in (23).

(22) forðon sona   gif he ænigne þearfan   nacodne gemette, þonne wæs he
      because at-once if he any   poor-man naked met,   then was he
      hine sylfne ungyrdende, & mid his hrægle he þone þearfan   gescrydde.
      himself   ungirding   and with his clothes he the poor-man clothed
      To þon₁ he þis dyde, **þæt₂** he him sylfum geearnode mede beforan
      to that   he this did that he him himself earn-SUBJ reward before
      Godes   eagum <GD 1 (C) 9.68.8–13>
      God-GEN eyes-DAT

      'because if he met any naked poor man, he would at once ungird
      himself and clothe the poor man with his clothes. To that end did he
      this, that he himself might earn a reward before God's eyes.'

(23) & þa wæs he ablænded mid þam þystrum þære   ylcan æfæste,
      And then was he blinded   with the darkness of-that same devotion

oþ   þæt he wæs **to þon**₁ getihted &   **on þon**₁ gebroht, **þæt**₂ he wæs
until that he was to that urged   and into that brought that it was

þæs   ælmihtigan Godes   þeowe   onsended to lace,
the-GEN almighty-GEN God-GEN servant-DAT sent   as offering

swylce hit his bletsung wære,   beweledne hlaf &   mid attre gemengedne.
as   hit his adoration was-SUBJ polluted bread and with poison mixed
<GD (C) 8.118.1>

'And then he was blinded with the darkness of that same devotion, until he was
urged and impelled to send it to the servant of the almighty God as an offering,
as if it was a sign of his adoration, that polluted bread, mixed with poison'

This shows that such PPs are independent constituents, just like the
anticipatory demonstratives in the previous section.

Þa 'then'-correlatives as in (24) are by far the most frequent type of
correlative adverbial in Old English, which is not suprising as we have
seen that the *þa₁*-V construction plays an important role in foregrounding, and in some texts peak marking, main events.

(24) **ða₂** he on his wege rad, **þa₁** beseah he on þæt eadigan mæden,
      then he on his way rode, then looked he on that blessed maiden

      þær þe hi sæt wlitig   and fæger onmang hire geferan.
      there that she sat beautiful and fair among her companions

      ða₁ cwæð he to his cnihtum: Ridað hraþe to þære fæmnan and axiað hire,
      then said he to his servants ride quickly to that girl   and ask her

      gif hi seo frig. <LS 14 (MargaretAss) 53–4>
      if she is   free

      'When he was riding on his way, he beheld that blessed maiden where she
      was sitting among her companions, beautiful and fair; then he said to his
      servants: 'Ride quickly to that girl and ask her if she is free.''

The two *þa*-V clauses contain the foregrounded events of the main storyline: *He catches sight of the girl; He has his servants ask her whether she is free.*
The first *þa*-clause provides background information only, in the shape
of a durative time-frame, but, apparently, without creating much in the
way of suspense, although this may well have been one of its functions
earlier. A construction with three *þa*s is also common: *þa₁ þa₂ . . ., þa₁*-V
'then, when . . ., then. . .'. This may have been an attempt to restore the
suspense function. Such doubling seems to have developed into a device
to mark subordination: *swa swa*, lit. 'so so', always denotes the conjunction 'as', not the adverb *swa* 'so'.

8.5.4 Relative clauses

Relative clauses in Old English are either expressed by the demonstratives ('*se*-relatives'), by *þe*, or by a combination of a demonstrative followed by *þe* ('[*se*] *þe*-relatives'). The 'universal embedder' *þe* is a sign of hypotaxis, which makes the syntactic status of these relatives clear. It is the *se*-relatives where things get murky.

The correlative nature of Old English *se*-relatives can be exemplified by the *se*-series in examples like (25):

(25)   **se**₁ awyrgde feond, **se**₂ to þe   wæs sprecende þurh   þinne geferan on wege,
       that accursed devil that to you was speaking   through your companion on way

       se   þe   æne gelæran   ne mihte, ne eac   æt þam æftran siþe ne mihte,
       that that once persuade not could nor also at the   next time not could

       ac æt ðam þriddan cyrre he þe gelærde & oferswiðde to þon þe he wolde.
       but at the third time he you persuaded and overcame to that that he wanted.
       <GD 2 (C) 13.129.27>

       'That accursed devil, it was he that was speaking to you through the mouth
       of your companion on the road, he who could not persuade you the first time,
       nor the second time, but persuaded you the third time and got you to do as he
       wanted.'

The context of (25) is that the protagonist of the story has just arrived at a monastery, an annual occasion which it is his custom to honour by not eating or drinking during the journey. On his arrival, the abbot perceives immediately that he has violated this custom. The protagonist explains that he was tempted by a stranger whom he met on the way. The utterance in (25) is the abbot's way of explaining to the protagonist that the stranger was the devil; *se*₂ has its full demonstrative force of picking out a particular referent – 'that one' – and is probably best translated by a PDE cleft (*it was he*, or possibly *he was it*). The second *se* is accompanied by the 'universal embedder' *þe*, after which the abbot calms down, which is reflected by the fact that he refers to the stranger as *he*.

The form of such *se*-relatives is identical to main clauses that have a pronoun in Spec,CP referring back to a referent in the previous clause, in the standard way of pronominal reference. Consider *se* in (26), from a previous narrative unit of the same story:

(26) witodlice hit gelamp sume dæge þa þa   se broðor   on þone weg ferde
      truly   it happened one day   then when the brother on the way went

to Benedictes mynstre,   þæt oþer wegferend₁ hine sylfne to him geþeodde
to Benedict's monastery that other traveller   him self   to him attached

se₂   bær   mid him mettas to þicgenne in þam wege
that-one carried with him food   to eat   on the way.
<GD (C), 13.127.30–13.128.6>

'Truly, it happened one day, when the brother travelled on the way to
Benedict's monastery, that another traveller attached himself to him, who
had some food with him to eat on the way.'

Personal pronouns can fill the same slot as demonstratives here – we
could have had *he* instead of *se*, although Old English, like Dutch and
German, can use demonstratives to coerce a reading that the pronoun
refers to the newly introduced referent of the previous clause rather
than the topic, the nameless 'brother' who is the protagonist. As in (25),
there is the additional possibility of contrast: the traveller has food to
eat on the way, while the brother does not, and this fact is central to
the story.

Adverbial *se*-relatives can also be found, and have the same problems
of interpretation:

(27)   ðære sawle mihta syndon þas   feower fyrmestan and sælestan; *prudentia*,
       of-the soul powers are   those four   first   and best   *prudentia*

       þæt is snoternysse, **þurh þa**   heo sceal hyre scippend understandan
       that is intelligence through that she shall her   creator   understand

       and hine lufian, and tosceaden god fram yfele. <ÆLS (Christmas) 157>
       and him love, and distinguish good from evil

       'the powers of the soul are those four, first and best: *prudentia*, that
       is intelligence. Through that/through which she [i.e. the soul] shall
       understand her creator, and love him, and distinguish good from evil.'

This example was discussed as example (30) in section 7.7.2.1, because
of the problems of the interpretation of *se*-relatives: are they embed-
ded/hypotactic/subordinate or are they paratactic main clauses? The
order of the constituents conforms to the V-to-F main clauses: *þurh þa*
'through that' in Spec,CP, the pronominal subject *heo* 'she' in Spec,FP
and *sceal* 'shall' in F. The referential status of *þurh þa*, as a constituent
encoding a link to the immediately previous discourse, also fits this
main clause profile.

The semantics are unlikely to help us decide what exactly we
are dealing with here, as non-restrictive relative clauses can express
foregrounded events (as they can in PDE; see (10)) and hence fit the

semantic profile for main clauses. The observation that *se*-relatives tend to be non-restrictive, and hence possible foregrounders, while *þe*-relatives tend to be restrictive (van Kemenade 1987; cf. the *þe*-relatives in *Cynewulf and Cyneheard* in (12b–d)) further emphasise the special status of *se*-relatives.

8.6 From parataxis to hypotaxis

The question whether the correlatives we discussed are syntactically more paratactic or more hypotactic depends on criteria such as how integrated the embedded event clause is with respect to the main clause, the degree of independence, and the form of the correlative element that introduces the embedded event clause.

The presence of anticipatory pronouns has consequences for the syntactic status of the following clause, as the argument structure of the higher verb (*bodedon* 'told' in (18), *gefægnode* 'rejoiced' in (19), *sæde* 'said' in (20)) does not require this clause: its object-slot is already filled by the anticipatory element. In (21) and (22), the *to*-PP and *on*-PP encode the purpose adjunct of the main-event-clause (see section 5.4.4), and in (23) the GOAL-argument of *getihtian* and *gebringan*, verbs of persuading and urging (see the subcategorisation frames of (62) in section 5.4.4). In all these cases, the presence of an anticipatory element does not leave a slot for the embedded-event-clause to fill in the main-event-clause, and its degree of integration into that higher clause is consequently low. The *se*-relatives, as relative clauses, cannot be expected to have a function in the main-event-clause, but postmodify a noun in that clause. The degree of integration depends on whether they are part of the NP or not, which we cannot test. Postmodifying phrases and clauses may freely extrapose (see Chapter 6) so the fact that relative clauses can be separated from the noun head cannot be taken as evidence for them being less integrated.

The next consideration is the degree of independence of the embedded-event-clause. There are Old English complement clauses and purpose clauses that do not appear to have a main-event-clause, but they can usually be construed as dependent on a main clause that has occurred much earlier in the text, or on a main-event-clause that can be inferred from the context (Mitchell 1997). *þæt₂* has no function – subject, object or adverbial – in its own clause, either; semantically, its origins appear to connect with the main-event-clause rather than with the embedded-event-clause, along the lines of (28):

(28) They told him that, i.e. that the girl was ill.> They told him that the girl was ill.

On balance, *þæt*-clauses cannot stand alone. For *se*-relatives, the situation is more problematic as they are formally indistinguishable from main clauses with clause-initial constituents that contain a demonstrative. The fact that they are mostly non-restrictive and can contain foregrounded events makes many of these clauses compatible with main clause readings. There is, however, a structural difference between *se*-relatives and *þe*-relatives in that the latter allow preposition stranding as in (29) (see also section 6.5.3), whereas the former do not:

(29) ðonne ætyweð Drihten ða   rode, þe he on þrowade <HomS 33, 115>
      then   showed Lord   the cross that he on suffered
      'Then the Lord showed the cross on which he suffered'

The *þe*-clause cannot stand on its own, as it has a gap: the NP-complement of the preposition *on* is missing. The fact that this is not possible with *se*-relatives supports the hypothesis that they are more independent, less embedded than *þe*-relatives.

The third consideration is that the correlative element that introduces the embedded event clause is invariant, and hence more likely to be a 'bespoke' C-element. The 'universal embedder' *þe* may be added to *þæt*, in which case we often find the combination *þæt þe* written as a single word, *þætte*.

In terms of modelling, a $þæt_2$-clause at the extreme end of the parataxis/hypotaxis cline in a correlative pair would be a separate CP, in apposition with the preceding CP. It is connected to another clause by means of $þæt_2$ in C, in the same way pronouns generally make connections with other referents in the discourse. Without the anticipatory demonstrative, the second clause can be assigned a slot in the higher clause, and it becomes an embedded, more hypotactic, subclause. The embedded clause in (30b), here shown in the preverbal object slot, will automatically extrapose to a position to the right of V because of its weight (see Chapter 6).

(30)

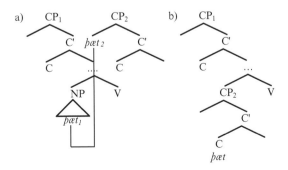

Note that *þæt₂* in (30a) has been positioned in Spec,CP₂ rather than in C. This would be an analysis suitable for a referential pronoun – cf. the discourse-linking adverbials in Spec,CP in section 7.4 – but we would expect such a pronoun to start out somewhere else in clause CP₂, as Spec,CP is a derived position; we saw in (28), however, that there is no such position for *þæt₂* to be found in the CP₂.

For the *þa*-correlatives, we show CP₁ and CP₂ in the commonest order, which is CP₂-first; Mitchell (1984: 276) shows that this is the order of about 95 per cent of the *þa*-correlatives in his sample. The function of CP₂ is that of providing a time-frame for the action in CP₁. After the demise of the correlative system, such time frame clauses have a conjunction *when* that no longer links to a corresponding *then* in CP₁ (see 31b).

(31)

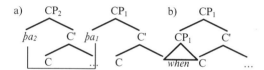

Is *when* a C-element or still in Spec,CP? For PDE, *wh*-complementisers are usually analysed as in Spec,CP; they show clear links with interrogatives in that they encode indirect questions, as in (32a–d), and are moved to Spec,CP from elsewhere in the clause; their form varies to agree with certain aspects of their referent (*who* versus *what*), their syntactic function (*who* versus *whom*) and their semantics (*why* for reason-adverbials, *when* for time-adverbials, etc.).

(32) a. Should we go there?   a'. He wondered whether we should go there.
      b. When did Darcy leave?   b'. He wondered when Darcy left.
      c. Where did Darcy go?   c'. He wondered where Darcy went.
      d. Who did Darcy prefer?   d'. He wondered who Darcy preferred.

Such an analysis is supported by the fact that the non-finite version of (32b) does not allow *if*, only *whether*.

(33) He wondered *if/whether* to go there.

This difference points to different positions for *whether* and *if* in PDE. *Whether, what, who, when*, etc., are not selective about the IP that follows – it can be finite or non-finite. They are not selective because they cannot

'see' the finiteness-information in the I-head. But *if* in the C-head can
see the information in the next head down (cf. the way heads share
information in V-to-I movement or I-to-C movement in Chapter 4),
which is why *if* can be selective. The PDE complementiser *that*, also
in C, can similarly be selective about finiteness – like *if*, it only accepts
finite clauses. Old English also uses interrogative pronouns to introduce
indirect questions, but non-finite indirect questions are too recent a
phenomenon to be used as evidence for their position in Old English.

The positional distinction between *wh-* and *that* is also relevant to
PDE relatives. Structure (34) shows an analysis in which a relative
clause (CP) is embedded in an NP (which will be part of a higher CP,
not shown here, but cf. (36b)). As relative clauses are usually analysed
as syntactic adjuncts, the CP is shown as a sister of an intermediate
N'-level rather than of the head N that is the antecedent of the relative
clause:

(34)

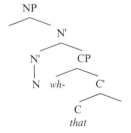

PDE relativisers can be *wh-*forms or *that*. *That* (and its 'silent' counterpart, the zero-relativiser) is in C, and the *wh-*relativisers are in Spec,CP,
for the same reasons as above, i.e. that they show agreement with their
antecedent, and have been moved to Spec,CP from elsewhere. *That*, on
the other hand, is invariant.

Although PDE requires the speaker to make a choice – either express
the *wh-*relativiser, or the C-element – this is not a requirement when
*wh-*relativisers make their first appearance in Middle English:

(35)   And of the secte of which þat he was born He kepte his lay to
       which þat he was sworn. (*OED, c.*1386 CHAUCER Sqr.'s T. 17,
                                                                    18)

The *se-*relatives we have seen so far show that as a demonstrative, *se*
exhibits agreement with the gender of its referent (*oþer wegferend* (m.)
'another traveller' . . . *se* (m.) in (25), *snoternysse* (f.) 'intelligence' . . . *þurh
þa* (f.)). *Se-*relatives at the paratatic end of the cline are independent

clauses where the se_2 pronoun has moved to Spec,CP from elsewhere in its clause, in the usual manner (see section 7.4, and also below).

The relativiser *that*, then, started out as an element in Spec,CP, and grammaticalised into a C-head when it became an invariant particle, bleached of deictic meaning, and primarily functioning as a sign of embedding. The grammaticalisation of *þæt* from a demonstrative pronoun into a complementiser is reflected in X'-structures as a Spec,CP constituent, a phrase, that is increasingly analysed as a word, and a C-head.

(36)

Such a re-analysis is often seen in grammaticalisation; for more examples, see van Gelderen (2004). Van Gelderen connects this type of grammaticalisation with a bias in language acquisition in which the default assumption of young children being exposed to linguistic items is that they are heads rather than phrases. Items will only be given a more complex analysis than 'head' if there is positive evidence in the child's data that they warrant it. Compare also the analysis of Roberts and Roussou (1999), who discuss the various morphosyntactic options of how functional heads can be expressed in languages (summarised at the end of section 4.8), and who hypothesise that, of these options, the option *merge* (base-generate in a function head) is the most economical one, and will be the preferred analysis in acquisition if the data allow it. Items that become invariant are prime candidates to be re-analysed as 'bespoke' elements to express functional heads.

Like *se*-relatives, complement-clauses and reason-clauses show 'early verbs' much more frequently in Old English than indirect questions or other adverbial clauses (Pintzuk 1999: 228). As complement-clauses and reason-clauses are also more likely to be found with main-clause-like orders in other languages, it is possible that the V-to-F there marks assertion versus non-assertion.

8.7 V-to-C in *þa*-correlatives

Discourse functions of correlatives may shed light on the mystery of V-to-C after *þa* or *þonne* as adverbs. Remember from section 7.2 and 7.4 that there is a basic distinction in Old English between V-in-C and V-in-F. V-in-C appears to have been motivated originally by a need to demarcate focused constituents, while V-in-F appears to have been motivated by a need to demarcate given information from new. For Old English, this can be summarised by *hw*-elements in Spec,CP versus *s/þ*-elements: *hw*-elements correlate with V-in-C, while *þ*-elements correlate with V-in-F. *Þ*-elements include the demonstrative *se*-paradigm, *þær* 'there', *þus* 'thus' but also *nu* 'now' and *swa* 'so'. Note that this leads to correlatives like (37), both with V-to-F:[2]

(37) **þær** Paulus ne mihte mid scipe faran, **þær** Petrus eode mid drigum fotum.
   there Paul not could with ship go,   there Peter went with dry feet
   \<GD (C) 1 12.91.8–10\>
   a. 'Paul could not cross with a ship, where Peter went with dry feet'
   b. 'Where Paul could not cross with a ship, Peter went with dry feet'

Modern translators, who have to make a choice between main and sub-clause, can either go for translation (a) or (b). The choice depends on the context. If Peter's crossing was in the past, and we have now arrived at Paul's crossing as the foregrounded event, translation (a) will be the most appropriate one, with Paul's crossing as the main clause. But if Paul's crossing was in the past and we have now arrived at Peter's crossing as our foregrounded event, this would call for translation (b).

   Now consider again (24), here repeated as (38):

(38) **ða₂** he on his wege rad, **þa₁** beseah he on þæt eadigan mæden,
   then he on his way rode, then looked he on that blessed maiden

   þær þe hi sæt wlitig and fæger onmang hire geferan.
   there that she sat beautiful and fair among her companions

   ða₁ cwæð he to his cnihtum: Ridað hraþe to þære fæmnan and axiað hire,
   then said he to his servants ride quickly to that girl and ask her

   gif hi seo frig. \<LS 14 (MargaretAss) 53–4\>
   if she is free

'When he was riding on his way, he beheld that blessed maiden where she was sitting among her companions, beautiful and fair; then he said to his servants: "Ride quickly to that girl and ask her if she is free."'

Example (38) marks the foregrounded event very clearly by having the finite verb in C after $þa_1$; we can tell it is not in F because the pronominal subject follows rather than precedes the verb. This behaviour is unexpected as *þa* belongs to the *s*/*þ*-set. Why does *þa*, as well as *þonne*, another item from the *s*/*þ*-set that means 'then', consistently trigger V-to-C rather than V-to-F when in Spec,CP? One way to account for this anomaly is to consider again the function of *þa*/*þonne*-clauses in discourse, as well as the frequency with which *þa* appears in correlative constructions, and the important role of *þa*-clauses in narrative discourse.

Where it is the timeline of the events that allows the audience to make out which of the two *þær*-clauses in (37) is the foregrounded one, this will not work for *þa* in (38), as it is itself a time adverbial. And unlike the *þær* correlatives, the subject of correlative *þa*-clauses is much more likely to refer to the same protagonist, because the backgrounded *when*-clause is quite likely to specify another action of the protagonist that grounds the main event, as it does in (38). This means that both clauses in the correlative pair will have pronominal subjects, as indeed does (38), so that they may end up with the same order of the subject and finite verb if that verb only moves to F. The combination of *þa*/*þonne* in Spec,CP and V-in-C is a clear signal of a foregrounded action.

A second piece of the puzzle is that $þa_2$-clauses in a $þa_2$-$þa_1$-V correlative overwhelmingly have a time-frame function. The configuration of $þa_2$-$þa_1$-V correlative comes as a package, to mark a foregrounded event in its time-frame, a narrative device that may originally have been introduced as a suspense-and-peak unit. We speculated in section 7.2 that V-to-C may have arisen to mark off a focus domain; and V-to-C may originally have been introduced after *þa*/*þonne* when these elements had intonational focus. PDE *then* can still be a peak marker, but it requires a stressed-focus *it*-cleft as in (39) to add the required focus (see also (9a–c) in the introduction):

(39)   The house was sold very quickly and the new owner immediately gave us all notice to quit. Many of the residents moved out shortly after Mrs Hill announced her intention to sell, and in fact there were only four of us left when the new landlord took possession. Another two moved on shortly afterwards and **it was then** that the intimidation began. (BNC, A0F w-fict-prose. Part of the furniture. Falk, Michael. London: Bellew Pub. Ltd, 1991, pp. 1–146.)

The *It was then*-construction in (39) gives you an idea of what the effect of focused *þa* may have been, and how this effect may have proved a useful device in narrative discourse. *Þa*-V lost some of its force through overuse, as is usual for such functions; Ælfric, writing at the end of the Old English period, has to rope in various other means, including adverbs with meanings of 'at once, straightaway', to mark his peaks. V-in-C after *þa* provided focus, and offered a solution to the local problem of marking the foregrounded member of a correlative *þa₂-þa₁*-pair. Other adverbs that build correlatives with important discourse functions, *nu* 'now' and *swa* 'as, so', may also mark the main clause of the pair by verb movement to C:

(40) **Nu** mote we habban maran rihtwisnysse, **nu** us synd behatene þa
     now may we have   more righteousness now us are   promised the

     heofonlican speda, þæt we moton sona   siþian to Criste on urum forðsiþe...
     heavenly   powers that we may   at-once travel to Christ on our death
     <ÆHom16, 120>

'Now may we have more righteousness now we have been promised the heavenly powers, so that we may travel to Christ at once after our death'

8.8 Summary of points

- The semantic concept of assertion and the discourse notion of foregrounding overlap to some extent, and both can be the main event of a pair of clauses, and hence any marking they develop may come to be used for marking main clauses.
- Typical discourse functions to be expressed linguistically in narratives are suspense, narrative peaks, and episode boundaries. Foregrounding and backgrounding are also important, and are likely to be marked.
- Suspense can be created by linguistic expressions that imply duration.
- Old English has correlative constructions of pairs of clauses that may offer clues as to how subordinate marking developed; on the paratactic pole of the cline both clauses of the pair are equally independent, with minimal integration, and only linked by the presence of a pronoun or adverb that is able to make a cataphoric or anaphoric connection; on the hypotactic end of the cline, one of the pair will be less independent, more integrated and more embedded, with the pronoun or adverb a conjunction.
- *Se*-relatives show main clause characteristics (no preposition stranding, high rates of 'early verbs', foregrounding) and derive from independent clauses with *se* in Spec,CP and V-to-F.

- Like *se*-relatives, complement-clauses and reason-clauses show 'early verbs' much more frequently in Old English than indirect questions or other adverbial clauses (Pintzuk 1999: 228). As complement-clauses and reason-clauses are also more likely to be found with main-clause-like orders in other languages, it is possible that some of these 'early verbs' are due to V-to-F as well, to mark assertion.

Exercises

1. DISCOURSE FUNCTION OF SLIPPING. A sudden change to direct speech in narratives without any introductions like 'she said' in historical texts is called 'slipping'. Identify an instance of slipping in the following text, and describe the linguistic element(s) that indicate that we are dealing with direct speech here (see also section 4.5.2). What effect does this instance of slipping have in the narrative?

   (i) Wulfstan sæde that he gefore of Hæðum, þæt he wære on Truso on syfan dagum & nihtum, þæt þæt scip wæs ealne weg yrnende under segle. Weonoðland him wæs onsteorbord & on bæcbord him wæs Langaland & Falster & Sconeg, & þas land eall hyrað to Denemearcan. & þonne Burgenda land wæs us on bæcbeord, & þa habbað him sylf cyning. [. . .] Ðæt Estland is swyðe mycel, & þær bið swyðe manig burh, & on ælcere byrig bið cyning, & þær bið swyðe mycel hunig & fiscað, & se cyning & þa ricostan men drincað myran meolc, & þa unspedigan & þa þeowan drincað medo (Bately 1980: 16–17)

   'Wulfstan said that he travelled from Hedeby and that he was in Truso within seven days and nights, since the ship was running under sail all the way. Wendland was on his starboard, and to his port was Laaland and Falster and Skane; and all these lands belong to Denmark. And then to our port was the land of the Burgundians, and they have their own king. [. . .] Estonia is very large, and there are many towns, and there is a king in every town. And there is very much honey and fishing; and the king and the richest men drink mare's milk, and the poor and the slaves drink mead.' (Translation: Swanton 1993: 66)

2. SUSPENSE-AND-PEAK MARKING. Appendix 2 of this book contains the description of Grendel's second coming to the hall of Heorot (lines 702–49 from *Beowulf*). Give examples of suspense-and-peak marking, and describe in as much linguistic detail as possible which devices are used to create these effects.

3. FOREGROUNDING. Compare the sentential relative clause in (ia) with the adverbial clause *as* in (ib) (both from Huddleston and Pullum [2002: 1147]):

(i) a. He'd phoned home every day, which he'd promised to do.
     b. He'd phoned home every day, as he'd promised to do.

The apparent equivalence between (ia) and (ib) is due to an overlap between the semantics of the two constructions. As explained by Huddleston and Pullum (2002: 1148), *as*-clauses as in (ib) ultimately derive from an expression denoting two variables x and y that are compared. X is 'he phoned home every day'; y is what he promised to do; and (ib) compares x to y. Relative clauses work by having a gap, a variable x, that links to an antecedent. In (ia), this variable x is 'he phoned home every day'; the relative clause is 'he promised to do x'. Where the overlap between these constructions stops is when the relative clause encodes information that is foregrounded (ibid.). As *as*-parentheticals cannot be foregrounded, such relatives do not have *as*-alternatives. Test this hypothesis by collecting examples of sentential relatives from a PDE corpus, preferably one that allows you to look at the context. Collect five examples which can also be phrased as *as*-clauses, and five which cannot. Do your examples support the hypothesis?

4. CORRELATIVES. Consider the following passage from the *Cynewulf and Cyneheard* episode:

(i)   ða   on morgenne gehierdun þæt þæs cyninges þegnas
       then in morning   heard   that the king's   retainers
       þe   him beæftan wærun þæt se cyning ofslægen wæs,
       who him behind   were   that the king killed   was
       þa   ridon hie þider. . . . <ChronA 755>
       then rode they thither

a. Provide a translation of this passage in idiomatic PDE.
b. Note any correlative constructions and say what the position of each correlative item is in the structure, using the clausal templates of Tables 6.4 and 7.2.
c. Decide, on linguistic grounds, whether the comma (which has been inserted by the editor of this text; Old English manuscripts do not have punctuation in the modern sense) is felicitous or not.

Further reading

The seminal work on discourse functions in historical texts is Brinton (1996). The labels main event and embedded event used in this chapter have been taken from Cristafaro (2003), who in turn takes them from Langacker (1991). For studies about foregrounding, see Hopper (1979), and about Old English *þa*, see Enkvist (1986) and van Kemenade amd Los (2006). This chapter has only fleetingly touched on the development of individual conjunctions, but see López-Couso (2007) on *lest*, Molencki (2007) on *since*, Lenker (2007) on *forwhi*, and Kortmann (1998: 5) and Fischer (1992b: 359) on *as*. For correlatives, see Mitchell (1984). The correlative system of clause linking shows a steep decline from about 1200, as is described in Lenker (2010). The demonstrative *se*-paradigm (Table 2.4) breaks down in Early Middle English (Smith 1996; McColl Millar 2000) and the decline of correlatives may well be one of its consequences. Referential – anaphoric and cataphoric – *that* is increasingly replaced by non-referential *it* (Ball 1991). There is a vast literature on the history of relative clauses in English that cannot be done justice here. For a discussion of the status of the various types of Old English relatives see Allen (1980), Mitchell (1985: §§2130ff.), Traugott (1992: 232), Fischer et al. (2000: 59ff.), and Suarez-Gomez (2006). For (discourse functions of) reported speech in Old English, see Mitchell (1985: §§1941ff.) and Moloney (1979); for subclauses that do not seem to be associated with a main clause, see Mitchell (1997). For subclauses with main clause behaviour in other languages, see Hooper & Thompson (1973), Givón (1990: 528–30), Cristofaro (2003: 229), and Schlachter (2012) for Old High German. For discourse and syntactic change in the history of English, see van Kemenade et al. (2008) and van Kemenade (2009). For the decline of first-position adverbials with a discourse-linking function, see Los and Dreschler (2012). For the rise of clefts, see Ball (1991), Los and Komen (2012), and Komen (2013).

Notes

1. Stein (1990) suggests this function for some of his examples of non-emphatic *do* in Early Modern English (see section 4.6).
2. The negator *ne* is a clitic on the finite verb, and has moved with that verb to F (see section 4.4.2).

Appendix 1:
Cynewulf and Cyneheard

FROM THE ANGLO-SAXON CHRONICLE, <CHRONA.PLUMMER 755.1–38>

Her Cynewulf benam Sigebryht his rices & West Seaxna wiotan for unryhtum dædum, buton Hamtunscire; & he hæfde þa oþ he ofslog þone aldormon þe him lengest wunode; & hiene þa Cynewulf on Andred adræfde, & he þær wunade oþ þæt hiene an swan ofstang æt Pryfetes flodan; & he wræc þone aldor mon Cumbran; & se Cynewulf oft miclum gefeohtum feaht uuiþ Bretwalum; & ymb xxxi wintra þæs þe he rice hæfde, he wolde adræfan anne æþeling se was Cyneheard haten, & se Cyneheard wæs þæs Sigebryhtes broþur; & þa geascode he þone cyning lytle werode on wifcyþþe on Merantune, & hine þær berad, & þone bur utan beeode ær hine þa men onfunden þe mid þam kyninge wærun; & þa ongeat se cyning þæt, & he on þa duru eode, & þa unheanlice hine werede, oþ he on þone æþeling locude, & þa utræsde on hine, & hine miclum gewundode.

& hie alle on þone Cyning wærun feohtende oþ þæt hie hine ofslægenne hæfdon; & þa on þæs wifes gebærum onfundon þæs cyninges þegnas þa unstilnesse, & þa þider urnon swa hwelc swa þonne gearo wearþ & radost; & hiera se æþeling gehwelcum feoh & feorh gebead, & hiera nænig hit geþicgean nolde. Ac hie simle feohtende wæran oþ hie alle lægon butan anum Bryttiscum gisle, & se swiþe gewundad wæs. ða on morgenne gehierdun þæt þæs cyninges þegnas þe him beæftan wærun þæt se cyning ofslægen wæs, þa ridon hie þider, & his aldormon Osric, & Wiferþ his þegn, & þa men þe he beæftan him læfde ær, & þone æþeling on þære byrig metton þær se cyning ofslægen læg, & þa gatu him to belocen hæfdon & þa þær to eodon; & þa gebead he him hiera agenne dom feos & londes gif hie him þæs rices uþon, & him cyþdon þæt hiera mægas him mid wæron þa þe him from noldon; & þa cuædon hie þæt him nænig mæg leofra nære þonne hiera hlaford, & hie næfre his banan folgian noldon, & þa budon hie hiera mægum þæt hie gesunde from eodon; & hie cuædon þæt tæt ilce hiera geferum geboden wære, þe ær mid þam cyninge wærun; þa cuædon hie þæt hie hie þæs ne onmunden þon ma þe

eowre geferan þe mid þam cyninge ofslægene wærun. & hie þa ymb
þa gatu feohtende wæron oþþæt hie þær inne fulgon, & þone æþeling
ofslogon, & þa men þe him mid wærun alle butan anum, se wæs þæs
aldormonnes godsunu, & he his feorh generede & þeah he wæs oft
gewundad.

Appendix 2: *Beowulf*

ll.702–749, Digitised from Elliott van Kirk Dobbie (ed.) (1953)

Com on wanre niht
scriðan sceadugenga. Sceotend swæfon,
þa þæt hornreced healdan scoldon,
ealle buton anum. þæt wæs yldum cuþ
þæt hie ne moste, þa metod nolde,
se scynscaþa   under sceadu bregdan;
ac he wæccende   wraþum on andan
bad bolgenmod   beadwa geþinges.
ða com of more   under misthleoþum
Grendel gongan,   godes yrre bær;
mynte se manscaða manna cynnes
sumne besyrwan in sele þam hean.
Wod under wolcnum to þæs þe he winreced,
goldsele gumena,   gearwost wisse,
fættum fahne.   Ne wæs þæt forma sið
þæt he Hroþgares   ham gesohte;
næfre he on aldordagum   ær ne siþðan
heardran hæle,   healðegnas fand.
Com þa to recede   rinc siðian,
dreamum bedæled.   Duru sona onarn,
fyrbendum fæst, syþðan he hire folmum æthran;
onbræd þa bealohydig,   ða he gebolgen wæs,
recedes muþan.   Raþe æfter þon
on fagne flor   feond treddode,
eode yrremod;   him of eagum stod
ligge gelicost   leoht unfæger.
Geseah he in recede   rinca manige,
swefan sibbegedriht   samod ætgædere,
magorinca heap.   þa his mod ahlog;
mynte þæt he gedælde,   ærþon dæg cwome,
atol aglæca,   anra gehwylces
lif wið lice,   þa him alumpen wæs
wistfylle wen.   Ne wæs þæt wyrd þa gen
þæt he ma moste   manna cynnes
ðicgean ofer þa niht.   þryðswyð beheold
mæg Higelaces,   hu se manscaða
under færgripum   gefaran wolde.
Ne þæt se aglæca   yldan þohte,
ac he gefeng hraðe   forman siðe
slæpendne rinc,   slat unwearnum,
bat banlocan,   blod edrum dranc,
synsnædum swealh;   sona hæfde
unlyfigendes   eal gefeormod,
fet ond folma.   Forð near ætstop,
nam þa mid handa   higeþihtigne
rinc on ræste,   ræhte ongean
feond mid folme;   he onfeng hraþe
inwitþancum   ond wið earm gesæt

Came on twilit night
stride-INF darkness-warrior. warriors slept
those that pinnacled house guard-INF should
all but one. That was to-men known
that him not could, (if) God did-not-allow-it,
the evil spirit under shadows bring-INF;
but he awake to-cruel-ones in hatred,
bided in-angry-mood battle's outcome.
Then came from moor under cloudy-cliffs
Grendel go-INF, God's anger bore;
intended the monster of mankind
one capture-INF in hall the high
Went under welkin to where he wine-joyous
goldhall of-men most-equipped knew,
with-plating brilliant. Not was that first time
that he Hrothgar's home (had) sought:
Never he in life-days earlier or later
(a) hardier hero, hall-thanes found.
Came then to building, warrior march-INF,
of his joy bereft. Door (f.) quickly opened
On-hinges fastened, when he her with-hands touched;
Flung-open then evil-minded-one while he angry was
hall's entrance. Quickly after that
on shining floor foe trod
went angry-in-mind; him from eyes stood
to-a-flame most-like light unlovely.
Beheld he in hall heroes many,
sleep-INF kinsmen-company all together,
of retainers a-heap: then his thoughts laughed;
intended that he sundered before day came
horrible demon from-each
life from body, since him happened was
plenty-of-food hopes. Not was the Fate then yet
that he more could of mankind
eat-INF in that night. Powerful-one saw
kinsman of-Higelac how the wicked spoiler
during sudden-assaults proceed-INF meant.
not that the monster delay-INF intended,
but he took quickly at-the-first occasion
sleeping warrior, tore unhindered,
bit bone-prison[1], blood in-streams drank,
swallowed in-huge-mouthfuls;straightaway had
lifeless-one's all eaten
feet and hands. Forth nearer stooped,
took then with hand stout-hearted
warrior in slumber, reached forward
the foe with hand; he captured quickly
feigning-one[2], and against arm rested...

---

[1] i.e. his body
[2] this is Beowulf, who is feigning sleep

Bibliography

Aarts, B. (2006), *Syntactic Gradience: The Nature of Grammatical Indeterminacy*, Oxford: Oxford University Press.

Aarts, B. (2012), The subjunctive conundrum, *Folia Linguistica* 46 (1), 1–20.

Allen, C. A. (1980), *Topics in Diachronic English Syntax*, New York: Garland.

Allen, C. A. (2006), Case syncretism and word order change, in A. van Kemenade and B. Los (eds), *The Handbook of the History of English*, Oxford: Blackwell, 201–23.

Allen, C. A. (2012), Why a determiner? The possessive + determiner + adjective construction in Old English, in A. Meurman-Solin, M. J. López-Couso and B. Los (eds), *Information Structure and Syntactic Change in the History of English*, New York: Oxford University Press, 245–70.

Attenborough, D. (2011), *New Life Stories*, London: HarperCollins.

Austen, Jane ([1807] 1997), *Letters*, 3rd edn, ed. Deirdre le Faye, Oxford: Oxford University Press.

Ball, C. N. (1991), The historical development of the it-cleft, PhD dissertation, University of Pennsylvania.

Bately, J. M. (ed.) (1980), *The Old English Orosius*, EETS Second Series 6, London: Oxford University Press.

Baugh, A. C. and T. Cable (2002), *A History of the English Language*, 5th edn, London: Routledge.

Bech, K. (2012), Word order, information structure, and discourse relations: a study of Old and Middle English verb-final clauses, in A. Meurman-Solin, M. J. López-Couso and B. Los (eds), *Information Structure and Syntactic Change in the History of English*, New York: Oxford University Press, 66–86.

Bergen, L. D. van (2013a), Early progressive passives, *Folia Linguistica Historica* 34, 173–207.

Bergen, L. D. van (2013b), Let's talk about *uton*, in A. H. Jucker, D. Landert, A. Seiler and N. Studer–Joho (eds), *Meaning in the History of English: Words and Texts in Context* (Studies in Language Companion Series 148), Amsterdam/Philadelphia: John Benjamins, 157–83.

den Besten, H. and J. A. Edmondson (1983), The verbal complex in continental West Germanic, in W. Abraham (ed.), *On the Formal Syntax of the Westgermania. Papers from the 3rd Groningen Grammar Talks* (Linguistik Aktuell 3), Amsterdam/Philadelphia: John Benjamins, 155–216.

Beths, F. (1999), The history of *dare* and the status of unidirectionality, *Linguistics* 37 (6), 1069–110.

Biber, D., S. Johansson, G. Leech, S. Conrad and E. Finegan (1999), *Longman Grammar of Spoken and Written English*, Harlow: Longman.

Birner, B. and G. Ward (1998), *Information Status and Canonical Word Order in English*, Amsterdam/Philadelphia: John Benjamins.

Birner, B. and G. Ward (2002), Information packaging, in R. Huddleston and G. K. Pullum (eds), *The Cambridge Grammar of the English Language*, Cambridge: Cambridge University Press, 1363–447.

Bittner, M. and K. Hale (1996), The structural determination of case and agreement, *Linguistic Inquiry* 27 (1), 1–68.

Bock, H. (1931), Studien zum präpositionalen Infinitiv und Akkusativ mit dem to-Infinitiv, *Anglia* 55, 115–249.

Bolinger, D. (1977), *Meaning and Form*, London/New York: Longman.

Booij, G. E. (2002), *The Morphology of Dutch*, Oxford: Oxford University Press.

Bosworth, J. and T. N. Toller (1882), *An Anglo-Saxon Dictionary*, Clarendon Press: Oxford. Idem. (1921), *Supplement.*

Breban, T. (2012), Functional shifts and the development of English determiners, in A. Meurman-Solin, M. J. López-Couso and B. Los (eds), *Information Structure and Syntactic Change in the History of English*, New York: Oxford University Press, 271–300.

Brinton, L. J. (1988), *The Development of English Aspectual Systems: Aspectualizers and Post-verbal Particles*, Cambridge: Cambridge University Press.

Brinton, L. J. (1996), *Pragmatic Markers in English: Grammaticalization and Discourse Functions* (Topics in English Linguistics 19), Berlin: Mouton de Gruyter.

Bromhead, H. (2009), *The Reign of Truth and Faith: Epistemic Expressions in 16th and 17th Century English* (Topics in English Linguistics 62), Berlin/New York: Mouton de Gruyter.

Brontë, E. ([1847] 1965), *Wuthering Heights*, Harmondsworth: Penguin Books.

Brown, P. and S. C. Levinson (1987), *Politeness: Some Universals in Language Usage*, Cambridge: Cambridge University Press.

Burnley, D. (1983), *A Guide to Chaucer's Language*, London: Macmillan.

Bybee, J. (1985), *Morphology: A Study of the Relation between Meaning and Form*, Amsterdam: John Benjamins.

Bybee, J. (2001), Main clauses are innovative, subordinate clauses are conservative: consequences for the nature of constructions, in J. Bybee and M. Noonan (eds), *Complex Sentences in Grammar and Discourse: Essays in Honor of Sandra A. Thompson*, Amsterdam and Philadelphia: John Benjamins, 1–17.

Bybee, J., R. Perkins and W. Pagliuca (1994), *The Evolution of Grammar: Tense, Aspect, and Modality in the Languages of the World*, Chicago: The University of Chicago Press.

Callaway, M. (1913), *The Infinitive in Anglo-Saxon*, Washington, DC: Carnegie Institution of Washington.

Campbell, L. (2004), *Historical Linguistics: An Introduction*, 2nd edn, Edinburgh: Edinburgh University Press.

Carey, K. (1994), The grammaticalization of the perfect in Old English, in W. Pagliuca (ed.), *Perspectives on Grammaticalization*, Amsterdam/Philadelphia: Benjamins, 103–17.

Chafe, W. L. (1976), Givenness, contrastiveness, definiteness, subjects, topics and point of view, in C. N. Li (ed.), *Subject and Topic*, New York: Academic Press, 27–55.

Chafe, W. L. (1994), *Discourse, Consciousness, and Time: The Flow and Displacement of Conscious Experience in Speaking and Writing*, Chicago: The University of Chicago Press.

CHEL (*The Cambridge History of the English Language*) (1992) vols I–VI, gen. ed. R. Hogg, Cambridge: Cambridge University Press.

Chomsky, N. (1980), On Binding, *Linguistic Inquiry* 11, 1–46.

Clarkson, J. (2007), *Indo-European Linguistics: An introduction*, Cambridge: Cambridge University Press.

Cole, M. (2012), The Old English origins of the Northern Subject Rule: evidence from the Lindisfarne gloss to the Gospels of John and Mark, in M. Stenroos, M. Mäkinen and I. Særheim (eds), *Speakers and Texts Around the North Sea: Reassessing the Historical Evidence*, Amsterdam/Philadelphia: John Benjamins, 141–68.

Cooper, W. E. and J. R. Ross (1975), World order, in R. E. Grossman, L. James San and T. J. Vance (eds), *Papers from the Parasession on Functionalism; April 17, 1975*, Chicago: Chicago Linguistic Society, 63–111.

Crawford, C. (1911), *The Marlowe Concordance*, vol. 1 (repr.), New York: Burt Franklin.

Crawford, C. ([1906–10] 1967), *A Concordance to the Works of Thomas Kyd*, Nendelin, Liechtenstein: Kraus Reprint.

Cristofaro, S. (2003), *Subordination* (Oxford Studies in Typology and Linguistic Theory), Oxford: Oxford University Press.

Cutler, A. (1988), The perfect speech error, in L. Hyman and C. Li (eds), *Language, Speech and Mind: Studies in Honor of Victoria A. Fromkin*, London: Croom Helm, 209–33.

Cuyckens, H. and M. Verspoor (1998), On the road to *to*, in J. van der Auwera, F. Durieux and L. Lejeune (eds), *English as a Human Language*, Munich: Lincom Europa, 57–72.

Danchev, A. (1988), Language change, typology and adjectival comparison in contact situations, *Folia Linguistica Historica* 9 (2), 161–74.

Davis, N. (1971), *Paston Letters and Papers of the Fifteenth Century*, vol. 1, Oxford: Oxford University Press.

Denison, D. (1990), 'Auxiliary + impersonal in Old English', *Folia Linguistica Historica* 9 (1), 139–66.

Denison, D. (1993), *English Historical Syntax*, London: Longman.

Denison, D. (1998), Syntax, in S. Romaine (ed.), *CHEL*, vol. IV, 1776–1997, Cambridge: Cambridge University Press, 92–329.

Denison, D. (2006), Category change and gradience in the determiner system, in A. van Kemenade and B. Los (eds), *The Handbook of the History of English*, Oxford: Blackwell, 279–304.

Denison, D. and M. Hundt (2013), Defining relatives, *Journal of English Linguistics* 41, 135–67.

De Smet, H. (2010), English -*ing*-clauses and their problems: the structure of grammatical categories, *Linguistics* 48 (6), 1153–93.

De Smet, H. (2013), *Spreading Patterns: Diffusional Change in the English System of Complementation* (Oxford Studies in the History of English), New York: Oxford University Press.

Dickens, C. ([1865] 1919) *Our Mutual Friend*, London: Dent.

Dixon, R. M. W. and A. Y. Aikhenvald (eds) (2006), *Complementation: A Crosslinguistic Typology* (Explorations in Linguistic Typology 3), Oxford: Oxford University Press.

Duffley, P. J. (1994), *Need* and *dare*: the black sheep of the modal family, *Lingua* 94, 213–43.

Eitler, Tamás (2006), Some sociolectal, dialectal and communicative aspects of word order variation in Late Middle English, PhD dissertation, University of Budapest.

Ellegård, A. (1953), *The Auxiliary Do: The Establishment and Regulation of its Use in English*, Stockholm: Almqvist & Wiksell.

Elsness, J. (1994), On the progression of the progressive in early Modern English, *ICAME Journal* 18, 5–25.

Enkvist, N. E. (1986), More about the textual functions of the Old English adverbial Þa, in D. Kastovsky and A. Szwedek (eds), *Linguistics across Historical and Geographical Boundaries: In Honour of Jacek Fisiak on the Occasion of his Fiftieth Birthday* (Trends in Linguistics: Studies and Monographs 32), vol. 1, Berlin: Mouton de Gruyter, 301–9.

Erman, B. and B. Warren (2000), The idiom principle and the open choice principle, *Text* 20 (1), 29–62.

Eythórsson, Th. (1995), Verbal syntax in the early Germanic languages, PhD dissertation, Cornell University.

Fanego, T. (1992), *Infinitive Complements in Shakespeare's English*, Santiago de Compostela: Universidade de Santiago de Compostela (Servicio de Publicacións e Intercambio Científico).

Fanego, T. (1996a), On the historical development of English retrospective verbs, *Neuphilologische Mitteilungen* 97, 71–9.

Fanego, T. (1996b), The development of gerunds as objects of subject-control verbs in English (1400–1760), *Diachronica* 13, 29–62.

Fanego, T. (1996c), The gerund in Early Modern English: evidence from the Helsinki Corpus, *Folia Linguistica Historica* 17, 97–152.

Fanego, T. (2004), On reanalysis and actualization in syntactic change: the rise and development of English verbal gerunds, *Diachronica* 21 (1), 5–55.

Fanselow, G. (1989), Coherent infinitives in German: restructuring vs. IP-complementation, in C. Bhatt, E. Löbel and C. Schmidt (eds), *Syntactic Phrase Structure Phenomena in Noun Phrases and Sentences* (Linguistik Aktuell 6), Amsterdam/Philadelphia: John Benjamins, 1–16.

Fennel, B. A. (2001), *A History of English: A Sociolinguistic Approach* (Blackwell Textbooks in Linguistics), Malden, MA: Blackwell.

Fielding, K. J. (1988), *The Speeches of Charles Dickens: A Complete Edition*, Hemel Hempstead: Harvester Wheatsheaf.

Fischer, O. C. M. (1989), The origin and spread of the accusative and infinitive construction in English, *Folia Linguistica Historica* 8, 143–217.

Fischer, O. C. M. (1990), Syntactic change and causation: developments in infinitival constructions in English, PhD dissertation, University of Amsterdam.

Fischer, O. C. M. (1991), The rise of the passive infinitive in English, in D. Kastovsky (ed.), *Historical English Syntax*, Berlin: Mouton de Gruyter, 141–88.

Fischer, O. C. M. (1992a), Syntactic change and borrowing: the case of the accusative-and-infinitive construction in English, in M. Gerritsen and D. Stein (eds), *Internal and External Factors in Syntactic Change* (Trends in Linguistics: Studies and Monographs), Berlin: Mouton de Gruyter, 17–88.

Fischer, O. C. M (1992b), Syntax, in N. Blake (ed.), *The Cambridge History of the English Language*, vol. 2, Cambridge: Cambridge University Press, 207–408.

Fischer, O.C.M. (1996), The status of *to* in Old English *to*-infinitives: a reply to Kageyama, *Lingua* 99, 107–33.

Fischer, O., A. van Kemenade, W. Koopman, and W. van der Wurff (2000), *The Syntax of Early English* (Cambridge Syntax Guides), Cambridge: Cambridge University Press.

Fludernik, M. (1996), Linguistics and literature: prospects and horizons in the study of prose, *Journal of Pragmatics* 26, 583–611.

Foster, T. and W. van der Wurff (1997), From syntax to discourse: the function of object-verb order in late Middle English, in J. Fisiak (ed.), *Studies in Middle English Linguistics* (Trends in Linguistics: Studies and Monographs 103), Berlin: Mouton de Gruyter, 135–56.

Francis, G. and J. McH. Sinclair (1994), I bet he drinks Carling Black Label: a riposte to Owen on corpus grammar, *Applied Linguistics* 15, 190–200.

Francis, W. (ed.) (1942), *Book of Vices and Virtues* (EETS 217).

Freed, A. F. (1979), *The Semantics of English Aspectual Complementation*, Dordrecht: Reidel.

Fridén, G. (1948), Studies on the tenses of the English verb from Chaucer to Shakespeare with special reference to the late sixteenth century, PhD dissertation, Uppsala University.

Furnivall, F. J. (ed.) (1901–3), *Robert of Brunne's Handlyng Synne* (EETS 119, 123).

Furnivall, F. J. (ed.) (1922), *Hali Meidenhad: An Alliterative Homily of the Thirteenth Century*, Oxford: Oxford University Press.

Fuß, E. (2005), *The Rise of Agreement: A Formal Approach to the Syntax and Grammaticalization of Verbal Inflection* (Linguistik Aktuell), Amsterdam/ Philadelphia: John Benjamins.

Gaaf, W. van der (1934), The connection between verbs of rest (*lie, sit*, and *stand*) and another verb, viewed historically, *English Studies* 16 (1), 81–99.

Gelderen, E. van (1993), *The Rise of Functional Categories*, Amsterdam/ Philadelphia: John Benjamins.

Gelderen, E. van (2004), *Grammaticalization as Economy*, Amsterdam/Philadelphia: John Benjamins.

Gelderen, E. van (2006), *A History of the English Language*, Amsterdam/Philadelphia: John Benjamins.

Gelderen, E. van (2011), Valency changes in the history of English, *Journal of Historical Linguistics* 1 (1), 106–43.

Getty, M. (2000), Differences in the metrical behavior of Old English finite verbs: evidence for grammaticalization, *English Language and Linguistics* 4, 37–67.

Givón, T. (1971), Historical syntax and synchronic morphology: an archaeologist's field trip, *Chicago Linguistic Society* 7, 394–415.

Givón, T. (ed.) (1983), *Topic Continuity in Discourse: A Quantitative Cross-language Study*, Amsterdam/Philadelphia: John Benjamins.

Givón, T. (1990), *Syntax: A Functional-Typological Introduction*, vol. 2, Amsterdam/Philadelphia: John Benjamins.

Godfrey, J., E. Holliman and J. McDaniel (1992), SWITCHBOARD: telephone speech corpus for research and development, in *Proceedings of the IEEE International Conference on Acoustics, Speech and Signal Processing* (ICASSP).

Görlach, M. (1997), *The Linguistic History of English: An Introduction*, Basingstoke: Macmillan.

Gregory, M. L. and L. A. Michaelis (2001), Topicalization and left-dislocation: a functional opposition revisited, *Journal of Pragmatics* 33, 1665–706.

Gussenhoven, C. (2011), Of migrant men, shifting sounds and stagnant waters, valedictory lecture, Radboud University Nijmegen, <http://ubn.ruhosting.nl/aanwinst/ne/aanwinstxx_3.html#17.54>.

Gutzmann, D. and E. Castroviejo Miró (2011), The dimensions of Verum, in O. Bonami and P. Cabredo Hofherr (eds), *Empirical Issues in Syntax and Semantics* 8, 143–65, <http://www.cssp.cnrs.fr/eiss8/index_en.html>.

Haas, N. de (2011), *Morphosyntactic Variation in Northern English: The Northern Subject Rule, its Origins and Early History*, Utrecht: LOT Dissertations.

Haeberli, E. (1999), Features, categories and the syntax of A-positions. Synchronic and diachronic variation in the Germanic languages, Doctoral dissertation, University of Geneva.

Haeberli, E. (2002), Observations on the loss of verb second in the history of English, in C. Jan-Wouter Zwart and W. Abraham (eds), *Studies in Comparative Germanic Syntax: Proceedings from the 15th Workshop on Comparative Germanic Syntax*, Amsterdam/Philadelphia: John Benjamins, 245–72.

Haegeman, L. M. V. (1994), *Introduction to Government and Binding Theory*, 2nd edn, Oxford: Blackwell.

Haegeman, L. and H. van Riemsdijk (1986), Verb projection raising, scope and the typology of rules affecting verbs, *Linguistic Inquiry* 3, 417–66.

Halliday, M. (1973), *Explorations in the Functions of Language* (Explorations in Language Study Series), London: Edward Arnold.

Hawkins, J. A. (1986), *A Comparative Typology of English and German: Unifying the Contrasts*, London: Croom Helm.

Healey, A. D. and R. L. Venezky ([1980] 1985), *A Microfiche Concordance to Old English*, Toronto: The Pontifical Institute of Mediaeval Studies.

Heine, B. and T. Kuteva (2002), *World Lexicon of Grammaticalization*, Cambridge: Cambridge University Press.

Heine, B. and T. Kuteva (2006), *The Changing Languages of Europe*, New York: Oxford University Press.

Hock, H. H. ([1986] 1991), *Principles of Historical Linguistics*, 2nd edn, Berlin/ New York: Mouton de Gruyter.

Hogg, R. and D. Denison (eds) (2006), *A History of the English Language*, Cambridge: Cambridge University Press.

Höhle, T. (1992), Über Verum-Fokus im Deutschen, *Linguistische Berichte*, Sonderheft 4, 112 141.

Hooper, J. B. and S. A. Thompson (1973), On the applicability of root transformations, *Linguistic Inquiry* 4, 465–97.

Hopper, P. J. (1979), Aspect and foregrounding in discourse, in T. Givón (ed.), *Syntax and Semantics 12: Discourse and Syntax*, New York: Academic Press, 213–41.

Hopper, P. J. and S. A. Thompson (1980), Transitivity in grammar and discourse, *Language* 56 (2), 251–99.

Hopper, P. and E. C. Traugott (2003), *Grammaticalization*, 2nd edn, Cambridge: Cambridge University Press.

Horobin, S. (2010), *Studying the History of Early English*, Basingstoke: Palgrave Macmillan.

Horstmann, C. (ed.) (1887), *The Early South-English Legendary* (EETS 87), London: Trübner & Co.

Huddleston, R. (1976), Some theoretical issues in the description of the English verb, *Lingua* 40, 331–83.

Huddleston, R. and G. K. Pullum (2002), *The Cambridge Grammar of the English Language*, Cambridge: Cambridge University Press.

Hundt, M. (2007), *English Mediopassive Constructions: A Cognitive, Corpus-Based Study of Their Origin, Spread, and Current Status*, Amsterdam: Rodopi.

Hurst, J. (1972), *Ælfric*, New York: Twayne.

Ingham, R. (2000), Negation and OV order in Late Middle English, *Journal of Linguistics* 36, 13–38.

Iyeiri, Y. (2001), *Negative Constructions in Middle English*, Fukuoka: Kyushu University Press.

Jespersen, O. (1940), *A Modern English Grammar*, vol. 5, London: Allen & Unwin.

Jolly, J. (1873), *Geschichte des Infinitivs im Indogermanischen*, München: Theodor Ackermann.

Kehler, L. K., H. Rohde and J. Elman (2008), Coherence and coreference revisited, *Journal of Semantics*, special issue on Processing Meaning, 25, 1–44.

Kemenade, A. van (1987), *Syntactic Case and Morphological Case in the History of English*, Dordrecht: Foris.

Kemenade, A. van (1997), V2 and embedded topicalisation in Old and

Middle English, in A. van Kemenade and N. Vincent (eds), *Parameters of Morphosyntactic Change*, Cambridge: Cambridge University Press, 326–52.

Kemenade, A. van (2000), Jespersen's cycle revisited: formal properties of grammaticalization, in S. Pintzuk, G. Tsoulas and A. Warner (eds), *Diachronic Syntax: Models and Mechanisms*, Oxford: Oxford University Press, 51–74.

Kemenade, A. van. (2009), Discourse relations and word order change, in R. Hinterhölzl and S. Petrova (eds), *Information Structure and Language Change*, Berlin: Mouton de Gruyter, 191–20.

Kemenade, A. van and B. Los (2006), Discourse adverbs and clausal syntax in Old and Middle English, in A. van Kemenade and B. Los (eds), *The Handbook of the History of English*, Oxford: Blackwell, 224–48.

Kemenade, A. van, T. Milicev and R. H. Baayen (2008), The balance between discourse and syntax in Old English, in M. Dossena and M. Gotti (eds), *Selected Papers from the 14th International Conference on English Historical Linguistics*, Amsterdam: John Benjamins, 3–22.

Kemenade, A. van, and M. Westergaard (2012), Syntax and information structure: Verb–Second variation in Middle English, in A. Meurman-Solin, M. J. López-Couso and B. Los (eds), *Information Structure and Syntactic Change in the History of English*, New York: Oxford University Press, 87–118.

Kerkhof, J. (1966), *Studies in the Language of Geoffrey Chaucer*, Leiden: Universitaire Pers.

Kerouac, J. (1959), *The Dharma Bums*, London: Deutsch.

Killie, K. (2008), From locative to durative to focalized? The English progressive and 'PROG imperfective drift', in M. Gotti, M. Dossena and R. Dury (eds), *English Historical Linguistics 2006, Vol. 1: Syntax and Morphology*, Amsterdam/Philadelphia: John Benjamins, 69–88.

Kilpiö, M. (1989), *Passive Constructions in Old English Translations from Latin: With Special Reference to the OE Bede and the Pastoral Care* (Mémoires de la Société Néophilologique de Helsinki 49), Helsinki: Société Néophilologique.

Kiparsky, P. (1995), The Indo-European origin of Germanic syntax, in A. Battye and I. Roberts (eds), *Clause Structure and Language Change*, Oxford: Oxford University Press, 140–69.

Köhler, A. (1867), Der syntaktische Gebrauch des Infinitivs im Gotischen, *Germania* 12, 421–62.

Komen, E. (2013), Finding Focus: A Study of the Historical Development of Focus in English (LOT Dissertations in Linguistics), Utrecht: LOT.

Koopman, W. (1990), Word order in Old English, PhD dissertation, University of Amsterdam.

Koopman, W. (1995), Verb-Final main clauses in Old English prose, *Studia Neophilologica* 67, 129–44.

Koopman, W. (2005), Transitional syntax: postverbal pronouns and particles in Old English, *English Language and Linguistics* 9 (1), 47–62.

Kortmann, B. (1998), The evolution of adverbial subordinators in Europe, in M. S. Schmid et al. (eds), *Historical Linguistics 1997*, Amsterdam: John Benjamins, 213–28.

Koster, J. (1975), Dutch as an SOV language, *Linguistic Analysis* 1, 111–36.

Kranich, S. (2008), The progressive in Modern English: a corpus-based study of grammaticalization and related changes, PhD dissertation, Freie Universität Berlin; published as Kranich (2010).

Kranich, S. (2010), *The Progressive in Modern English. A Corpus–Based Study of Grammaticalization and Related Changes* (Language and Computers. Studies in Practical Linguistics 72), Amsterdam: Rodopi.

Krifka, M. (2007), Basic notions of information structure, in C. Féry, G. Fanselow and M. Krifka (eds), *The Notions of Information Structure* (Interdisciplinary Studies on Information Structure 6; Working Papers of The Sonderforschungsbereich 632), Potsdam: Potsdam Universitätsverlag, 13 55.

Kroch, A. (1989), Reflexes of grammar in patterns of language change, *Language Variation and Change* 1, 199–244.

Kroch, A. and A. Taylor (1997), Verb movement in Old and Middle English: dialect variation and language contact, in A. van Kemenade and N. Vincent (eds), *Parameters of Morphosyntactic Change*, Cambridge: Cambridge University Press, 297–325.

Kroch, A. and A. Taylor (2000a), Verb-object order in early Middle English, in S. Pintzuk, G. Tsoulas and A. Warner (eds), *Diachronic Syntax: Models and Mechanisms*, Oxford: Oxford University Press, 132–63.

Kroch, A. and A. Taylor (2000b), *Penn-Helsinki Parsed Corpus of Middle English*, 2nd edn, <http://www.ling.upenn.edu/hist–corpora/PPCME2–RELEASE–2/>.

Kroch, A., B. Santorini and A. Diertani (2004), *Penn-Helsinki Parsed Corpus of Early Modern English*, <http://www.ling.upenn.edu/hist–corpora/PPCEME–RELEASE–2/index.html>.

Kroch, A., B. Santorini and A. Diertani (2010), *Penn Parsed Corpus of Modern British English*, <http://www.ling.upenn.edu/hist–corpora/PPCMBE–RELEASE–1/index.html>.

Kroch, A., A. Taylor and D. Ringe (2000), The Middle English Verb-Second constraint: a case study in language contact and language change, in S. C. Herring, P. v. Reenen and L. Schøsler (eds), *Textual Parameters in Older Languages*, Amsterdam/Philadelphia: John Benjamins, 353–91.

Krug, M. G. (2000), *Emerging English Modals: A Corpus-Based Study of Grammaticalization* (Topics in English Linguistics 32), Berlin/New York: Mouton de Gruyter.

Kusters, C. W. (2003), *Linguistic Complexity: The Influence of Social Change on Verbal Inflection*, Utrecht: LOT.

Kuteva, T. (2001), *Auxiliation: An Enquiry into the Nature of Grammaticalization*, Oxford: Oxford University Press.

Kytö, M., ed. (1993), *Manual to the Diachronic Part of the Helsinki Corpus of English Texts: Coding Conventions and Lists of Source Texts*, 2nd edn, Helsinki: University of Helsinki, English Department.

Kytö, M. (1997), BE/HAVE + past participle: the choice of the auxiliary with intransitives from Late Middle to Modern English, in M. Rissanen, M. Kytö and K. Heikkonen (eds), *English in Transition: Corpus-based Studies in Linguistic Variation and Genre Styles* (Topics in English Linguistics 23), Berlin: Mouton de Gruyter, 17–85.

Labov, W. (1972), *Language in the Inner City*, Philadelphia: University of Pennsylvania Press.

Ladefoged, P. and I. Maddieson (1996), *The Sounds of the World's Languages*, Blackwell: Oxford.

LAEME, Laing, M., and R. Lass (2008–), *A Linguistic Atlas of Early Middle English 1150–1325*, version 1.1, <http://www.lel.ed.ac.uk/ihd/laeme1/laeme1. html>, Edinburgh: University of Edinburgh.

LALME, McIntosh, A., M. L. Samuels, M. Benskin, with M. Laing and K. Williamson (eds), (1986), *A Linguistic Atlas of Late Mediaeval English*, vol. I, Aberdeen: Aberdeen University Press.

Lambrecht, K. (1994), *Information Structure and Sentence Form*, Cambridge: Cambridge University Press.

Langacker, R. W. (1991), *Foundations of Cognitive Grammar*, vol. II: Descriptive Applications, Stanford: Stanford University Press.

Lass, R. (1990), How to do things with junk: exaptation in language evolution, *Journal of Linguistics* 26, 79–102.

Lecki, A. M. (2010), *Grammaticalisation Paths of Have in English* (Studies in English Medieval Language and Literature 24), Frankfurt am Main etc.: Peter Lang.

Lenker, U. (2000), *Soþlice* and *witodlice*: discourse markers in Old English, in O. Fischer, A. Rosenbach and D. Stein (eds), *Pathways of Change: Grammaticalization in English* (Studies in Language Companion Series 53), Amsterdam/Philadelphia: John Benjamins, 229–49.

Lenker, U. (2007), *Forhwi* 'because', Shifting deictics in the history of English causal connection, in U. Lenker and A. Meurman-Solin (eds), *Connectives in the History of English* (Current Issues in Linguistic Theory 283), Amsterdam/Philadelphia: John Benjamins, 193–227.

Lenker, U. (2010), *Argument and Rhetoric: Adverbial Connectors in the History of English* (Topics in English Linguistics 64), Berlin: Mouton de Gruyter.

Lewis, M. P. (ed.) (2009), *Ethnologue: Languages of the World*, 16th edn, Dallas: SIL International <http://www.ethnologue.com/>.

Lightfoot, D. W. (1979), *Principles of Diachronic Syntax*, Cambridge: Cambridge University Press.

Lightfoot, D. W. (1991), *How to set Parameters: Arguments from Language Change*, Cambridge, MA: MIT Press.

Lindemann, J. W. R. (1965), Old English preverbal *ge–*: a re-examination of some current doctrines, *Journal of English and Germanic Philology* 64, 65–84.

Lloyd, A. L. (1979), *Anatomy of the Verb: The Gothic Verb as a Model for a Unified Theory of Aspect, Actional Types, and Verbal Velocity*, Amsterdam: John Benjamins.

Loey, A. van ([1959] 1970), *Schönfeld's Historische Grammatica van het Nederlands*, Zutphen: Thieme.

Longacre, R. E. (1983), *The Grammar of Discourse*, New York: Plenum Press.

López-Couso, M. J. (2007), Adverbial connectives within and beyond adverbial subordination: the history of *lest*, in U. Lenker and A. Meurman-Solin (eds), *Connectives in the History of English*, Amsterdam/Philadelphia: John Benjamins, 11–29.

López-Couso, M. J. and B. Mendez Naya (1996), On the use of the subjunctive and modals in Old and Middle English dependent commands and requests: evidence from the Helsinki Corpus, *Neuphilologische Mitteilungen* 97, 411–22.

Los, B. (2000), *Onginnan/Beginnan* + *to*-infinitive in Ælfric, in O. Fischer, A. Rosenbach and D. Stein (eds), *Pathways of Change: Grammaticalization in English* (Studies in Language Companion Series 53), Amsterdam/ Philadelphia: John Benjamins, 251–74.

Los, B. (2005), *The Rise of the* to-*infinitive*, Oxford: Oxford University Press.

Los, B. (2012), The loss of Verb-Second and the switch from bounded to unbounded systems, in A. Meurman-Solin, M. J. López-Couso and B. Los (eds) *Information Structure and Syntactic Change in the History of English*, New York: Oxford University Press, 21–46.

Los, B. and G. Dreschler (2012), The loss of local anchoring: from adverbial local anchors to permissive subjects, in T. Nevalainen and E. C. Traugott (eds), *The Oxford Handbook of the History of English*, New York: Oxford University Press, 859–72.

Los, B. and E. Komen (2012), Clefts as resolution strategies after the loss of a multifunctional first position, in T. Nevalainen and E. C. Traugott (eds), *The Oxford Handbook of the History of English*, New York: Oxford University Press, 884–98.

Los, B., C. Blom, G. Booij, M. Elenbaas and A. van Kemenade (2012a), *Morphosyntactic Change: A Comparative Study of Particles and Prefixes*, Cambridge: Cambridge University Press.

Los, B., M. J. López-Couso and A. Meurman-Solin (2012b), On the interplay of syntax and information structure: synchronic and diachronic considerations, in A. Meurman-Solin, M. J. López-Couso and B. Los (eds), *Information Structure and Syntactic Change in the History of English*, New York: Oxford University Press, 3–18.

Loureiro-Porto, L. (2009), *The Semantic Predecessors of* Need *in the History of English* (Publications of the Philological Society 43), Chichester: Wiley-Blackwell.

Macaulay, G. C. (1899–1902), *The Complete Works of John Gower*, 4 vols, Oxford: Clarendon Press.

McColl Millar, R. (2000), *System Collapse System Rebirth: The Demonstrative Pronouns of English 900–1350 and the Birth of the Definite Article*, Oxford: Lang.

McFadden, Th. and A. Alexiadou (2013), Auxiliary selection and counterfactuality in the history of English and Germanic, in J. M. Hartmann and László Molnárfi (eds), *Comparative Studies in Germanic Syntax*, Amsterdam/ Philadelphia: John Benjamins, 237–63.

McIntyre, D. (2009), *History of English: A Resource Book for Students* (Routledge English Language Introductions), Abingdon: Routledge.

Macleod, M. (2012), The perfect in Old English and Old Saxon: the synchronic and diachronic correspondence of form and meaning, PhD dissertation, Cambridge University.

Macleod, M. (2013), Synchronic variation in the Old English perfect, *Transactions of the Philological Society* 111, 1–25.

McWhorter, J. H. (2002), What happened to English? *Diachronica* 19 (2), 217–72.

Mair, C. (1990), *Infinitival Complement Clauses in English: A Study of Syntax in Discourse*, Cambridge: Cambridge University Press.

Majid, A., A. J. Sanford and M. J. Pickering (2007), The linguistic description of minimal social scenarios affects the extent of causal inference making, *Journal of Experimental Social Psychology* 43, 918–32.

Mayor, J. E. B. (1876), The English Works of John Fisher, (EETS Extended Series 27).

MED (*Middle English dictionary*), (1956–), ed. H. Kurath and S. M. Kuhn. From 1984: editor-in-chief R.E. Lewis, Ann Arbor: University of Michigan Press.

Meillet, A. (1903), *Introduction l'étude comparative des langues indoeuropëennes*, Paris: Librairie Hachette et Cie.

Michaelis, L. A. (2004), Type shifting in construction grammar: an integrated approach to aspectual coercion, *Cognitive Linguistics* 15, 1–67.

Mills, S. (2003), *Gender and Politeness*, Cambridge: Cambridge University Press.

Mitchell, B. (1984), The origins of Old English conjunctions: some problems, in J. Fisiak (ed.), *Historical Syntax* (Trends in Linguistics, Studies and Monongraphs 23), Berlin: Walter de Gruyter & Co., 271–300.

Mitchell, B. (1985), *Old English Syntax*, 2 vols, Oxford: Clarendon Press.

Mitchell, B. (1997), Unexpressed principal clauses in Old English?, in T. Nevalainen and L. Kahlas-Tarkka (eds), *To Explain the Present: Studies in the Changing English Language in Honour of Matti Rissanen* (Mémoires de la Société Néophilologique de Helsinki 52), Helsinki: Société Néophilologique, 124–34.

Mitchell, B., C. Ball and A. Cameron (eds) (1975), Short titles of Old English texts, *Anglo-Saxon England* 4, 207–21.

Mitchell, B., C. Ball and A. Cameron (eds) (1979), Addenda and corrigenda, *Anglo-Saxon England* 8, 331–3.

Mitchell, B. and F. C. Robinson (1982), *A Guide to Old English*, rev. edn, Oxford: Blackwell.

Mithun, M. (1989), The subtle significance of the locus of morphologization, *International Journal of American Linguistics* 55, 265–82.

Mittwoch, A. (1990), On the distribution of bare infinitive complements in English, *Journal of Linguistics* 26, 103–31.

Moens, M. and M. Steedman (1988), Temporal ontology and temporal reference, *Journal of Computational Linguistics* 14, 17–28.

Moessner, L. (1997), -ing-constructions in Middle English, in J. Fisiak (ed.), *Studies in Middle English Linguistics*, Berlin/New York: Mouton de Gruyter, 335–49.

Moessner, L. (2003), *Diachronic English Linguistics: An Introduction*, Tübingen: Gunther Narr Verlag.

Möhlig-Falke, R. (2012), *The Early English Impersonal Construction: An Analysis of Verbal and Constructional Meaning*, New York: Oxford University Press.

Molencki, R. (1999), *A History of English Counterfactuals*, Katowice: Wydawnictwo Uniwersytetu Śląskiego.

Molencki, R. (2007), The evolution of *since* in medieval English, in U. Lenker and A. Meurman-Solin (eds), *Connectives in the History of English*, Amsterdam/ Philadelphia: John Benjamins, 97–115.

Moloney, B. (1979), A Further Anglo-Saxon Trait in the Narrative Style of Ælfric's 'Lives of Saints', *Notes and Queries* 224, 498–500.

Morris, R. (1874–92), *Cursor Mundi (The Cursor of the World)*, 6 vols (EETS 57, 59, 62, 66, 68, 99), London: Kegan Paul, Trench, Trübner.

Mossé, F. (1938), *Histoire de la Forme Périphrastique* être + *Participe Présent en Germanique*, 2 vols, Paris: Klincksieck.

Mustanoja, T. F. (1960), *A Middle English Syntax. Part I: Parts of Speech*, Helsinki: Société Néophilologique.

Napier, A. S. (ed.) (1894), *History of the Holy Rood-Tree: A Twelfth Century Version of the Cross-Legend* (EETS Original Series 103), published for the Early English Text Society by K. Paul, Trench, London: Trübner & Co.

Nevalainen, T. (1997), Recycling inversion: the case of initial adverbs and negators in Early Modern English, in J. Fisiak (ed.), *A Festschrift for Roger Lass on his Sixtieth Birthday*, Studia Anglica Posnaniensia 31, Poznan: Wydawnictwo Nakom, 203–14.

Nevalainen, T. (2006), *An Introduction to Early Modern English* (Edinburgh Textbooks on the English Language), Edinburgh: Edinburgh University Press.

Noonan, M. (1985), Complementation, in T. Shopen (ed.), *Language Typology and Syntactic Description*, vol. 2, Cambridge: Cambridge University Press, 42–140.

OED Online (*Oxford English Dictionary* Online), <http://www.oed.com>.

Ogawa, H. (1989), *Old English Modal Verbs: A Syntactical Study* (*Anglistica* 26), Copenhagen: Rosenkilde and Bagger.

Ohkado, M. (2004), Coordinate clauses in Old English with special reference to Ælfric's Catholic Homilies, *Folia Linguistica Historica* 25 (1–2), 155–76.

Petré, P. (2010), On the interaction between constructional & lexical change: copular, passive and Related Constructions in Old and Middle English, PhD dissertation, University of Leuven.

Pinker, S. and D. Birdsong (1979), Speakers' sensitivity to rules of frozen word order, *Journal of Verbal Learning and Verbal Behavior* 18 (4), 497–508.

Pintzuk, S. (1999), *Phrase Structures in Competition: Variation and Change in Old English Word Order* (Outstanding Dissertations in Linguistics), New York: Garland Publishing.

Pintzuk, S. (2002), Verb-object order in Old English: variation as grammatical competition, in D. Lightfoot (ed.), *Syntactic Effects of Morphological Change*, Oxford: Oxford University Press, 276–300.

Pintzuk, S. and A. Taylor (2006), The loss of OV-order in the history of English, in A. van Kemenade and B. Los (eds), *The Handbook of the History of English*, Oxford: Blackwell, 249–78.

Plank, F. (1984), The modals story retold, *Studies in Language* 8, 305–64.

Pollock, J. Y. (1989), Verb movement, universal grammar, and the structure of IP, *Linguistic Inquiry* 20, 365–424.

Poussa, P. (1982), The evolution of Early Standard English: the creolization hypothesis, *Studia Anglica Posnaniensia* 14, 69–85.

Pratt, L. and D. Denison (2000), The language of the Southey-Coleridge circle, *Language Sciences* 22, 401–22.

Prince, E. F. (1978), A comparison of wh-clefts and it-clefts in discourse, *Language* 54, 883–906.

Quirk, R., S. Greenbaum, G. Leech and J. Svartvik (1985), *A Grammar of Contemporary English*, Harlow: Longman.

Radford, A. (2004), *English Syntax: An Introduction*, Cambridge: Cambridge University Press.

Richardson, P. (1994), Imperfective aspect and episode structure in Beowulf, *Journal of English and Germanic Philology* 93, 313–25.

Ringe, D. (2006), *A Linguistic History of English. Volume I. From Proto-Indo-European to Proto-Germanic*, Oxford: Oxford University Press.

Rissanen, M. (1967), *The Uses of 'One' in Old and Early Middle English*, (Mémoires de la Société Néophilologique de Helsinki 31), Helsinki: Société Néophilologique.

Rissanen, M. (1999), Syntax, in *CHEL*, vol. III, ed. R. Lass, Cambridge: Cambridge University Press, 187–233.

Roberts, I. G. (1985), Agreement parameters and the development of the English modal auxiliaries, *Natural Language and Linguistic Theory* 3 (1), 21–58.

Roberts, I. G. and A. Roussou (1999), A formal approach to 'grammaticalization', *Linguistics* 37, 1011–41.

Roberts, I. G. and A. Roussou (2003), *Syntactic Change: A Minimalist Approach to Grammaticalization*, Cambridge: Cambridge University Press.

Robinson, F. N. (1957), *The Complete Works of Geoffrey Chaucer*, 2nd edn, Boston, MA: Houghton Mifflin.

Rosenbach, A. (2002), *Genitive Variation in English: Conceptual Factors in Synchronic and Diachronic Studies* (Topics in English Linguistics 42), Berlin/New York: Mouton de Gruyter.

Ross, J. R. (1968), *Constraints on Variables in Syntax*, Bloomington: Indiana University Linguistic Club.

Royster, J. F. (1918), The causative use of 'Hatan', *The Journal of English and Germanic Philology* 17, 82–93.

Rudanko, J. (1996), *Prepositions and Complement Clauses: A Syntactic and Semantic Study of Verbs Governing Prepositions and Complement Clauses in Present-Day English*, Albany: State University of New York Press.

Russom, J. H. (1982), An examination of the evidence for OE indirect passives, *Linguistic Inquiry* 13: 677–80.

Rutten, J. (1991), *Infinitival Complements and Auxiliaries* (Amsterdam Studies in generative Grammar 4), PhD dissertation, University of Amsterdam.

Rydén, M. (1966), *Relative Constructions in Early Sixteenth Century English* (Acta

Universitatis Upsaliensis; Studia anglistica upsaliensia 3), Stockholm: Almqvist and Wiksell.

Rydén, M. and S. Brorström (1987), *The Be/Have Variation with Intransitives in English, with Special Reference to the Late Modern Period* (Acta Universitatis Stockholmiensis 70), Stockholm: Almqvist and Wiksell.

Sairio, A. (2006), Progressives in the letters of Elizabeth Montagu and her circle in 1738–1778, in C. Dalton-Puffer, D. Kastovsky, N. Ritt and H. Schendl (eds), *Syntax, Style and Grammatical Norms*, Bern: Peter Lang, 167–89.

Sato, K. (2012), Ælric's linguistic and stylistic alterations in his adaptations from the Old English *Boethius*, *Neophilologus* 96, 631–40.

Scheffer, J. (1975), *The Progressive in English*, Amsterdam: North Holland Publishing Company.

Schlachter, E. (2012), *Syntax und Informationsstruktur im Althochdeutschen: Untersuchungen am Beispeil der Isidor-Gruppe*, Heidelberg: Winter.

Siewierska, A. (1999), From anaphoric pronoun to grammatical agreement marker: why objects don't make it, *Folia Linguistica* 33 (2), 225–51.

Smith, C. S. (1983), A theory of aspectual choice, *Language* 59, 479–501.

Smith, C. S. (1997), *The Parameter of Aspect*, 2nd edn, Dordrecht: Kluwer Academic Publishers.

Smith, J. J. (1996), *An Historical Study of English: Function, Form and Change*, London and New York: Routledge.

Smith, L. (ed.) (1885), *York Plays*, Oxford: Clarendon Press.

Sorace, A. (2000), Gradients in auxiliary selection with intransitive verbs, *Language* 76, 859–90.

Spevack, M. (1969), *A Complete and Systematic Concordance to the Works of Shakespeare*, vol. 4, Hildesheim: Olms.

Stankiewicz, E. (1991), The concept of structure in contemporary linguistics, in L. R. Waugh and S. Rudy, *New Vistas in Grammar: Invariance and Variation* (Current Issues in Linguistic Theory 49), Amsterdam/Philadelphia: John Benjamins, 11–32.

Stein, D. (1990), *The Semantics of Syntactic Change: Aspects of the Evolution of 'Do' in English* (Trends in Linguistics, Studies and Monographs 47), Berlin/New York: Mouton de Gruyter.

Stockwell, R. P. (1977), Motivations for exbraciation in Old English, in Ch. N. Li (ed.), *Mechanisms of Syntactic Change*, London/Austin: University of Texas Press, 291–314.

Streitberg, W. (1965), *Die Gotische Bibel*, Heidelberg: Carl Winter Universitätsverlag.

Suarez-Gomez, C. (2006), *Relativization in Early English (950–1250): The Position of Relative Clauses*, Bern: Peter Lang.

Swanton, M. J. (1993), *Anglo-Saxon Prose*, 2nd edn, London: Dent.

de Swart, P. (2007), *Cross-linguistic Variation in Object Marking* (LOT Dissertation Series 168), Utrecht: LOT.

Tajima, M. (1985), *The Syntactic Development of the Gerund in Middle English*, Tokyo: Nan'un-do.

Tajima, M. (1996), The common-/objective-case subject of the gerund in Middle English, *NOWELE* 28/29, 569–78.

Taylor, A. (2005), Prosodic evidence for incipient VO order in Old English, *English Language and Linguistics* 9, 139–56.

Taylor, A.S. and S. Pintzuk (2012), The effect of information structure on object position in Old English: a pilot study, in A. Meurman-Solin, M. J. López-Couso and B. Los (eds), *Information Structure and Syntactic Change in the History of English*, New York: Oxford University Press, 47–65.

Taylor, A., A. Warner, S. Pintzuk and F. Beths (2003), *The York-Toronto-Helsinki Parsed Corpus of Old English Prose*, <http://www–users.york.ac.uk/~lang22 / YCOE/YcoeHome.htm>.

Tennyson, A. (1842), *Poems in Two Volumes*, London: Edward Moxon.

Thomason, S. G. (2001), *Language Contact: An Introduction*, Edinburgh: Edinburgh University Press.

Thomason, S. G. and T. Kaufman (1988), *Language Contact, Creolization, and Genetic Linguistics*, Berkeley: University of California Press.

Thompson, E. (2005), A cross-linguistic look at VP-ellipsis and verbal speech errors, *Proceedings of DiSS'05* (Disfluency in Spontaneous Speech Workshop, ISCA Archive), 163–4, <http://www.isca–speech.org/archive>.

Thráinsson, H. (1985), V1, V2 V3 in Icelandic, in H. Haider and M. Prinzhorn (eds), *Verb Second phenomena in Germanic Languages*, Dordrecht: Foris, 169–94.

Toyota, J. (2008), *Diachronic Change in the English Passive*, Basingstoke: Palgrave Macmillan.

Traugott, E. C. (1972), *The History of English Syntax* (Transatlantic Series in Linguistics), New York: Holt, Rinehart and Winston.

Traugott, E. C. (1992), Old English syntax, in R. M. Hogg (ed.), *The Cambridge History of the English Language*, vol. I, Cambridge: Cambridge University Press, 168–289.

Trips, C. (2002), *From OV to VO in early Middle English* (Linguistik Aktuell), Amsterdam/ Philadelphia: John Benjamins.

Trudgill, P. J. (2011), *Sociolinguistic Typology: Social Determinants of Linguistic Complexity*, Oxford: Oxford University Press.

Updike, J. (1990), *Rabbit is Rich*, in *Rabbit Angstrom: A Tetralogy*, New York: Knopf.

Van Kirk Dobbie, E. (ed.) (1953), *Beowulf and Judith* (Anglo-Saxon Poetic Records 4), New York: Columbia University Press.

Van linden, A. (2010), The rise of the *to*-infinitive: evidence from adjectival complementation, *English Language and Linguistics* 14 (1), 19–51.

Vendler, Z. (1957), Verbs and times, *The Philosophical Review* 66, 143–60.

Visser, F. T. (1969), *An Historical Syntax of the English Language*, vol. 3, Leiden: Brill.

Warner, A. R. (1982), *Complementation in Middle English and the Methodology of Historical Syntax*, London: Croom Helm.

Warner, A. R. (1993), *English Auxiliaries: Structure and History*, Cambridge: Cambridge University Press.

Warner, A. R. (1995), Predicting the progressive passive: parametric change within a lexicalist framework, *Language* 71, 533–57.

Warner, A. R. (2004), What drove *do*?, in C. J. Kay, S. Horobin and J. J. Smith (eds), *New Perspectives on English Historical Linguistics I: Syntax and Morphology*, Amsterdam/Philadelphia: John Benjamins, 229–42.

Warner, A. R (2006), Variation and the interpretation of change in periphrastic *do*, in A. van Kemenade and B. Los (eds), *The Handbook of the History of English*, Oxford: Blackwell, 45–67.

Warner, A. R. (2007), Parameters of variation between verb-subject and subject-verb order in late Middle English, *English Language and Linguistics* 11, 81–111.

Wårvik, B. (2013), Peak-marking strategies in Old English narrative prose, *Style* 47, 168–84.

Wilson, H. ([1825] 1957), *The Game of Hearts: Harriette Wilson and Her Memoirs* (edited and introduced by Lesley Blanch), London: Gryphon Books.

Wischer, I. (2004), The *have*-perfect in Old English, in Chr. J. Kay, S. Horobin and J. Smith (eds), *New Perspectives on English Historical Linguistics*, Amsterdam/Philadelphia: John Benjamins, 243–55.

Wright, J. ([1954] 1910), *Grammar of the Gothic Language*, 2nd edn, Oxford: Clarendon Press.

Wurff, W. van der (1997), Deriving object–verb order in late ME, *Journal of Linguistics* 33, 485–509.

Wurmbrand, S. (2001), *Infinitives: Restructuring and Clause Structure*, Berlin/New York: Mouton de Gruyter.

Yerkes, D. (1982), *Syntax and Style in Old English: A Comparison of the Two Versions of Wærferth's Translation of Gregory's Dialogues*, Binghamton: Center for Medieval and Early Renaissance Studies.

Zeitlin, J. (1908), *The Accusative with Infinitive and Some Kindred Constructions in English*, New York: Columbia University Press.

Answers to the Trivial Pursuit questions on pages 26 to 27: (a) Thieves (b) Grapes (c) Brothels (d) Pluto (e) The tank (f) Minute hands.

Index

Printed and bound by CPI Group (UK) Ltd, Croydon, CR0 4YY

24/01/2025

01825366-0004